MERCY
REIGNS

A DAILY DEVOTIONAL OF
COMPASSION, COMFORT & HEALING

To Alberta.
Peace & blessings!

Bill

A Message to the Reader

This book is my gift in thanksgiving to all who have supported me, taught me, and loved me over the years, especially my late father, my mother, and brother. Also, to all my school teachers without whom I would never have become the writer that I am. My utmost gratitude goes to my greatest teacher, Jesus of Nazareth, as well as the living Christ.

If you are reading these words now, know that I wrote this book especially for *you* in the hopes that you would find compassion, comfort, and healing. Here is how to use the book effectively. As you start each day (or if you prefer...as you *end* each day), sit comfortably in the silence of God's loving presence for a minute or two acknowledging the One who is always with you. Then read the day's entry. Each begins with a title and then a scripture verse or two. Read them slowly and let them *soak in*. This will lead you into the practice of *Lectio Divina* whereby you silently reflect on the words and find rest there. Following a minute or two of rest... slowly read the reflection and again allow the words to speak to your heart. At the end of each reflection there is a suggested original song of mine to listen to. That is completely optional, but, if you are a musical person, it will add another layer to your spiritual experience. Finally, thank God for the gift of life and for the healing you are receiving.

In my former life as a radio news journalist, I delivered far too much *bad news*. When I followed the voice in my heart asking me to leave radio for ministry, I had already been writing songs. But I had a strong desire to continue the routine of writing daily to deliver news, but this time it would be the *Good News* of God's unconditional love. It began in 2008 as a daily devotional sent by email to the kids in my youth ministry and then expanded to an email to many of their parents and friends as well, before turning into a daily blog at billtonnismusic.wordpress.com/todays-contemplation. Those posts are what led to this book you are holding!

Reading and reflecting silently on the words of scripture helped change my life for the better. It will do the same for *you*...but you must find a *quiet* place to do it. As Jesus instructed, "When you pray, go to your inner room, close the door, and pray to your Father in secret" (Matthew 6:6).

The voice of God is never harsh, always merciful and compassionate. It will be a voice that tenderly says, "You are loved." May you hear that voice with each day's reflection...and find *rest*.

Bill Tonnis
Cincinnati, Ohio
6 July 2018

"Go and learn the meaning of the words,

'I desire mercy, not sacrifice.'"

Matthew 9:13

LOVE NEVER FAILS | I

The way we came to know love was that he laid down his life for us; so we ought to lay down our lives for our brothers and sisters. If someone who has worldly means sees a brother or sister in need and refuses them compassion, how can the love of God remain in him? Children, let us love not in word or speech, but in deed and truth.

Jesus *showed* us what pure Unconditional Love *is* by responding to persecution and even a torturous death with love and forgiveness.
He showed us that death does *not* have the *final say*,
but that it leads to *transformation*, *resurrection*, and *new life*.
While on the cross, even though *no one asked for forgiveness or deserved it*,
Jesus *freely gave it!*
Gaze for a moment upon Jesus hanging on the cross,
while still extending unconditional love.

This is how much God loves *each* of us.
You do *not* have to *earn* it.
It's given.
It's Grace.
Accept it.
Allow it to *saturate* your heart.
Allow it to transform you.
Love wins!

Listen to the song of the day "Salvation" on the *Live to Love* album.

2 GOD SAVES

Mark 6:50-51

"Take courage, it is I, do not be afraid!"
He got into the boat with them
and the wind died down.
They were completely astounded.

The disciples were already afraid as their boat was being tossed about by heavy winds.
That's when they saw Jesus walking on the sea.
The sight *terrified* them.

**The storms of life *will come*.
That is a *certainty*.**

Perhaps you have already endured some difficult storms.
Perhaps you are in the midst of one now.

The one *constant* in life is the fact that God *loves us* and will *not* let us go.

Jesus is the manifestation of this Unconditional Love in human form.
He was with his followers in times of joy, sorrow, and terror.

**His message *was* and *still is*...
that we have *nothing to be afraid of*.**

When times get tough and the winds are howling...
lean into the Love that made you.
The winds *will calm*.
Inner peace is *assured*.

Listen to the song of the day "I Will Give You Rest" on the *Live to Love* album.

FOLLOW JESUS | 3

1 John 4:9

In this way, the love of God was revealed to us:
God sent his only son into the world
so that we might have life through him.

Scripture says that God *is* Love...
a Love that is *incomprehensible* and *unconditional*.
This Love took *flesh* in Jesus.

**His whole life was to show us the true nature of God
as love, mercy, forgiveness, and compassion...
as well as to show God's equal acceptance and inclusivity of all people.**

Inevitably, this brought him persecution and crucifixion.

But *resurrection* and *new life* followed.

Let this knowledge set you free!

**That same new life is promised to *each* of us...
not only at death but through *each daily struggle*,
each "little dying" to ourselves.**

If you want to have life and have it more abundantly (John 10:10)...
then follow Jesus *now*...
and *forever*.

**Listen to the song of the day "Pour Me Out" on the *Give Praise and Thanks*
album.**

4 ALPHA AND OMEGA

Mark 1:11

And a voice came from the heavens,
"You are my beloved son;
with you I am well pleased."

Jesus shows us the way to *abundant life*...
as in a life *full of love*.

"I came so that they might have life and have it more abundantly" (John 10:10).
We are children of God (1 John 3:2).

When Jesus was baptized by John the Baptist,
he heard the voice of God call him the "beloved son."

Each of us is meant to also hear God's voice call *us* the "beloved son or daughter."

This is *not* a *merited* status.
It is *given*.

It is your *original blessing*.

Don't let other voices tell you otherwise!

**God is "well pleased" with *you*...
simply based on you being a *unique reflection* of Love *itself*...
for "God is love" (1 John 4:8).**

Hear God speak these words to you: "You are my beloved son/daughter."

Now... *live each moment in the awareness of your preciousness.*

Listen to the song of the day "The Way You Are" on the *Mercy Reigns* album.

PERFECT LOVE

1 John 4:18

There is no fear in love, but perfect love drives out fear because fear has to do with punishment, and so one who fears is not yet perfect in love.

Since God *is* love... God has *no intention to punish you*.

Human existence is *not* a "reward-punishment" scenario at all, but an opportunity for each of us to *know* and *experience* God's *unconditional* love.

God's justice is not *retributive* but *restorative*.

God intends for each of us to experience an unconditional love that will *transform* and *redeem* us.

When we fear... we know we are off base.

God's *only* desire is to *love* us.

God's perfect love was personified in Jesus, who loved and forgave from the cross.

That *same* forgiveness is for *you*.

It is not something that is earned.

It is a *gift*.

Simply accept it into your heart.

Listen to the song of the day "God's Love Is All You Need" on the *Listen to Your Heart* album.

6 REDEMPTION IN PROGRESS

Luke 5:12-13

Now there was a man full of leprosy in one of the towns where he was; and when he saw Jesus, he fell prostrate, pleaded with him, and said, "Lord, if you wish, you can make me clean." Jesus stretched out his hand, touched him, and said, "I do will it. Be made clean." And the leprosy left him immediately.

Notice how Jesus was always trying to restore *wholeness*.
He did not shy away from the man who was considered "unclean"
in the eyes of not only the society, but also the religious leaders.
The man with leprosy had been totally *excluded*.
Notice how Jesus did *not seem concerned at all* about the man's *religious beliefs*.

All we know is that the man demonstrated total faith that Jesus could heal him.
And with no test of his beliefs...
no assurances from the man that he would follow any set of doctrines in the future... Jesus healed him.
Jesus demonstrated what St. Paul would later write: "As a body is one though it has many parts, and all the parts of the body, though many, are one body, so also Christ.
If [one] part suffers, all the parts suffer with it;
if one part is honored, all the parts share its joy" (1 Corinthians 12:12, 26).
The true *reality* is that *we are all one*.

Where and how do *you* feel excluded? Where and how do *you* feel rejected by others?
Jesus wants to be with you *in that place*...
to let you know you *are* loved and that you *do belong* in the kingdom of God!
You are a *beloved daughter or son of God!*

Listen to the song of the day "All Are Welcome" on the *Give Praise and Thanks* album.

AWAKEN

1 Samuel 2:6

The Lord puts to death and gives life.

Death and life are part of *one* whole.
You can't have *one* without the *other*.
It's not an *"either-or"* but a *"both-and"* scenario.

This is our "blueprint" for how God operates.

Life and death is the pattern for each day
with the rising and setting of the sun.
It's the pattern of the seasons...
from spring to winter.

**It's the pattern Jesus showed us
in his life and death on the cross.**

But remember:
Each night is followed by a new dawn;
each winter is followed by a new spring;
the crucifixion was followed by the resurrection.

**Death does *not* win.
Christ lives!**

All our struggles will lead to new life
if we trust in the flow of Goodness.

**There is a bigger picture in which all suffering
will be transformed to *new birth*.**

Listen to the song of the day "Make Your Way" on the *Mercy Reigns* album.

8 ALL IS WELL

Psalm 94:18-19

> When I say, "My foot is slipping," your love,
> Lord, holds me up. When cares increase
> within me, your comfort gives me joy.

Does today's scripture reflect *your* image of God?

Or is your image of God that of a *judging ogre* who, instead of helping you,
is ready to *push* you and *ridicule* you when you slip?
From what we know of the Pharisees (the religious leaders of Jesus' time),
when they saw someone struggling and falling away from God,
they strictly held that person to the rules without offering a helping hand.
They were all about "law and order". It was an "*either-or*" proposition.
Either you kept the law and were in or you broke the law and were out.

Jesus was a "*both-and*" kind of guy.
This enabled him to *both* embrace the rules...
***and* uplift those who were "slipping" *without condemning or judging* them.**

While his *head* upheld the *rules*... his *heart* dictated his *actions*.
**That's because Jesus' heart had been transformed by the
unconditional love and *mercy* of God.
This Love will *not* be defeated.**
The 14th century mystic and theologian Julian of Norwich wrote that
Jesus had told her in a vision that "All shall be well."

Rules will *never* transform a person's heart. *Love will.*

And since God *is* Love (1 John 4:8)...
we have reason to feel *comfort* and *joy*.

Listen to the song of the day "Radically Okay" on the *Mercy Reigns* album.

SIGN OF JONAH |

Psalm 44:24-25

Awake! Why do you sleep, O Lord? Rise up! Do not reject us forever! Why do you hide your face; why forget our pain and misery?

Sometimes it *feels like* God has abandoned us.
**If you are suffering in some way and feel as though God is far away...
remember that Jesus felt such pain in the most extreme way.**

On the cross he cried out to God, "Why have you abandoned me?"
But God was *not* gone.
**Our Loving Creator is always there...
holding us silently and eventually leading us to new life.**

Suffering seems to be the *great mystery*.
**But it also seems to be the one thing that leads us to *let go* of *one thing*...
so that *another can begin*.**

Jesus *questioned*... but also *surrendered to what was happening*.
"Father, if you are willing, take this cup away from me;
still, not my will but yours be done" (Luke 22:42).
**As Jesus hung on the cross...
he hung between life and death...
arms outstretched embracing it all.**

And when all was said and done, the crucifixion was *not* the end.
Following the death of Jesus... was the resurrection of the Christ!

Jesus showed us the way to *transformation* and *new life*.
Look to him... and *follow*!

Listen to the song of the day "Love Will Always Lead You Home" on the *Mercy Reigns* album.

10 WONDROUS LOVE

1 Samuel 8:6-7

Samuel was displeased when they asked
for a king to judge them. He prayed to the
Lord, however, who said in answer:
"Grant the people's every request.
It is not you they reject,
they are rejecting me as their king."

It is the same story repeated throughout thousands of years.
The sons and daughters of God *reject* the God who made them.

They again and again choose gods of power, prestige, and possessions instead.
They... or should I say we...
choose to place ourselves at the center of the universe.

Each of us mistakenly believes that *we*... our individual *egos*... are the *center* of *all that is*.
God allows this... allows us to *choose*.

But this is *not* so that we can feel God's wrath and punishment...
but so that we can experience the *loving embrace*
of a God who loves unconditionally.

What better way to be *transformed* by Love...
than to *reject* the One who loves us...
and in return *be loved anyway!*

This is a Love that causes our hearts to melt...
and to then yearn to serve such a wondrous God with our lives.

Listen to the song of the day "God Is" on the *Give Praise and Thanks* album.

LOVE – FOREVER AND FREE

II

Mark 2:1-2

When Jesus returned to Capernaum after some days, it became known that he was at home. Many gathered together so that there was no longer room for them, not even around the door, and he preached the word to them.

People flocked to Jesus just to hear him preach "the Word."
What would cause so many to come to hear him speak?
What was he saying that was so *attractive*?
We know it *wasn't* about how to gain *fame, fortune,* and *power*.

Since God *is* love (1 John 4:8) and since in the beginning "the Word was God" (John 1:1) and "the Word became flesh" (John 1:14) *in* Jesus... then the Word must *be* Love.

Jesus' message was about God's *unconditional* Love and forgiveness for *all* people.

This was *THE* truth...
that God *is* Love and loves each of us infinitely *just as we are*.

This *cannot change* due to our behavior.
The "Word" was always about love...*not* punishment.
Jesus' words brought people peace, hope and freedom.
They *drove out* fear.
They do the same for us two thousand years later.

Read his words.
Get to know the Prince of Peace... and be free.

Listen to the song of the day "The Way You Are" on the *Mercy Reigns* album.

12 LET GO AND LET GOD

Mark 1:23-25

In their synagogue was a man with an
unclean spirit; he cried out, "What have you to
do with us, Jesus of Nazareth? Have you come
to destroy us? I know who you are–the Holy
One of God!" Jesus rebuked him and said,
"Quiet! Come out of him!"

What *unclean spirit* has its grips on you today?

Is it *fear... worry... envy...jealousy...*
or some *unhealthy attachment,* whether it be to
a *relationship, your job,* a *material possession, nationalism, politics...*
or perhaps even to *religion*?

Or is it some illness that you just can't shake?
Call on God.

**Allow the Light of God's Presence to shine on the darkness enfolding you...
keeping you from living in the freedom of the *naked now*.**

In this Presence you are unconditionally loved.
In it you are whole and your *true self.*

Humbly bask in the rays of God's light.

While the healing may not come in *your* timing and may not be exactly how *you* want it...
a healing is *already in the works* when you *ask, let go, trust and allow.*

Listen to the song of the day "Heal Me" on the *Live to Love* album.

LOVE WINS NOW AND ALWAYS

Hebrews 2:18

Because he himself was tested through what he suffered, he is able to help those who are being tested.

What is testing you now?
What trial are you going through?

Whatever it is...
Jesus has already walked through greater trials...
all the way to the cross...
to show you that there is *nothing to fear*.

**In the end...
there is resurrection and new life.**

Fear of rejection, failure, loss, or death...
dissolves in the light of the truth of
God's *unconditional love* and *eternal hope* shown fully in Jesus.

Whatever is testing you now...
remember:
"This, too, will pass."

God's unconditional love prevails.

Allow Jesus to bring you comfort.

Listen to the song of the day "Come to Jesus" on the *Live to Love* album.

14 GOD'S LOVE IS ALL YOU NEED

Hebrews 3:13

Encourage yourselves daily while it is still "today", so that none of you may grow hardened by the deceit of sin.

"Sin" is basically when we *turn away* from *God's* desires and
choose *our self-centered*, *ego-satisfying* desires.
Sooner or later we need *more* and *more* to be satisfied...
and it's *never* enough.

Today... *this* **moment...**
is a brand new opportunity to *turn back* **to God and**
away **from the** *self-gratifying* **ways that leave us** *empty.*

It's more a *"letting go"* than *"doing"* anything.
It's *accepting the moment* for what it is and *allowing* God to move in your life...
and then taking action.

Each time we revert to our old ways...
the *next moment* **is the opportunity to change directions.**

The beautiful thing is that God holds no grudges and is
always ready to *forgive* you and to *love* you.

That's what *unconditional* **love** *is.*

Today is the time.
Right *now.*

Accept it!

Listen to the song of the day "God's Love Is All You Need" on the *Listen to Your Heart* album.

GRACE | 15

Hebrews 6:11-12

We earnestly desire each of you to demonstrate the same eagerness for the fulfillment of hope until the end, so that you may not become sluggish, but imitators of those who, through faith and patience, are inheriting the promises.

We all need *hope*.
But it's hard to keep hope alive when we are assailed by the struggles of this world, our egos' *endless* self-centered demands, our human weaknesses and the actions of those in the grips of a *low-level consciousness*.

Jesus proclaimed a God of *unconditional* love, mercy, grace, forgiveness, and compassion for *everyone*... no matter how *misguided* or *imperfect* they were.

He continued to do this... even *on his way* to the cross.
Even *on* the cross.
"Father, forgive them, they know not what they do" (Luke 23:34).
**Jesus showed us the promise of *new life*...
a *gratuitous gift* of Grace.**

That is *truly* hope.
**Despite the world's opposition...
it is *yours now*.**

The ways of the world will *try* you and *persecute* you...
but if you *let go* into the *flow of Love*...
you *will* find *peace, wholeness,* and your *true self* in each *step*,
each *moment* of your journey.

Listen to the song of the day "Make Your Way" on the *Mercy Reigns* album.

16 GOD LOVES YOU

Psalm 111:1

I will praise the Lord with all my heart.

Have you ever praised God with *all your heart*?

It has happened spontaneously with me...
such as when seeing an amazing sunset or sunrise...
or when witnessing an incredible act of mercy
or listening to the incredible voice of a gifted singer.

How about when a mother joyfully cradles her baby?

There are moments when time seems to stand *still* and all is *intensely well*.

They are the moments when we are just
being who we are in *oneness* with *all that is*.

Take a moment to *stop*...
let go of all the things that are weighing you down...
and know that the God Who *is*,
Who *was*,
and Who *will be*...
has us *all* in an embrace that will *never* end...
no matter what.

Praise God!

Alleluia!

Listen to the song of the day "Give Praise and Thanks" on the *Give Praise and Thanks* album.

Psalm 56:3

O, Most High, when I am afraid, in you I place my trust.

God is always there for you, even when it *feels* otherwise.
Feelings of God's Presence are beautiful.
But there are *many times* when those feelings are *absent*.

Mother Teresa and many other mystics experienced this void as the "dark night of the soul."

Even Jesus experienced this feeling on the cross when he cried out,
"My God, my God, why have you forsaken me?"
But God had *not* abandoned Jesus.

Every *dark night* is eventually followed by the *light of dawn*.

New life is being *birthed*.
Death did not have the final say with Jesus.

The resurrection of the Christ followed.
This is the pattern for *everyone* and *all* things.

You are *included* in this *transforming process*.
God is Love.
Love has *no end*.
So *trust...*
let go...
and *awaken*.

Listen to the song of the day "Make Your Way" on the *Mercy Reigns* album.

18 | COMPASSION RULES

Mark 3:2

They watched him closely to see if they might accuse him.

It was the Sabbath and so under the religious laws...
work was *forbidden.*
The law's purpose was to help people focus on their relationship with God.

**But when Jesus was confronted with the situation of
whether to cure a man with a withered hand on the Sabbath...
he knew that extending God's love would be
more important than following the law.**

The Pharisees were *blind* to this.
The religious leaders of the day saw everything as *black* or *white.*
Their hearts were *hardened.*

**Sometimes when encountering the *gray* areas of life,
the "rule book" must be put aside.**

Jesus said the *greatest commandments* were to
love God and *love your neighbor as yourself.*
Love is the *lens* you must look through.

**It's the lens through which God looks
at *you and me* (*thank God!*).**

Allow God's unconditional love to
open your heart in a new way today.

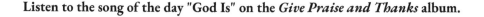

Listen to the song of the day "God Is" on the *Give Praise and Thanks* album.

AWESTRUCK

Psalm 57:6

Be exalted above the heavens, O God; above all the earth be your glory!

**If you can look past the *delusions* and *misery*
caused by *human greed* for *power, prestige,* and *possessions*...
God's *glory* is indeed showing *everywhere*.**

Not just within our earthly bubble...
but *far, far* beyond.

The universe...
at an estimated 92 billion light-years in diameter...
is *too vast* to *comprehend* and appears to be *still expanding*.
It is estimated to be around 14 billion years old.
The numbers *boggle the mind*.

If you look up at a clear night sky at the amazing array of stars and galaxies...
you will find your mouth dropping open in awe and wonder.

At the same time, gaze at the sweet, smiling face of a baby and feel your heart warm.
Look upon the intricate yet delicate beauty of a tiny flower.

**Now stop and ponder this:
The Creator of it all...
also created *you* and *me*.**

How *magnificent,*
wondrous,
and *glorious* is God!

**Listen to the song of the day "How Magnificent, Wondrous and Glorious" on the
Mercy Reigns album.**

20 | SOLIDARITY

Mark 3:35

"For whoever does the will of God is my brother and sister and mother."

In today's scripture, Jesus made this statement right after being told
that his mother and family were at the door.
His response would seem to have been somewhat insulting to them...
but we know that this is not the case, since Jesus adhered to the Commandment
"Honor your father and mother."

**We know that Jesus sometimes made statements to
jar his listeners and *awaken* them to a *deeper truth*.
The only way we can be doing God's will...
is by *being present to the Divine Presence*.**

When we are *truly present to another*...
we offer them the *sacrament of the present moment*...
to quote a phrase used 300 years ago by a Jesuit priest Jean-Pierre de Caussade.

***This moment* is the *only time* when we can meet God, who is always *present*.**

It is *we* who are *not* present... often lost in our thoughts of the *past* and *future*.

**Since "God is love" (1 John 4:8)...
then when we are *present*, we are also *one with Love* and *everyone around us*.**

All divisions fall away and we are one human family.

It is then that we are *in the flow of God's will*.

Be present to the Love that sustains *everything*.

Listen to the song of the day "All Are One" on the *Mercy Reigns* album.

Acts 22:4

LOVE NEVER FAILS

I persecuted this Way to death, binding both men and women and delivering them to prison.

Before becoming Saint Paul, he was known as Saul,
a persecutor of Christians in the name of God.
Saul *thought* he was doing *God's work* by rounding up followers of the "Way",
the name of the early Christian movement and throwing them into prison.
Some were undoubtedly *put to death*.
Saul was basically a *terrorist*.

**This was when he encountered the resurrected Christ in some
mystical way and his heart was *changed*.**

No wonder Jesus tells us to *love our enemies*.
If Saul had been killed, it would have prevented
one of the greatest conversions *in history* from taking place and
we would not have the writings of one of the *greatest* evangelists to ever live.
What other amazing conversion stories are waiting to take place in God's *time*?

Could it be *yours*?

We're all *on the path* to conversion...
completion...
and salvation...
no matter how young or old we are.

Let it begin *now*.

Listen to the song of the day "Mercy Reigns" on the *Mercy Reigns* album.

22 | GOOD NEWS OF GREAT JOY

Mark 16:15

Jesus said to them, "Go into the whole world and proclaim the gospel to every creature."

God loves you *unconditionally*.

That is the *good news*... the "gospel" message.

Jesus wanted his followers to not only *proclaim* that message,
but to *be* that message to "every creature."
He modeled that message perfectly...
giving himself in love, mercy, and compassion...
even when faced with unjust persecution and execution.

Jesus showed us that death is *not final*.

It always leads to resurrection and new life.
It was the risen Christ who told the apostles to spread this good news.

God's love for us is *infinite!*.

That is hard to comprehend until you truly *experience* it.
It's the Love that transformed Saul from a persecutor of Christians
to one of the greatest proclaimers of the Christian message.
Information about Jesus and God's love is practically meaningless...
until you experience it at the *heart-level*.
That's when *transformation* happens.

***Each* of us is called to be a part of a great Love story *in progress*.**

It's never too late to join in!

Listen to the song of the day "Shall We Sing" on the *Listen to Your Heart* album.

TRANSFORMATION IN PROGRESS

2 Timothy 1:7-8

For God did not give us a spirit of cowardice,
but rather of power and love and self-control.
So do not be ashamed of your
testimony to our Lord, nor of me,
a prisoner for his sake;
but bear your share of hardship for the gospel
with the strength that comes from God.

St. Paul's encounter with the risen Christ totally
transformed him from a *persecutor* of Christians
(which he was doing because he thought he was doing God's will!)
to totally dedicating himself to *spreading Christ's message* of *unconditional love*.

Things were not going well for Paul at the time of today's scripture reading...
he was in prison being persecuted himself for following Christ.
But amidst the struggle Paul had an inner peace and strength.

**If you are going through tough times,
it does *not* mean that God has *abandoned* you.
On the contrary...
God has you in a *sacred place of transformation*.**

If you *trust* and *persevere*...
then God will lead you to *new life*.
Allow the risen Christ to show you the way to *wholeness*.

**Listen to the song of the day "You'll Lead Me" on the *Listen to Your Heart*
album.**

24 LOOK AND LISTEN

Mark 4:18-19

"Those seeds sown among thorns
are another sort. They are the people
who hear the word, but worldly anxiety,
the lure of riches, and the craving for other
things intrude and choke the word,
and it bears no fruit."

God's word will *always* communicate
unconditional love, mercy, forgiveness, and *compassion*.
It comes to us in many ways:
in scripture, in silence, in music, in nature, through other people, etc.
There are many "seeds" being sown...
but what is the condition of our "soil"?

Are we *cultivating* our soil so that the seeds of Love take *root*?

What words, music, entertainment, social media, or people
might be poisoning our soil and choking God's seeds?

***Stop* for a moment.**
***Be* aware.**
Listen.

God is speaking words of love *all around you...*
and *in your heart.*

**Listen to the song of the day "Turn Off the Noise" on the *Listen to Your Heart*
album.**

DIVINE GUIDE 25

Psalm 25:4-5

Make known to me your ways, Lord;
teach me your paths.
Guide me in your truth and teach me,
for you are God my savior.

Do you ever feel *lost*...
like you just really have *no idea* what your next step should be
in dealing with a situation...
a relationship...
or your life's direction?

Who would have a better idea of the best next-step...than *God*?

Loving God, make known to me *your* will.
There is so much NOISE distracting me!

Help me to hear your gentle voice in silent prayer...
through reading scriptures...
through your wondrous creation and through the words and actions of others.

As I stray...
I *trust* that you will lead me back to the right path.

As Thomas Merton prayed,
"I will trust you always,
though I may seem to be lost and in the shadow of death.
I will not fear, for you are ever with me,
and you will never leave me to face my perils alone."

**Listen to the song of the day "You'll Lead Me" on the *Listen to Your Heart*
album.**

26 HAPPY FAULTS

Mark 4:21-22

He said to them, "Is a lamp brought in to be placed under a bushel basket or under a bed, and not to be placed on a lampstand? For there is nothing hidden except to be made visible; nothing is secret except to come to light."

Jesus certainly wants us to channel the light of God's unconditional love to the world and not keep it hidden.

But first *you* must experience that love for *yourself*.

Jesus wants us not to be afraid of the darkness inside of us... the things we struggle with and aren't proud of.

God *knows* these things about us and does *not* reject us.

What if we didn't try to *hide* those things... but instead lifted our defenses and allowed God's Light to shine into those areas? Those are the areas where we can truly experience God's *unconditional love*!

Jesus *never* condemned or accused those who brought their struggles to him... but instead *reached out* to them in love and *transformed* them.

God wishes to do the same for *you*.

Listen to the song of the day "I Stand in the Light" on the *Mercy Reigns* album.

LOVE NEVER FAILS

Psalm 31:23

Once I said in my anguish,
"I am shut out from your sight."
Yet you heard my plea,
when I cried out to you.

We all go through times of darkness and suffering.
It seems it is a *necessary* part of this mysterious journey.
Many times, it appears that we need the *suffering* to *force us to let go*
so that we can experience the *new life that is coming.*
***Suffering* inevitably happens when we refuse to *go with the flow* of what *is*.**
Even *Jesus suffered* as he *wrestled* with his apparent fate on the cross.
He said to God, "If you are willing, take this cup away from me;
still, not my will but yours be done" (Luke 22:42).
Jesus was our *ultimate model* of how to live our lives.
In times of trouble and darkness, he showed us how to *let go* and accept *what is*.
But he also showed us to then place our trust in a Higher Power.
Trust that *Love* will lead you.
He showed us how to follow that path of Love.
Jesus showed us what "unconditional" love is by loving and forgiving others
even when being persecuted and put to death.
Death does not win! There is always *resurrection*.
God *will save you*.
So when the tough times come, do not to label them as "bad"
because God will surely allow those times to *transform* you *if you are open to it*.
Christ will be there *with you in your struggles...*
and *all the way through them*.
It's the *way of the cross*. New life *is* coming.
Count on it!

Listen to the song of the day "Love Will Always Lead You Home" on the *Mercy Reigns* album.

28 | BE STILL

Psalm 3:6-7

Whenever I lay down and slept, the Lord preserved me to rise again. I do not fear, then, thousands of people arrayed against me on every side.

Sometimes life is tough and it can feel like there are so many people against us.
It can feel like *life* is *against* us.
Jesus experienced this in the *worst possible way* and *continued to respond in love*.
The truth is, life *will* deliver *difficulties*.
It is not to make you miserable but to *wake you up*.
The difficulties may be obstacles to deal with,
but they only cause *suffering* when your mind starts telling you
unpleasant stories about them.
The truth is...
your *truest self* at your *deepest core*...
is always *safe* and *secure* in the Love of God.

When you *rest in the moment*...
even though life is handing you struggles...
all is well.
God is with you and *cannot let you go*.
When you *let go*...
turning over your need to control the situation...
and allow God to lead you...
you *will* experience *peace* amidst the storms.
If you are going through something difficult this day, invite God to help.
***Wake up* and rise again.**

Do not fear.
Trust that you are being led by Love to *New Life*!

Listen to the song of the day "Make Your Way" on the *Mercy Reigns* album.

DEATH TO LIFE | 29

Mark 5:41-43

Jesus took the child by the hand and said to her, "Talitha koum," which means, "Little girl, I say to you, arise!" The girl, a child of twelve, arose immediately and walked around. At that they were utterly astounded. He gave strict orders that no one should know this and said that she should be given something to eat.

Can you imagine being present in that room when Jesus brought this girl *back to life?*
I'm sure we would all be *"utterly astounded"*!

We all go through various *"deaths"* as we take our spiritual journeys.
It seems the pain and sorrows we encounter are *necessary* so that we
let go of our ego-*centered* selves and enter into a bigger story...
God's story for our lives.
It seems to be the *only way* our egos will *willingly let go.*
Otherwise, our lives become all about gratifying the insatiable desires of this ego...
or as the famous monk Thomas Merton called it, our "false selves."
**Jesus showed us that his concern was for the
healing and *wholeness* of the person.**

Notice how he wants the miracle to remain a total *secret!*
It is not about *him...* but about the *wholeness of the girl and her family.*
Jesus has that *same concern* for *you!*
If you need new life... do not fear.
Turn* to Jesus and hear his voice say, *"Arise!"

Listen to the song of the day "Heal Me" on the *Live to Love* album.

30 | SAVED BY GRACE

Psalm 51:3

Have mercy on me, God,
in your goodness;
in your abundant compassion ,
blot out my offense.

We tend to beat ourselves up over mistakes and transgressions.
But when we turn back to God... instead of punishment and chastisement...
we receive *loving acceptance*.
This encounter with Love is *transforming*!

Just look at the parable Jesus told of the *prodigal son* (Luke 15:11-32).
The son totally rejects his father, runs off and
spends his entire inheritance on an immoral life...
and ends up in total depravity.
So with no other recourse...
he goes home hoping his father might let him
join the ranks of his servants.
But *instead*... the father (who is the "God" figure) totally
accepts him and *throws him a party*
without a *word* of *scolding* or *ounce* of *punishment*!
And the son *never* actually says he's "sorry!"
This is how Jesus describes *God*.

This is the *Great Compassion*,
who created you from nothing as a beloved son or daughter,
who wants to draw you *deeper and deeper* into a Love that will *fill* you,
change you, *complete* you...
and *have no end*!

Listen to the song of the day "Changed" on the *Give Praise and Thanks* album.

Romans 10:14

But how can they call on him in whom they have not believed? And how can they believe in him of whom they have not heard? And how can they hear without someone to preach?

I take these words of St. Paul to heart.
Listening to the words of Jesus in scripture and hearing him speak to my heart while sitting in quiet contemplative prayer has *totally changed my life.*

If you try it...
your life *will change* for the better, too.
I *guarantee* it.

But a "Christ-connection" will *not* mean the end of struggles.
No... *far from it.*

Life will still hand you challenges.
But for me...
my connection with Christ is what allows me to
go with the flow* and *be transformed in the process.

That, my friend, is Grace.
It's what leads you to *new life* and to a place where one day you will look back and be thankful for the *very struggle* that seemed to be so horrible when it happened.

God is not causing your difficulties...
but is the Grace leading you through them.

Listen to the song of the day "May I Be Light" on the *Listen to Your Heart* album.

I LIFE CHANGING LOVE

Hebrews 12:3-4

Consider how Jesus endured such opposition
from sinners, in order that you may not grow
weary and lose heart. In your struggle against
sin you have not yet resisted to the
point of shedding blood.

Jesus showed us how *far* God would go to show us unconditional love.

This is our God...
not a *harsh disciplinarian* ready to *punish* us...
but a *tender nurturer* who will go to *any length* to *love* us!

Whatever you are struggling with now...
turn to Jesus for help.
He knows what you are going through and will walk *with you*.

When you reach the end of your rope...
God is *waiting there*...
***not* to *scold* you...**
but to *embrace you*!

This is where God says,
"I *know* you can't do it *on your own. Let me help.*"
Why wait until the end of your rope?

Turn to the risen Christ now...
and *allow* him to *share* your journey to wholeness and new life.

Listen to the song of the day "God Is" on the *Give Praise and Thanks* album.

KEEP HOPE ALIVE

Hebrews 2:18

Because he himself was tested through what he suffered, he is able to help those who are being tested.

Since God *is* love (1 John 4:8), then I can't believe that God *inflicts* us
with suffering as some kind of *test*. That would be *cruel*.
Hardships seem to be part of life.
Jesus experienced all the joys and sorrows of being human.
God becoming flesh shows us that *flesh*... is *good*... as is *all creation*.
Indeed, *everything* is *sacred*.
St. Irenaeus said, "The glory of God is the human fully alive."
All of human experience is sacred... the joys and sorrows.
Through the sorrows we learn *compassion*.
It seems to be the *only way* that we are awakened from the
***delusion* that life is all about *me*.**
As Richard Rohr puts it: "*Suffering is the most effective way whereby humans learn to trust, allow, and give up control to Another Source. I wish there were a different answer, but Jesus reveals on the cross both the path and the price of full transformation into the divine.*"
We are *all* meant to be *transformed*.
Whatever pain and suffering you are going through...know that Jesus went through the
pain of total rejection, extreme persecution, and what appeared to be total defeat.
But he did so while responding with love, mercy, forgiveness, and compassion.

And in the end, total *defeat* was *transformed* into
total *victory* in the resurrection.
This path is *your* path as well!

Trust that God is with you in your struggle.
Allow it to transform you.

Listen to the song of the day "Changed" on the *Give Praise and Thanks* album.

3 LET GO AND LIVE

Hebrews 2:14-15

Through death he might destroy the one who has the power of death, that is, the devil, and free those who through fear of death had been subject to slavery all their life.

By becoming human, Jesus showed us the path to freedom: *Letting go*.
When we do not *cling* to things of this world...
a Greater Love leads us to freedom.
Following Jesus while loving God and our neighbor frees us from the
worldly attachments that we sometimes cling to due to our fear of death.

Nothing can separate us from the *Oneness* of all things.

As St. Paul says, "For I am convinced that neither death, nor life, nor angels, nor
principalities, nor present things, nor future things, nor powers,
nor height, nor depth, nor any other creature will be able to separate us
from the love of God in Christ Jesus our Lord" (Romans 8:38-39).
All possessions, power, and prestige in this life come to an *end*.

**But through Jesus' life, death, and resurrection...
we see that there is *nothing* to fear in death.**

Eternal life is *promised*.

In the end... *love wins*... not death.

By living a life of love, we will simply move freely into the joy of God when this life ends.
Let this knowledge *set you free*!

Listen to the song of the day "Pour Me Out" on the *Give Praise and Thanks* album.

BE FREE

Psalm 27:1

The Lord is my light and my salvation;
whom do I fear?
The Lord is my life's refuge;
of whom am I afraid?

We get so caught up in the struggles and challenges of life that we start giving in to *fear*.
We lose sight that God *is* Love (1 John 4:8) and love *drives out* fear (1 John 4:18).

**God... or *Love*... will ultimately save us...
even when things appear out of control.**

Love wins in the end.
Jesus gave us the ultimate example.

You are loved *eternally* and *unconditionally*.

God will *never* abandon you...
and no matter how a particular situation in your life turns out...
God will still love you.

**You are part of an *unfolding love story* in which God aims to bring *you* and *all
things* to their *fullest expression* of Love.**

So *persevere* and *engage confidently* in *each moment* of your life,
no matter the circumstances.
Relax in the knowledge that whatever today's struggle is... it will pass.

But the Light of Love shining upon you will *never be extinguished!*

Listen to the song of the day "Make Your Way" on the *Mercy Reigns* album.

5 GRACE UPON GRACE

Psalm 32:5

Then I declared my sin to you; my guilt I did not hide. I said, "I confess my faults to the Lord," and you took away the guilt of my sin.

God is *not* an angry tyrant waiting to punish.
When I admit my wrongdoings and times I acted selfishly...
as if *I* was the *center of the universe*...
God *forgives* and *extends mercy*.
That's because God *is* love.
What *else* would Love *do*?

Turn back to your Loving Creator and allow yourself to be held.

**As a mother cradles a baby in her arms...
this is how God wants to hold *you*...
with *no* condemnation...
only Love.**

It's *not* a matter of *worthiness*...
but Grace!

It is simply a *choice* to open yourself to a Love that is *never* withheld.

**God's justice is not *retributive*...
but *restorative*.**

Feel the embrace of Unconditional Love...
and watch your guilt and pain...
fall away.

Listen to the song of the day "How Wonderful to Me" on the *Live to Love* album.

ETERNAL HELP

Psalm 46:2

God is our refuge and our strength, an ever-present help in distress.

If you're like me, you call on God almost automatically
when confronted with trouble.
I remember vividly the phone call from the hospital
in the middle of the night when a voice told me that
my father was dying and that I needed to come immediately.
I remember driving the short distance down the highway to the hospital
invoking God's name *over and over* to be with my dad.

**I was totally focused on the *present moment*...
which seems to be the case whenever we are
confronted by such a *distressing* situation.**

I had no doubt that God was *indeed* with my dad,
my mom who was at his bedside...
and me.

**God is *always* as keenly present to *us*...
but *we* are *not* always as keenly *present* to *God*.**

It seems it takes these times of distress for us to fully *awaken* to the *sacred now*.
Whether or not *you* are in distress...
awaken...
and *be* in the *presence* of the Divine Presence...
right *now*.

God is *always* right *here* with you.

Listen to the song of the day "Slow Me Down" on the *Mercy Reigns* album.

7 SOUL CRAVING

Psalm 84:3

My soul yearns and pines for the courts of the Lord.
My heart and flesh cry out for the living God.

This is *profoundly true* but most are probably quite *unaware of it.*

Everyone is *yearning*... *pining* for something.

Our hearts and flesh are *crying out* for something to satisfy us!
Isn't this true for you?
The problem is that most people try to satisfy and fulfill this
yearning and longing with the three "P's":
possessions, power, and prestige.
These things will only satisfy the constant craving *temporarily*
before it continues to *yearn* for more.
That's because the yearning isn't for something
physical, emotional, or psychological...
but for something spiritual.

God made each of us with a *yearning* that *only* God can fill.

When we *empty* ourselves of our egos' desires...
God has the opportunity to fill us.
When we *die to ourselves*...
we paradoxically *find ourselves.*

**This is about *impossible* without *practicing* contemplative prayer.
God is as *close* as your very breath.**

Take a few minutes to simply be silent and to be aware of your breathing.
See what happens.

**Listen to the song of the day "Breathe On Me" on the *Listen to Your Heart*
album.**

BECOMING WHOLE

Mark 6:56

Whatever villages or towns or countryside he entered, they laid the sick in the marketplaces and begged him that they might touch only the tassel on his cloak; and as many as touched it were healed.

Can you imagine what it was like for Jesus
as everyone came to him expecting to be healed?
How overwhelming!
And yet this was his mission...
to heal and to preach the unconditional love of God.
Let's face it. We *all* have need of healing.

We all have wounds...
whether physical, psychological, emotional, or spiritual.
Our wounds are sacred...
places where we meet the healing, unconditional love of God.
Our wounds are not places to conceal and be ashamed of...
but places to invite God to be with us.
These are the places where we are not in control...
the places where we need help and can't fix ourselves.
These are the places where we have no choice but to "die"
to our "false selves" and to be truly honest and vulnerable with God.

God's desire is *not* to punish or criticize us but to *comfort* and *redeem* us.
God wants to make us whole.

Sometimes our wounds are the only places where we can truly experience the
unconditional, unmerited, and transformational love of God.

Listen to the song of the day "God's Love Is All You Need" on the *Listen to Your Heart* album.

9 HAVE FAITH

Psalm 37:5

Commit your way to the Lord;
trust that God will act.

When you *let go* of your need for *control*...
when you *surrender* your *ego* and its *self-centered desires* and
turn yourself over to the will of God...
you will seldom get clear *answers*.
You will seldom see a *direct path*.
**That's what *faith* is about... *not* having the answers and *not* seeing the road in
front of you... but still *trusting* in the providence of God.**

There is an Infinite Love at the core of all that is.
If you allow this Love to lead you... you may not find answers but
you *will* find an *inner peace* as well as your *true self*.
**Love is leading you *to* Love so that you know that *you are loved*...
and so you *share* that Love with the world.**
Try journaling about what happens in your life.
Then look back and see the winding thread of Providential Direction.
Faith is about *not knowing*... and *still trusting*.

I'm reminded of the prayer of Thomas Merton:
*"MY LORD GOD, I have no idea where I am going. I do not see the road ahead of me. I
cannot know for certain where it will end. Nor do I really know myself, and the fact that I
think I am following your will does not mean that I am actually doing so. But I believe that
the desire to please you does in fact please you. And I hope I have that desire in all that I am
doing. I hope that I will never do anything apart from that desire. And I know that if I do
this you will lead me by the right road, though I may know nothing about it. Therefore, I
will trust you always though I may seem to be lost and in the shadow of death.
I will not fear, for you are ever with me,
and you will never leave me to face my perils alone."*

**Listen to the song of the day "Take the Road Less Traveled" on the *Live to Love*
album.**

ALL ARE WELCOME | 10

Psalm 104:24

How varied are your works, Lord! In wisdom you have wrought them all.

God has made all things and deemed them "good."
Scripture says that we are all made in God's image.

That means *you*!

But that also means the person that most annoys us.

**Could it be that *all* things *belong* and
are necessary for each of us becoming "whole"
and for God's Kingdom to come into being?**

God holds *all* things without *dividing*.

That means *you* are included.

Always.
We are called to include everyone.

*Loving God,
help me to reach out to and
pray for the people I would rather exclude.*

Listen to the song of the day "All Are Welcome" on the *Give Praise and Thanks* album.

II | LOVE ENDURES

Psalm 32:6-7

Then should all your faithful pray
in time of distress.
Though flood waters threaten,
they will never reach them.
You are my shelter;
from distress you keep me;
with safety you ring me round.

Jesus knows what you are going through.
He felt the pain and distress of being rejected...
of becoming the one *cast-out* and nailed to a cross.

Yet he never gave up on his mission of extending God's unconditional love, mercy, forgiveness, and compassion... of showing the *true* face of God.

From the cross Jesus said,
"Father, forgive them, they know not what they do" (Luke 23:34).

This **is the God Who created *you*...**
the One who forgives *even when being crucified!*

This is a Love that will *never* give up on you!

Never!

Listen to the song of the day "Lift Up Our Voices" on the *Give Praise and Thanks* album.

THE WAY TO HEALING

Mark 7:34-35

Then he looked up to heaven and groaned, and said to him, "Ephphatha!" (that is, "Be opened!") And immediately the man's ears were opened, his speech impediment was removed, and he spoke plainly.

Many of us find ourselves bound, stuck, struggling, or hurting in some way or *many* ways.

**Just as Jesus "groaned" in today's scripture reading...
God *groans* in *yearning* to heal us of our brokenness.**

Jesus healed this deaf man as he had healed many others of physical, emotional, and psychological problems.

He knows exactly the healing that you need.

Jesus is the *Divine Physician.*
Call out to him. Then... have faith that the healing you need *will happen.*

But remember... the healing you *want* might not be the healing you *need*.

God's objective is that each of us becomes the full, unique person that each of us was created to be.

You are on the path to *becoming* your "true self."

Trust that God knows best the *path*, the *experiences*, and the *healing* that you need to become *whole*.

Listen to the song of the day "Heal Me" on the *Live to Love* album.

13 GRATEFUL

Psalm 116:12

How can I repay the Lord for all the good done for me?

If we took an inventory of all our blessings...
we would be hard pressed to be able to "repay" God for all of them.
Thankfully, God does not want repayment.
God simply wants to shower us with *unconditional* love.

True love does not seek anything in return.
It's given to us *freely* with *no strings attached*.

That is a hard concept for us to fathom since we seldom experience such
gratuitous favor from other human beings.

The beautiful truth is... God loved you and me into existence.
It is a Love that is *always given* and *never withdrawn*.

God *is* Love (1 John 4:8).
There came a time when I experienced this Love in my heart... and it changed my life.
When *you know* that *you know* that *you know* you are loved by God
in your imperfection... just as you are... it changes everything.

I simply *had* to share that news with others.
Jesus said, "Go and learn the meaning of the words,
'I desire mercy, not sacrifice'" (Matthew 9:13).

God doesn't need our sacrifices or payments.
God simply wants us to pass on the love we've been freely given.
Open your heart and receive a Love that *was, is,* and forever *will be*.

Listen to the song of the day "The Way You Are" on the *Mercy Reigns* album.

GOD DELIVERS | 14

Psalm 34:5

I sought the Lord,
who answered me,
delivered me from all my fears.

The sooner you come to know God as an
un*conditional lover* and *forgiver*,
the sooner you will be able to live an authentic life.

**God does not love you because of *your goodness*,
but because of *God's* goodness.
You do not have to *prove* yourself *worthy*!**

God does not want to punish you,
but to see you whole and healed...
and God loves being the One restoring you and healing you!

Jesus *showed us this quite clearly*.

So why not *seek* Christ throughout the day?

**He will *never desert* you and
*promises to deliver you from all fears!***

Listen to the song of the day "Come to Jesus" on the *Live to Love* album.

15 | WAY OF CHRIST

Mark 8:27-28

Along the way Jesus asked his disciples, "Who do people say that I am?" They said in reply, "John the Baptist, others Elijah, still others one of the prophets." And he asked them, "But who do you say that I am?"

That's a good question. Who do *you* say Jesus is?
There was a time when I *mentally* knew who Jesus was.
I had all the *information* about him.
But what *effect* did that information have on my life?
I held a lot of beliefs and would generally critique others as to whether they had the "right" set of beliefs or not (by "right" I mean *my* beliefs *of course*).
This kind of thinking often results in forming a harsh, judgmental attitude that decides who's *in* and who's *out*.
But when I read the gospels... I did *not* find a *harsh, judgmental* Jesus. Instead...
I found a Jesus who *reached out* to the *rejects*, the *poor* and the *sick*.
He *didn't divide* based on *beliefs*.
Who were the harsh, judgmental ones? The Pharisees (religious leaders).
I was like the *Pharisees*!
It dawned on me that if Jesus was "the way, and the truth and the life" (John 14:6) as he claimed...then that knowledge should have a positive effect on my life. As I intensified my pursuit of knowing Jesus more deeply... my life started to change for the better.
My heart *softened*.
I realized that *information about Jesus* was a far cry from *transformation through him*.
My transformation came in the *process* of being *unconditionally loved* while humbly following him *in my imperfection*.
So... who do *you* say he is?

Listen to the song of the day "I Want to Follow You" on the *Listen to Your Heart* album.

ETERNAL ACCEPTANCE | 16

Mark 8:11-12

The Pharisees came forward and began to argue with him, seeking from him a sign from heaven to test him. He sighed from the depth of his spirit and said, "Why does this generation seek a sign?

Jesus' actions spoke for themselves...
and yet the religious leaders of the time wanted more signs of *proof* that
he was the incarnation of God.

Many are *still* blind to the truth of God's loving presence.

Just experience a beautiful sunrise,
singing birds,
blue skies,
the mind-boggling, expanding size of the universe,
a warm hug,
laughter with a friend,
the savory taste of your favorite food,
the fragrant aroma of flowers,
the emotional sounds of your favorite songs,
the feeling you get when someone reaches out to you with compassion or forgiveness.

What other *sign* do we need that there is a *Loving Source* behind it all?

Why not drop any cynicism and simply *believe*?
Deep down... there is a Love that refuses to let us go.
It is the source of our deep yearning for unconditional acceptance and love.
Abide in this *never-ending* wellspring of Goodness.

Listen to the song of the day "How Magnificent, Wondrous and Glorious" on the *Mercy Reigns* album.

17 | BE RENEWED

Psalm 51:12

A clean heart create for me, God; renew in me a steadfast spirit.

Whatever you have done to turn away from God...is in the *past*.
That includes something you did *seconds* ago.
That time *no longer exists*.
As St. Paul said, "Behold, now is a very acceptable time;
behold, now is the day of salvation" (2 Corinthians 6:2).
***Now* is the *only time* where *God is present*,
where the kingdom of God *comes alive*.
Now is when God is *always gazing at you with
unconditional love and acceptance*.**
God always looks at us with open arms.
There is *no* condemnation.
There is *no* question of *worthiness*.

You are loved and accepted *as you are*.
This Love *makes you worthy*.
Open your heart and allow *Compassion itself*...
your loving Creator...
to renew you.

Live in the knowledge that you are loved and accepted *as is*.

As Jesus said, "When you pray, go to your inner room, close the door, and pray to your
Father in secret. And your Father who sees in secret will repay you" (Matthew 6:6).
Spend some quiet time and *bask in that love and acceptance*.

Be renewed!

Listen to the song of the day "The Way You Are" on the *Mercy Reigns* album.

PROVIDENCE | 18

Mark 8:20-21

"When I broke the seven loaves
for the four thousand,
how many full baskets of fragments
did you pick up?"
They answered, "Seven."
He said to them,
"Do you still not understand?"

We often say, "Seeing is believing."
If we'd only see *proof*...
we'd *believe*.

Well... the apostles saw Jesus perform many miracles
(including the multiplication of loaves of bread)
and yet in today's scripture verse when they forgot to bring bread with them...
they still worried how they would be fed.

Think of all the rough times you've experienced and how...
somehow...
things happened to help you make it through.

Have faith!

God will *never* forsake you!

"Do you still not understand?"

Listen to the song of the day "God's Love Is All You Need" on the *Listen to Your Heart* album.

19 SALVATION

Psalm 130:3-4

If you, Lord, mark our sins, Lord, who can stand?
But with you is forgiveness and so you are revered.

If our loving Creator was actually a God marking our every fault and misstep...
we would *all* be in *deep trouble*!
But Jesus told us if we know him...
we also know *God* (John 8:19).

Did you *ever* see Jesus "marking" people's sins?

The Pharisees... the religious leaders themselves...
were the *only* ones Jesus openly criticized because of
their arrogance and self-righteousness.

As for all the rest...
we saw Jesus reaching out to them in love and forgiveness.

And as the ultimate example of who God is...
Jesus forgave his persecutors while nailed to a cross.
He looked on all those who had just brutalized him and said:
"Father, forgive them, they know not what they do."

Is this the God you know...
or has your 'God image' been of a punishing tyrant?

Scripture tells us:
"God is love, and whoever remains in love remains in God and God in him" (1 John 4:16).
That is *my* experience of the One who created me and all things.

Allow that understanding to settle into your soul.

Listen to the song of the day "Salvation" on the *Live to Love* album.

BREATHE 20

Psalm 23:1

The Lord is my shepherd; there is nothing I lack.

If we truly took this verse to heart and *lived* it... we would *know peace*.
If we truly let God lead us, guide us, and love us... we would have *all we need*.
We... and everything else... would be *enough*.

Unfortunately, many of us are living in the trance of a culture
that leads us to always yearn for more *stuff*.
We are constantly being told that we need *more* and *more* to be *happy*.
Advertisers and marketers *know well* what they are doing.
But the fact of the matter is... in *this moment*... right *now*... what is lacking?

Nothing.
You are breathing.
Life is pulsing through you.
You are a miraculous child of God.
Who or *what* is leading you in life?
***Who* or *what* is your *motivating source*?**
Are you trying to please your *ego* or *God*?
Did you ever hear that EGO stands for: Edge God Out?
**When we *let go* of our *attachment* to *worldly things*...
in a sense *emptying* ourselves,
we are *free* to experience the *Divine Presence*.**
When God (or Unconditional Love) is our primary focus and
we are totally *present* to God (or Unconditional Love)...
we *lack nothing*.
A contemplative prayer practice will help you immensely.
Try sitting quietly for 15 to 20 minutes...
allowing all your thoughts to slowly slip away.
**Be *present* to the *Divine Presence*...
breathe... and all will be quite *enough*.**

**Listen to the song of the day "Breathe On Me" on the *Listen to Your Heart*
album.**

21 THE TIME IS NOW

2 Corinthians 6:2

Behold, now is a very acceptable time;
behold, now is the day of salvation.

May each of us focus on *this moment...*
the only time that is *real*.
The past is *gone*.
The future is *yet to be*.

**Now is the *place* and *time*
where God *dwells* and *wants to be with you*
to bring you to completion and wholeness.**

That *is* salvation!

**So *be present* to the Divine Presence.
God is *everywhere*
and as close to you as your breath.**

May each of us *open our hearts* to God
who wants nothing more
than to be with us and guide us
to wholeness and peace.

Listen to the song of the day "Slow Me Down" on the *Mercy Reigns* album.

PRAYER OF PRESENCE | **22**

Matthew 6:7-8

"In praying, do not babble like the pagans, who think that they will be heard because of their many words. Do not be like them. Your Father knows what you need before you ask him."

Jesus gives us a very meaningful teaching today about how to pray,
but it has been *roundly ignored* by many of his followers.
Instead... they have done the *opposite* and have formulated written prayer after written prayer to recite endlessly... *over and over.*
Not that *all* written prayers are bad!
It's just that Jesus *specifically advised* his followers to pray by *saying little*.
In the only recited prayer Jesus is recorded as teaching (known as *The Lord's Prayer*), he told his followers to say to God, "Thy will be done"...
which of course means... *not my will.*
***We* need to *get out of the way*.**
By *we*... I mean our *egos*... and our *non-stop chattering minds.*
If, as Jesus told us, God *knows what we need before we ask*,
why not *ask God what that is?*
The only way "God's will" can be done is if we *hear* what it is
that God wants us to do to make it happen.
For this to happen... we must be *in tune* with our Loving Source.
One good way to be *in tune with God* is by following the instructions
Jesus gave just before today's verses:
"Go to your inner room, close the door,
and pray to your Father in secret" (Matthew 6:6).
Be *still*.
Be *present*.
Be. Listen.

Listen to the song of the day "Turn Off the Noise" on the *Listen to Your Heart* album.

23 | GOD SAVES

Psalm 31:5-6

Free me from the net they have set for me,
for you are my refuge.
Into your hands I commend my spirit;
you will redeem me, Lord, faithful God.

Sometimes it feels like *everyone* and *everything* is *conspiring against us*.
Sometimes we feel completely *abandoned*.

Jesus felt this.
When he was *thoroughly rejected* and hanging on the cross...
he quoted Psalm 31: "Into your hands I commend my spirit."
Life is a *moment-by-moment* "letting go."
It's a surrendering of the things we thought at one time were so important,
but which really aren't important at all.
It will feel like *dying*.

When we *let go* of these "attachments" and turn ourselves over
to the One who loves and sustains us...
God redeems us.
In other words...
God *restores* us and makes us *whole*.

Only *God* can give us what we truly *need*.
Jesus showed us the way to new life.
It's the path of *dying and rising*.

The path may be a lonely one...
but it's the only path to becoming your *true self*.

Listen to the song of the day "Take the Road Less Traveled" on the *Live to Love* album.

YOU ARE LOVED

Sirach 6:14-15

A faithful friend is a sturdy shelter;
he who finds one finds a treasure.
A faithful friend is beyond price,
no sum can balance his worth.

All the money in the world cannot bring you comfort
in times of sorrow or loss.
But a friend... ah....
a friend can.

A friend's presence is worth its weight in gold.

As Jesus said,
"For where two or three are gathered together in my name,
there am I in the midst of them" (Matthew 18:20).
In the loving presence of another...
Jesus shows up.

It's in the *relationship*.

Jesus brings this message:
"God is with you."

Allow that message to set you free.

Listen to the song of the day "There Is Three" on the *Mercy Reigns* album.

25 GRACE IS FREE

Luke 6:36-37

"Be merciful, just as [also] your Father is merciful. Stop judging and you will not be judged. Stop condemning and you will not be condemned. Forgive and you will be forgiven."

The world has not changed.
Humans continue to fight with each other and to kill each other.
Jesus said to "love your enemies" (Luke 6:27).
This is hard.
It also would *change the world*.

Some will never buy it.
What about *you*?

This is what Jesus told us to do.
When we *mirror* the mercy, forgiveness and compassion God gives us *to others*...
we are in the flow of the Trinity...
a never-ending outpouring of unconditional love.
Allow today's scripture verses to sink into your soul.

It's the path to *transformation*.
Mercy is yours *now*.

It's God's gift.
Pass it on to others.

The kingdom of God is at hand...
if we cooperate.

Listen to the song of the day "Salvation" on the *Live to Love* album.

BEAUTIFULLY BROKEN

Psalm 51:3

Have mercy on me, God,
in your goodness;
in your abundant compassion,
blot out my offense.

Who among us is without the need of forgiveness?
No one.
We were *made* with *flaws* and *imperfections*.
We are *all* broken.

If we were *perfect*...
we wouldn't *need* God.
**It's only *in our brokenness* that we can truly *experience*
the *unconditional love* of God.**

Jesus was always reaching out those who were
abandoned, cast out, or in need of healing.
This is what God does!

What *else* would Love do?
Wherever you are struggling or in need of forgiveness...
allow God to embrace you.
That's what God *wants* to do!

**God does not love you because *you* are good...
but because *God* is good!**

Pass this message on to someone who needs to hear it.

Listen to the song of the day "God Is" on the *Give Praise and Thanks* album.

27 ETERNAL GIVER

Matthew 7:7

"Ask, and it will be given you;
seek, and you will find;
knock, and the door will be opened for you."

When we *ask, seek, and knock...*
we are in the *process* of *receiving,*
finding, and having the door opened.

**The *inner desire* prompting our "seeking" is the *groaning* of
the *Spirit* in our very *soul.***

It is *in* the *asking, seeking,* and *knocking...*
that we are *present* to the *Divine Presence.*

**When we are truly *present...*
we are in *God's Presence.***

It is only *then* that God's *will* can be done... in the *now...*
where God is *eternally Present* and pouring out *unconditional* love.
It is only in the *now* that God can *give...*
and *is* giving to us.
Believe that you *are* receiving and finding and that the door *is* being opened.

For it is *in that process* that God is giving you what you truly *need.*

Stop for a moment and look back on all the ways
God has given you gifts beyond measure...
even when at the time you were quite unaware of what was coming to you.
Thanks be to God!

**Listen to the song of the day "Give Praise and Thanks" on the *Give Praise and
Thanks* album.**

WAKE UP | **28**

2 Corinthians 6:3

Behold, now is a very acceptable time; behold, now is the day of salvation.

We spend so much time either
carrying the weight of *past* hurts and injustice
or *worrying* about the *future*.

But, as St. Paul tells us, *now* is the only time that is *real*.

Now is where God resides.
Now is the time and place where God wants
to meet you and make you whole.

Are you *present* to *this moment*?

It's the only time to hear and see God's Presence.

**In each moment, God is telling you that
you are loved *beyond measure*.**

It has nothing to do with what you've *done* or what you *will do*...
but simply because of *who you are*...
God's *beloved son or daughter*.

**Live in that awareness...
and be free.**

Now is the day of *salvation*.

Listen to the song of the day "Slow Me Down" on the *Mercy Reigns* album.

I | BE FREE

Matthew 18:21-22

Then Peter came to Jesus and asked, "Lord,
how many times shall I forgive my brother
or sister who sins against me?
As many as seven times?"
Jesus answered, "I say to you,
not seven times but seventy-seven times."

Peter thought he was being very noble in extending forgiveness
to his brother as many as *seven* times.
Jesus countered by telling Peter that basically...
you must forgive your brother an *infinite number* of times.

This is exactly what our Loving Creator does with *each of us*.

Forgiveness *changes hearts* and *brings the kingdom of God to life* in the *present moment*.

**It also *frees you* from the *bondage* of the chains
that *grudges* and *resentments* cast upon you.**

So *let go* of any past transgressions against you.
Ask for forgiveness for any wrongdoings.

**Forgive *yourself*.
God does.**

Then... *bask in the freedom* of God's *unfolding* and *unending* unconditional Love.

Listen to the song of the day "Radically Okay" on the *Mercy Reigns* album.

ETERNAL PERSPECTIVE

Deuteronomy 4:9

"However, take care and be earnestly on your guard not to forget the things which your own eyes have seen, nor let them slip from your memory as long as you live, but teach them to your children and to your children's children."

God's constant message from the beginning of the Bible to the end is:
"I love you."
There are *no* strings attached.
But people seem to have short memories...
easily forgetting God's fidelity and care...
slipping away to worship other idols.
This continues today.
We all have our "idols" that we too often place first in our lives...
whether they are *money, sports, possessions, lust, power, control, our physical appearance...*
or even *religion itself.*
Whatever we put before loving God, neighbor, and self... is an idol.
But God still does *not* abandon us...
no matter how many times we turn away.
Just so we can't miss the message...
Jesus allowed himself to be crucified and then while hanging on the cross...
forgave his killers...
even when *no one had asked to be forgiven*!
***That's* Unconditional Love!**
That is Who God *Is.*
God's love is *constant.*
Think of how many times you have experienced this redemptive Love.
Experience it again *now*... and *pass it on*!

Listen to the song of the day "How Wonderful to Me" on the *Live to Love* album.

3 UNMERITED REDEMPTION

Matthew 5:21-22

"You have heard that it was said to those of ancient times, 'You shall not murder'; and 'whoever murders shall be liable to judgment.' But I say to you that if you are angry with a brother or sister, you will be liable to judgment."

Jesus takes the commandments to *another level*... basically saying that even if you get *angry* with someone you are *guilty* of *breaking the commandment against murder!*

In other words... it's an *impossible standard to keep*.

Did he say this so we'd all be afraid and feel horrible? *No!*
It is so we understand that it's not *our* goodness... but *God's* goodness that *saves us.*
You cannot merit or achieve your salvation.
It is a gift from God!

**God knows you cannot keep such an impossible standard
that demands perfection...
because God wants to be *with* you *in* your struggles...
embrace you *in* your imperfection...
forgive you and thereby *transform* you *so* that
you can be a more compassionate person!**

God does *not* want to *punish* you... but *redeem* you!
As it says in Psalm 130:7,
"For with the Lord is mercy, with him is full redemption."
Fall into the arms of God and open yourself to un*conditional* Love with no end.

Listen to the song of the day "God Is" on the *Give Praise and Thanks* album.

PRAISE YOUR CREATOR

Psalm 33:3, 9

Sing to God a new song;
skillfully play with joyful chant.
For he spoke, and it came to be,
commanded, and it stood in place.

**There is *reason* to sing for joy!
God loves all of creation...
and that includes *you*!**

God's Word *became* flesh in Jesus and it *became* flesh in *you* as well.

You are God's beloved *child*.

God will *never* forsake you,
never let you go,
no matter how shaky the circumstance
or how hard the struggle might *appear*.

**God, the Loving Source of all, *embraces* you always...
even when times seem dark.**

It is only in the darkest of times that God's light can make the most *dramatic difference*...
and *lead* you to the most *dramatic* transformation.

For when God's Light *breaks through* your darkest night...
you will have quite the story to *share*...
a new and *glorious song* to *sing*.

Listen to the song of the day "Sing a New Song" on the *Live to Love* album.

5 DO NOT FEAR

Psalm 46:2-3

God is our refuge and our strength, an
ever-present help in distress. Thus we do
not fear, though earth be shaken and
mountains quake to the depths of the sea.

"Ever-present."
Is that how *you* experience God?
For many people, God was always viewed as *far off*...
"watching us from a distance" as a popular song once said.
Or even *worse*... not even *watching* us...
but somewhere far off in a distant heaven ignoring us.
However, the psalmist says God is not only "ever-present" but also "help in distress."
God is *actively present* for our *good*.
When Moses asked for God's name, God said: "I Am."
God is "Always Here."
Are *you*?
Are you focused on living in the *now*...
or are you holding on to a *past* injury or worrying over something that is in the *future*?
**God is present to you *now* and wants nothing more than
to be with you *now* because *you* are God's *beloved child*.**
You are a *reflection* of the *Divine Light*.
And as St. Paul said, "For I am convinced that
neither death, nor life, nor angels, nor principalities, nor present things,
nor future things, nor powers, nor height, nor depth, nor any other creature
will be able to separate us from the love of God in Christ Jesus our Lord"
(Romans 8:38-39).
Jesus was the incarnation of God's love poured out for us.
So be at peace.

Listen to the song of the day "I Will Give You Rest" on the *Live to Love* album.

PRINCE OF PEACE

Psalm 112:7

They shall not fear an ill report;
their hearts are steadfast,
trusting the Lord.

Why do we *fear*?

How many things actually turn out to be
"the end of the world?"
I often repeat this phrase to myself
when in the midst of a *challenging* situation:
"This, too, will pass."

God will *never abandon* you no matter how *bleak* the situation may appear.
Even when Jesus *felt abandoned* on the cross...
he *wasn't*.
God *was there*!

On the *other side* of death was resurrection and new life!

I remember how *devastated* I was when a great friend of mine
was diagnosed with advanced cancer several years ago.
Sadly, he died seven months later.
But my friend is now experiencing the wonders of a *transformed* life in heaven.

One of Jesus' *most repeated* messages was that we should *not be afraid!*

Trust the One who showed us that even death is *not the end*...
but a new beginning.

Listen to the song of the day "Make Your Way" on the *Mercy Reigns* album.

7 YOU ARE THE BELOVED

Isaiah 49:15

Can a mother forget her infant,
be without tenderness for the child of her womb?
Even should she forget, I will never forget you.

When you feel like you're alone...
like you've been rejected...
take comfort that Jesus became the one *totally rejected*.
But in response, Jesus continued to mirror for us the true nature of God.

He *forgave* his persecutors.
He *forgave* all those who betrayed him.
God's love is not based on *conditions* or *expectations*.

This does not mean we won't face struggles in life.
As Julian of Norwich stated, "If there is anywhere on earth a lover of God who is always
kept safe, I know nothing of it, for it was not shown to me. But this was shown:
that in falling and rising again we are always kept in that same precious love."
Just as Jesus *spread God's love to the world... we are called to do the same.*

We are called to respond to persecution as *Jesus* did... with *forgiveness*.
And just as Jesus was transformed to new life... we, *too*, will be *transformed*.

As the prophet Isaiah tells us in today's scripture verses...
we are God's children.
God's love for each of us is as tender as a mother's love for her babies.

This love is meant to be shared *through us* with *everyone* and *all creation*.
It's a Love that will bring us safely from birth.... to death...
to New Life.

Listen to the song of the day "I Stand in the Light" on the *Mercy Reigns* album.

HOLD ON TO HOPE

Psalm 5:2-3

Hear my words, O Lord; listen to my sighing.
Hear my cry for help, my king, my God!

Sometimes we are *overwhelmed* with *painful situations*.
It is part of the human condition.
God showed us how intimately he is with us by becoming
completely *immersed* in our *pain* and *suffering* by becoming human.

**Jesus went through all of life's *struggles* and *sufferings* and even endured the
most *humiliating* and *unjust* death to show us that God *is* with us!**

God *is hurting* with us *in our pain*... *struggling* with us *in our struggles*...
and *laughing* with us *in our joy*.
I think sometimes we feel we are not being a "good Christian" when we cry out to God...
or we think we aren't *measuring up*.
**But Jesus himself *cried out* to God when *struggling*
with his impending crucifixion.**

It sometimes appears God is not there as Jesus no doubt felt
when he cried out on the cross to God,
"Why have you forsaken me?"
**But God is there *feeling our pain*...
and *promising to deliver us to* new life.**

Death did *not win* at the crucifixion.

**The resurrection showed us that despite all the pain and suffering...
love *wins* in the end.**

Trust in Jesus.

**Listen to the song of the day "Love Will Always Lead You Home" on the *Mercy
Reigns* album.**

9 GOD IS LOVE

Psalm 51:18-19

For you do not desire sacrifice; a burnt offering you would not accept. My sacrifice, God, is a broken spirit; God, do not spurn a broken, humbled heart.

We're *all* broken in some way...
messed-up somewhere inside.
But most people try to *hide* it... pretend it's not there...
and sometimes beat themselves up over it...
feeling like a failure...
feeling like God is pointing to it in disdain.
What if God wanted to love you *in* your brokenness?

What if God... knowing this brokenness... wanted nothing more than to be with you
precisely in that place to let you know that you are loved *unconditionally*?
Jesus demonstrated God's *ultimate* unconditional love when He said,
"Father, forgive them, they know not what they do" as he hung on the cross.
What more proof do you need?

Instead of trying to earn points with God by making sacrifices,
why not give up your ego?
Jesus said,
"Go and learn the meaning of the words,
'I desire mercy, not sacrifice'" (Matthew 9:13).
Why not offer to God your broken self?

Sacrifice your ego... *let it go*.

It is only then that you can live from your heart.
Allow God to love you *in your brokenness* and lead you to *healing and wholeness*.

Listen to the song of the day "Breathe On Me" on the *Listen to Your Heart* album.

Psalm 42:2-3

As the deer longs for streams of water,
so my soul longs for you, O God.
My being thirsts for God,
the living God.

We are all *thirsting*...
yearning inside for something to fill us...
fulfill us.

Pop culture tells us all kinds of stuff will satisfy that need.

But all that stuff will only bring
temporary satisfaction
before the *thirsting* intensifies.

That's because the *yearning* is not physical but *spiritual*.
God *yearns* to quench our thirst.

Why not take inventory of all our *activities* and *habits* and
see which ones improve our relationship with God and
which ones block that relationship?

God alone brings deep satisfaction.

Jesus discovered this for himself during his forty days in the desert.

Ask him to lead you.

Listen to the song of the day "You'll Lead Me" on the *Listen to Your Heart* album.

II | BE

Psalm 130:5-6

I wait with longing for the Lord, my soul
waits for his word. My soul looks for the Lord
more than sentinels for daybreak.

How *attentive* are you for God's word?
**Is your soul *looking* for God... with the *expectation of soldiers
on guard at night awaiting the break of dawn*?**
God is always Present... but it is we who often aren't.
It's hard to be present when we are lost in our *constant thoughts*.
Many people mistakenly believe that they *are* their *thinking*.
They are *attached* to their chattering minds.

But you are *not* your thoughts.
Sit and be *silent*.
Observe the *stream of thoughts* as they come.
Who is doing the *observing*?
It is the *real* you... your *true self*.

Take some quiet time to allow the thoughts to *drift away*.
Observe them without judgment.
Let them *dissolve*.
Cultivate a contemplative place in your soul.

Then as you live each day... *be present* to the *moment*.
As I walked this morning... the sound of the birds could have been meaningless *noise*...
unheard due to the din of *chattering thoughts* in my head.
**Instead... as I *calmed my mind* and focused on the present...
the beautiful chirping became God's *harmonious music* singing,
*"I Am here. I Am with you. I Am."***

Listen to the song of the day "God Is" on the *Give Praise and Thanks* album.

LET GO AND LIVE

Romans 4:13

It was not through the law that the promise was made to Abraham and his descendants that he would inherit the world, but through the righteousness that comes from faith.

In other words... *life* is *not about* our *doing* something...
following some particular rules...
so as to *earn* the world.
It's not about *earning*.
It's not about *achieving*.
It's not about *being worthy*.
It's not about a *check-off-list of righteousness*.
Our *precious lives* and *all things* have been *given* to us... by *Pure Grace*.
It's *all gift*.

And each of our lives is meant to be lived so as to *share* God's gift of love.
When you *give yourself away*... you *paradoxically inherit everything*.

All you have to do is *have faith*... or in other words... *believe*.
***Awaken* to the wonder that each breath you take is a wondrous gift of God.**

Go ahead... take a deep breath of Love.
Exhale life-giving carbon dioxide to the plants and trees...
which in turn release oxygen back to you and me.
It's one beautiful *cycle of life*... all fueled by a Source of *Eternal Love*.

May we all *surrender* to the joy of the great gift we have received and
are *continuing to receive each moment*.

**Listen to the song of the day "Breathe On Me" on the *Listen to Your Heart*
album.**

13 | LOVE WINS

Psalm 34:19

The Lord is close to the broken-hearted, saves those whose spirit is crushed.

Jesus was always going to those
who were on the outside looking in.
He went to be with the rejected,
those regarded as "sinners", and those who were physically sick.
**He didn't shun them but loved them
and returned them to wholeness.**

He accepted them without condemnation
and with *no* conditions.
**He never required others to adhere to any belief system
before he included them.**

Then... Jesus *became* the one *thrown-out and rejected*
to show us how *intimately* he relates to *all* of us
who have had our *hearts broken* and *spirits crushed.*

And then...
in return for such anguish and torture being inflicted upon him...
Jesus *forgave and showed compassion.*
This reflects Who God Is.

Trust in Jesus!
Come to him...
just as you are.

The risen Christ promises *you* new life.

Listen to the song of the day "Come to Jesus" on the *Live to Love* album.

EVERYONE IS A MASTERPIECE | 14

Psalm 139:1, 13-14

O Lord... you know me. You formed my inmost
being; you knit me in my mother's womb.
I praise you, so wonderfully you made me;
wonderful are your works!

King David is said to have written this psalm in praise to God around *3000* years ago.
It's the same God who brought the universe into *being*...
and who *wills everything to be*... or it would simply *disintegrate*.
That includes *you* and *me*.
We are part of a larger Life.
Scripture tells us that we are made in *God's image* (Genesis 1:27).
We have been created by Love *itself* ("God is love" 1 John 4:8).
You and I are *children* of this wonderful God.
**And since God looked on *all* of creation as "good" (Genesis 1:31),
then we are also innately good.**

If you don't *feel* like a *wonderful work* of God... take heart.
It is *not based* on your *feelings*, *behavior* or *achievements*.
It's based on your belovedness as a child of God.

Nothing can *change* that.
Our *goodness* comes from God... *not* from *anything we do*.

So whatever it is about you that you feel disqualifies you from being loved...
that is *exactly the place* where God wants to *love you* and *be with you*.
How else would you know and experience Love that is unconditional?

Open your heart and believe it!

Listen to the song of the day "How Wonderful to Me" on the *Live to Love* album.

15 DELIVERER

Psalm 18:3-4

I love you, Lord, my strength,
Lord, my rock, my fortress, my deliverer,
my God, my rock of refuge, my shield,
my saving horn, my stronghold!
Praised be the Lord, I exclaim!
I have been delivered from my enemies.

Sometimes we are persecuted in life...
but if we rely on God...
we *will be rescued!*

There comes a time when we realize that we are unable to save ourselves.

When we reach the end of our ropes...
God is there to catch us.

Why not turn to God *now*?

Jesus showed us the extent God was willing to go to show us unconditional Love.

If you are in the middle of a storm...
allow God to embrace you
like a father or mother would cradle a child while whispering into your ear,
"I love you... we're going to make it together!"

Follow *that* voice!

Listen to the song of the day "I Want to Follow You" on the *Listen to Your Heart* album.

ETERNAL HOPE

Psalm 23:4

Even when I walk through a dark valley, I fear no harm for you are at my side.

When you feel rejected...buried in troubles...*lost*...
remember that Jesus felt the *same* feelings in the most *extreme* way.

The Son of God chose to be *fully human* and
in the name of *love* and *justice*,
allow himself to *become the one rejected, cast-out, despised,* and finally
nailed to a cross to die in the most painful and humiliating way.

**This is so he could share in our humanity and show us that
no matter *how* bad our struggles...
all of them lead to *new life*.**

Jesus also shows us the true face of God in that Jesus had
no condemnation for his killers...
only forgiveness.

**It is like Jesus saying to each of us,
"Don't you see? No matter *what* you do...
I will hang with you and *not* reject you!"**

This is *unconditional* love poured out.
What seems *unbelievable*...
is *true*.

This is God's Love for us both *now and forever!*

The risen Christ invites us to take the *same path* to new life.

**Listen to the song of the day "Pour Me Out" on the *Give Praise and Thanks*
album.**

17 ALWAYS AND FOREVER

John 8:29

> "The one who sent me is with me.
> He has not left me alone,
> because I always do what is pleasing to him."

Jesus knew who he was.
He came to know this through his close relationship with God.

This way of *being* was no doubt modeled to him
by his father and mother, Joseph and Mary.

**Jesus then cultivated this relationship with God
through *quiet prayer*...
spending time in prayerful meditation alone.**

He allowed God to *name* him and *define* him:
"This is my beloved son,
with whom I am well pleased"
(Matthew 3:17).

Their relationship was *intimate*.

Are *you* in an *intimate relationship* with God?

Your Loving Creator *wants* to *commune* with you.
Set aside some special *one-on-one* time to simply
be present with the Divine Presence.

Listen to the song of the day "How Wonderful to Me" on the *Live to Love* album.

DEATH LEADS TO LIFE | 18

Psalm 31:6

Into your hands I commend my spirit;
you will redeem me,
Lord, God of truth.

Let go of all things that won't last and
allow the great Love of God to lead you to *new life*.

Respond to hate with love and kindness...
then watch as evil is *transformed* to Goodness.

Death is an *illusion of finality*.

In reality...
it is a pathway to *transformation*.
This is true in all of life's "little deaths" as well.

**All "dyings" when placed in the hands of Love...
lead to "risings."**

This is the great lesson of the crucifixion of Jesus.

Let it free you.

Listen to the song of the day "Make Your Way" on the *Mercy Reigns* album.

19 REJOICE

Psalm 30:12-13

You changed my mourning into dancing.
With my whole being, I sing endless praise to you.

Let's face it.
When we are at the top of our game and everything is going our way...
we have no *conscious need* of God.
We would likely not actually *say* that...
but we certainly are not thinking we need *any* help from *anyone*.
It's *only* when things are *not* going according to our plans...
when we encounter some form of *adversity*...
that we turn to our Maker.

I believe a Loving Force...
a Divine Benevolence...
has turned many of my *lowest* points into *highest* points in *due time*.
That's because God is in the *redemption* business.

That's what Love *does*.
God's glory is truly shown in transforming our apparent *defeats* into *victories*.

Jesus was always joining those on the fringes and margins of society...
those who counted as *nothing*...
so that they would know that they truly *did* count.
He healed the sick, restored sight to the blind, and freed the oppressed.
Jesus showed that God's love does not depend on *our* goodness... but *God's*.

Even when *we* ignore *God*... God does *not* ignore *us*.
It's like the unconditional love a parent has for a beloved daughter or son.
Kind of makes you want to *sing* and *dance*... doesn't it?

Listen to the song of the day "Lift Up Our Voices" on the *Give Praise and Thanks* album.

SURE THING

Psalm 18:2-3

I love you, Lord, my strength,
Lord, my rock, my fortress,
my deliverer, my God,
my rock of refuge, my shield,
my saving horn, my stronghold!

God is the thread that is wound through *all that is*.

**God, our Loving Source, is holding all things
and accepting all things as they are.**

God is constantly loving all...
drawing all things to be a part of an
on-going creative masterpiece.

Wherever and whenever we are weak and stumble...
God is with us...
ready to *strengthen* us and *lift* us,
embrace us,
redirect us and *carry* us.

**God is always *with* you and *for* you.
God *will* deliver you!**

Listen to the song of the day "Give Praise and Thanks" on the *Give Praise and Thanks* album.

21 | ETERNALLY GRATEFUL

Psalm 72:17

May his name be blessed forever; as long as the sun, may his name endure.

Jesus was described as the *alpha and the omega*.
His reign is *eternal*.
His love is *everlasting*.

**This is Who our God *is*...
an *Eternal Love*.**

There is no *beginning* and no *ending*.
It is a Love that *never* fails or depletes.

Anchor your life on that foundation.

You are from that Love...
in that Love...
and forever will be in that Love.
Amen.

Listen to the song of the day "Give Praise and Thanks" on the *Give Praise and Thanks* album.

GOD IS FOR YOU

Psalm 145:14

The Lord supports all who are falling and raises up all who are bowed down.

Our Creator is holding everything in a loving embrace.
Everything.

Love is *transforming* everything into the *fullness of being.*
Everything.

There is a *trajectory toward goodness* and *wholeness.*
You and ***I*** are ***included*** in this process. It's happening ***now.***

We need to trust that when things are not going the way we want...
that our Loving Source has *not* abandoned us.
As God told the prophet Isaiah:
"Can a mother forget her infant, be without tenderness for the child of her womb?
Even should she forget, I will never forget you" (Isaiah 49:15).

Usually it takes some form of suffering before we will
***stop clinging to control* and**
allow* ourselves to *fall into the arms of God.

You cannot ultimately save yourself or avoid loss. Eventually we all discover this.
In the end...
there is a loving Creator always wanting to raise you to New Life.
Jesus showed us this...
and it *saves me every day.*

I am called to *follow* his example.
Why not come to know this Loving Presence *now*?

Listen to the song of the day "Let It Be Done to Me" on the *Mercy Reigns* album.

23 GOOD NEWS

John 14:7

> "If you know me, then you will also
> know my Father. From now on,
> you do know him and have seen him."

We all have wrestled with the concept of "God".
Who is our Creator?
**This is all in the realm of mystery...
so beware of people who have it all figured out!**
We see how people tried to get a handle on God all throughout the Old Testament.
God seemed somewhat vindictive and harsh.
**This is because the people were mirroring their own
vindictiveness and harshness onto God.**

When horrible things happened... well then... *God* must have been responsible!
But then we have Jesus telling his followers that they can know God... if they know *him*.
Is Jesus vindictive, judgmental and harsh? *No.*
Is Jesus arrogant, critical, judgmental, and condemning? *No.*
Does Jesus smite people? *No.*
Is Jesus loving, merciful, forgiving, and compassionate? Yes!

He reaches out and spends time with those who are "sinners".
He also stands up for those treated unjustly.
The *only* ones Jesus routinely criticizes, quite pointedly, are the Pharisees...
the *religious leaders* who show no mercy and
who are always holding the people to the letter of the law.
If you are a sinner (and *who isn't?*), then *Jesus wants to be with you.*

That apparently is Who God Is.
This is *Good News!*

Listen to the song of the day "God Is" on the *Give Praise and Thanks* album.

FORGIVENESS IS THE KEY | **24**

John 13:21

Jesus was deeply troubled and testified, "Amen, amen, I say to you, one of you will betray me."

Before we look down on Judas and lay the blame on him...
let us remember that we are *all* Judas.
We have *all* turned our backs on Jesus and his teachings
over and over and over again.
Thankfully, God is an *unconditional lover*.

Jesus told his followers to forgive...
always.

Take a moment and contemplate the forgiveness you've been given so freely.

Now ask yourself,
"Who needs the same kind of forgiveness from me?"

**Could it be that besides someone else...
you need to forgive *yourself*?**

Invite Jesus...
the suffering servant and unconditional lover of all...
into your heart.

Receive forgiveness.

It's *that* easy...
and it's totally *free*!

Listen to the song of the day "Come to Jesus" on the *Live to Love* album.

25 TRANSFORMATION THROUGH LOVE

Psalm 34:2

I will bless the Lord at all times; praise shall be always in my mouth.

It's easy to praise God when things are wonderful...
but what about when things are seemingly *bad?*

God is only capable of loving us *unconditionally.*
("God is love" 1 John 4:8).

Jesus reflected this in the way he lived his life and the way he died as well —
"Father, forgive them, they know not what they do" (Luke 23:34).

So what if we continued to praise and bless the Lord *at all times...*
even in times of *darkness?*

**Our God of Love will *always* lead us to something
amazing and beautiful...
because *that's what Love does.***

Just trust the *process.*
In my life, the seemingly worst times have always turned
into profoundly *transforming* times thanks to the grace of God.
A new "birthing" is underway.

Deliverance and restoration is coming.

Believe that!
Love wins.
Praise God!

**Listen to the song of the day "Lift Up Our Voices" on the *Give Praise and
Thanks* album.**

GOD IS PRESENT | 26

Matthew 24:42

"Therefore, stay awake!
For you do not know on which day
your Lord will come."

More words of wisdom are offered today from the master teacher, Jesus.
This may sound like an ominous warning about
not knowing when our death will come.
But also remember that Jesus said *many* times that
we should *not be afraid*.

Given that, this statement *cannot* be based in *fear*.

Each *moment* is an *opportunity* to *encounter the risen Christ*.
But instead, many times we end up *sleep-walking through life...*
filling each day with meaningless pursuits.

Stay awake!

Each moment is a *gift* where God is *fully present...*
ready to be made known to us in ways we can't *imagine...*
if only we would *cooperate*.

But how often do we find ourselves too immersed in the *noise* of the world?

Take a few minutes of *silence* to allow God to embrace and enlighten you.

**For when you *seek*...
you *will* find.**

Listen to the song of the day "Slow Me Down" on the *Mercy Reigns* album.

27 | THE LOVE EVOLUTION

Romans 8:28

> We know that all things work for good
> for those who love God,
> who are called according to his purpose.

Be reluctant to label anything as "good" or "bad" because
what seems "good" or "bad" may end up being the *opposite*.
**Labels are generally not a good idea because God is not separating the field
but is *including all things* in the grand plan.**

Jesus said not to remove the weeds from the wheat (Matthew 13:29).
He also said not to call anyone "good" but *God* (Luke 18:19).

My ruptured appendix episode a number of years ago seemed like
the *worst* thing that ever happened to me when I was going through it.
At the time if I had been given the opportunity to avoid such a "bad" thing from
happening I would have done so in an instant.

**However, today I am forever grateful that I wasn't
given the opportunity to avoid what became one of the
most *transforming, God-filled, spiritual* experiences of my life.**

In the midst of your struggles and pain...
be present to the *Presence* of God
who will lead you *through* it to great growth and goodness.

Why? Because God *is* Love... and that's what *Love does!*

We only need to surrender to this Love... who will *never* abandon us.

Listen to the song of the day "How Wonderful to Me" on the *Live to Love* album.

SILENT PRESENCE | **28**

In those days he departed to the mountain to pray,
and he spent the night in prayer to God.

Even Jesus withdrew from the noise of everyday life and went into *isolation*...
or to his *"inner room"* as he put it (Matthew 6:6)...
to *pray* to God.

**Praying is opening up the *communication channel*
between you and your Loving Creator.**

It is *quieting* the *endlessly babbling* and *judging* mind...
so we can *hear* God's *voice* in our hearts.

**It is the practice of self-*emptying*...
creating a space for God to fill.**

To many it would seem like a *meaningless* practice...
like you are doing *nothing*.

**In reality...
it is a practice that will open you to the Presence of God and
will *utterly change* your life for the better.**

God wants to *be with you* and transform you.
Spend some time in the *silent* Divine Presence today.

**Listen to the song of the day "Turn Off the Noise" on the *Listen to Your Heart*
album.**

29 | BROKEN AND BLESSED

Matthew 18:12-14

If a man has a hundred sheep and one of them goes astray, will he not leave the ninety-nine in the hills and go in search of the stray? And if he finds it, amen, I say to you, he rejoices more over it than over the ninety-nine that did not stray. In just the same way, it is not the will of your heavenly Father that one of these little ones be lost.

We have all at one time or another (or perhaps *many* times) strayed...
and have made choices that take us away from God.
Isn't it wonderful that God does *not* hold grudges?
**Jesus says that God will *always* pursue us when we stray and
will rejoice when we come back.**

There is no talk of retribution or punishment...only *love*.
After all... God's love is *unconditional*.

And as a matter of fact...
we have *no concept* of what that kind of love *is*
until we *stray* and God finds us *in our brokenness*.
That's *grace*!

How else would we ever experience what Grace *is*?
**Let that thought...
settle into your soul!**

Listen to the song of the day "Radically Okay" on the *Mercy Reigns* album.

ENDLESS WORTH | **30**

Luke 12:6-7

"Are not five sparrows sold for two small coins?
Yet not one of them has escaped the notice of God.
Even the hairs of your head have all been counted.
Do not be afraid.
You are worth more than many sparrows."

God *knows* all and is *in* all.
God's very name is "I Am" (Exodus 3:14).
God is *being itself*.
God *Is*.

We cannot comprehend the One who created both the universe and the amoeba.
Yet Jesus says that God knows *you* intimately down to each hair on your head.
God knows each little sparrow intimately as well.
God's "Is-ness" is woven in everything
and so is God's love because "God is love" (1 John 4:8).
So why do we fear this God of Love?

Could it be all the years of being indoctrinated with the false teaching
that you had to prove your worthiness for God's love and acceptance?
Where do we get this... when Jesus told us *over and over*, "Do not be afraid"?

That's because each of us is a *precious daughter or son of God*.

All people are God's precious sons and daughters.
That means *you* are included.

Know that *deeply*... and remember... the same is true of *everyone else*.

Listen to the song of the day "God Is" on the *Give Praise and Thanks* album.

31 TRUST IN LOVE

Psalm 102:2-3

Lord, hear my prayer; let my cry come to you.
Do not hide your face from me now that
I am in distress. Turn your ear to me;
when I call, answer me quickly.

In the Psalms we see every human emotion expressed to God.
It is part of the human experience to call out to God for help in time of need.
Have you ever noticed how that seems *instinctual*?
**And thanks to the teaching of Jesus,
we believe that God actually *listens* and *cares*!**

Jesus called God "Abba" which is translated as an *intimate* term for father...
somewhat like "daddy". It's as though our Creator is the best of both *father* and *mother*.
**The God that Jesus spoke to was not *stern*, *critical* or *judgmental*.
God was not *far away* but *readily accessible*... and so it is *now*.**

But sometimes it seems as though God is *not* answering our calls.
Could it be that God is not absent... but that the silence *is an answer*?
We are all very impatient. I know *I am*. We want *quick fixes*.
**But let us trust that God *is* answering us because
we are *beloved sons and daughters*.**

As Rainer Maria Rilke wrote, "Live the questions now.
Perhaps you will then gradually, without noticing it,
live along some distant day into the answer."

**Perhaps the *waiting* is part of the Loving Process
that will lead us to a deeper trust, faith, healing, wholeness.**

**Listen to the song of the day "You'll Lead Me" on the Listen to Your Heart
album.**

LOVE IS THE ANSWER | I

Mark: 12:30-31

"You shall love the Lord your God
with all your heart,
with all your soul,
with all your mind,
and with all your strength.
The second is this:
You shall love your neighbor as yourself.
There is no other commandment
greater than these."

Jesus modeled perfect unconditional love for us.
He loved even when he was rejected, persecuted, and killed.
The ultimate demonstration was forgiving those who killed him
while hanging on the cross.
This is the kind of love God has for *you*.

Doesn't that just *melt your heart*?
Allow that feeling to envelope you.

We are incapable of loving perfectly...
but it is precisely *through that imperfection* that
we come to realize God's unconditional love.

To that... I can only say,
"Amen!"

Listen to the song of the day "God Is" on the *Give Praise and Thanks* album.

2 THANKS BE TO GOD

Psalm 118:1

Give thanks to the Lord, who is good, whose love endures forever.

Do you believe this?

Many people seem to have a *toxic* image of God as
a judgmental ogre looking to punish us.
But if God *is* love as scripture tells us (1 John 4:8)
and if God is like Jesus as Jesus was quoted as saying (John 14:7)...
then a 'punishing God' is certainly a *false* image.
Have we not all experienced the love and comfort of God in times of sorrow and pain...
as well as experienced the love of God in times of joy and pleasure?
Jesus showed us the true nature of God.

He shared in the joy and he shared in the suffering.
He untiringly reached out to heal those in need.

**When you feel the pain that comes along the path of life,
know that God *hangs* with you...
suffers with you...
cries with you...
and *comforts* you.**

Our loving Creator inspires others to come to our aid as well.
Perhaps *you* have been inspired to reach out to someone in need?
God's love does not depend on our response, beliefs, or actions.
It is *always freely given*.

It is eternally abundant.
Give thanks!

Listen to the song of the day "Give Praise and Thanks" on the *Give Praise and Thanks* album.

LET GO TO LIVE

Psalm 31:6

Into your hands I commend my spirit; you will redeem me, Lord, faithful God.

Jesus shows us the face of God throughout his ministry... all the way to the end.
He responds even to his persecutors and killers with love, mercy, and forgiveness.
He hangs on the cross *for* you and me (not *in place of*) and *with* you and me.
No matter what suffering or injustice you are going through...
Jesus is hanging there with you and showing you that this is *not* the end.
Love wins... not *death*.

Jesus also shows us that making someone the scapegoat...
trying to "get rid" of someone you have deemed the "problem" or a trouble-maker...
is wrong.
He *becomes* the one "thrown-out" and rejected... and then *forgives*.
Gaze upon him on the cross and see the result of engaging in this kind of "scapegoating"!
Jesus also shows us how to respond to life's struggles.
This is our model to live by... the "way and the truth and the life" (John 14:6).
This is the way that the Kingdom of God becomes *present*.
We must go *through* the struggle.

We must learn to *sit in the pain*.
It sounds so *counterintuitive*... but I have found it to be true.
Jesus shows us that it's the *way to new life*. A "birthing" is underway.
To borrow a line from author Brené Brown,
your religion should be a *midwife* not an *epidural*.
No matter what suffering or injustice you are going through...
Jesus is hanging there with you and showing you that this is *not* the end.

A *new beginning* is underway.
Your resurrection is coming!

Listen to the song of the day "Mercy Reigns" on the *Mercy Reigns* album.

4 PRESENCE DISSOLVES WORRY

2 Corinthians 6:2

Behold, now is a very acceptable time; behold, now is the day of salvation.

This whole business about *being present* and *being centered in the now*...
is *not* some *new age* concoction.

St. Paul was aware of the importance of the *moment*.

**Saints and mystics were all aware that the only time that is *real*...
the only time that you can connect with the Living God...
is *now*.**

What happened *yesterday* is a *shadow* and
what is to happen in the *future* is *unknown*.

**God is present *here* and *now* and it's the *only* place and time
where you can *connect* to your Loving Source.**

It's the *only* place and time where you can rest in a Love that is *unconditional*...
a Love that *completes* and *saves* you.

Stop and take a few *slow, deep* breaths.
Allow that Presence to fill you.

***Now* is a very *acceptable time*!**

Listen to the song of the day "Slow Me Down" on the *Mercy Reigns* album.

KEEP THE FAITH | 5

Psalm 34:19

The Lord is close to the brokenhearted, saves those whose spirit is crushed.

God *is* love and you are made in God's image.

**You are a *child of God*...
part of our Loving Creator's grand plan
from the beginning of time.**

If you are struggling...
if you feel you can't do it alone...
if something has happened that has caused you great pain...
call on God for help.

Your Maker *longs* to *free* you from fear, despair, and all pain.

**The way to transformation is by going
through the struggle with Jesus and
allowing God to raise you to *new life*.**

Jesus was always seeking out the lost...
reaching out to them with total acceptance and healing.

Call out to him!

He is always *with* you in your time of need.

Listen to the song of the day "Love Will Always Lead You Home" on the *Mercy Reigns* album.

6 PEACE OF CHRIST

Matthew 14:30-31

But when Peter saw how strong the wind was he
became frightened; and, beginning to sink,
he cried out, "Lord, save me!"
Immediately Jesus stretched out his hand and
caught him, and said to him,
"O you of little faith, why did you doubt?"

We all face times of struggle... when the seas of life are full of turmoil and toss us about.
These are the times that test our faith.
These are the times we are called to step out of the boat and trust.

These are the times that will build our character.
But, yes, these are also the times when we can falter from fear.
Have courage!

Jesus showed us that God is not a God who is poised to criticize,
punish, and seek retribution when we struggle or fail...
but a God who reaches out to lift us and embrace us.
It is *through* our struggles and failures that we learn and experience
the unconditional love of God.
How else would we ever experience it?

Jesus showed us that God wants each of us to be *redeemed, restored,* and *made whole.*
When Peter called out...
the response from Jesus was immediate.
So... *why be afraid*?
God will *never* abandon you!

Listen to the song of the day "Come to Jesus" on the *Live to Love* album.

NOW AND FOREVER

John 8:51

"Amen, amen, I say to you, whoever keeps my word will never see death."

This moment is *eternal*.
There will never be anything other than *this* moment...
now.

Jesus wants you to experience the wonders of God's love *right now* and says we *can*...
if we keep his word and remain in his word (John 8:31-32).
Christ *is* the Word...
the *blueprint* of all creation.

As St. Paul said, "Christ is all and in all" (Colossians 3:11).
Jesus said that he is "the way, the truth and the life" (John 14:6).
He showed us that no struggle or hardship...
even *crucifixion*...
can prevent New Life from happening!

The name "Jesus" literally means "Yahweh saves."
Open yourself to that salvation *now*... in *this* moment...
and *follow* where Jesus' word leads you.

New Life is at hand *now*...
and *now*...
and *now*...
as it *will be* at the *moment* of physical death.

Listen to the song of the day "Make Your Way" on the *Mercy Reigns* album.

8 AMAZING GRACE

Micah 7:18-19

Who is there like you,
the God who removes guilt and pardons
sin for the remnant of his inheritance;
And will again have compassion on us,
treading underfoot our guilt?

Isn't God *amazing*?

Our Loving Creator *constantly pours out* Love upon us...
accepting us *exactly who we* are in our imperfection...
yearns to be with us...
and who would *do anything* to be with us for eternity...
even becoming human and dying on a cross to say, *"I love you!"*

**God, from age to age,
you have loved each of us...
*before time began!***

As St. Paul said in Romans 8:38-39,
"For I am convinced that neither death, nor life,
nor angels, nor principalities,
nor *present things*, nor *future things*,
nor powers, nor height, nor depth,
nor *any other creature* will be able to *separate us* from the
love of God in Christ Jesus our Lord."

This is *Good News*!

Listen to the song of the day "God Is" on the *Give Praise and Thanks* album.

DEATH LEADS TO LIFE

John 20:15-16

Jesus said to her, "Woman, why are you weeping? Whom are you looking for?" She thought it was the gardener and said to him, "Sir, if you carried him away, tell me where you laid him, and I will take him." Jesus said to her, "Mary!" She turned and said to him in Hebrew, "Rabbouni," which means "Teacher".

How hard it is to lose someone we love.
Mary of Magdala had witnessed her beloved friend...
the one who had turned her life around... brutally killed on the cross.
**Mary of Magdala had been one of the few
who did not abandon Jesus when he was crucified.**

She was also one of the few who were there when his body was taken from the cross.
When Jesus' followers were all hiding in fear...
she had come to hold vigil at his tomb.
She must have been *crushed* by all that had happened.

What *amazing love* she must have had for him!
What joy she must have experienced...
and what joy we should *all* experience in realizing that the risen Christ *lives*!
Death is *not* the end.

Allow this to lift you!
Death leads to life! *Alleluia*!

Listen to the song of the day "Lift Up Our Voices" on the *Give Praise and Thanks* album.

10 | UNCONDITIONAL LOVE

Psalm 27:13-14

But I believe I shall enjoy the Lord's goodness
in the land of the living. Wait for the Lord,
take courage; be stouthearted, wait for the Lord!

Life is *not* some game in which we try to be *good enough*
to make the cut to get to heaven one day.
God's love *cannot be earned*. It's *freely given*!
"It's heaven all the way to heaven" as St. Catherine of Siena is quoted as saying.
**God wants us to experience love, mercy, forgiveness, and compassion *now*,
"in the land of the living,"**
so that we can be *transformed* and *share* that love with others.

That is how we take part in building the kingdom of God here on earth.
It's not about *our* goodness *earning* God's love...
but *God's* goodness poured out *generously* and *unconditionally* upon us *now*.
God does not love me because *I* am good but because *God* is good, generous and loving.
God *is* Love.

Allow that knowledge to *sink in*.
Rest in it.
And if you are not experiencing this amazing acceptance and love at the moment...
take courage!
Wait for the Lord!
Be *still*.
Be.
While you are consciously waiting...
you are *being present*.
In that Presence...
I guarantee that you will find the unconditional love and compassion of God.

Listen to the song of the day "Slow Me Down" on the *Mercy Reigns* album.

BE AT PEACE | II

Luke 24:36-37

Jesus stood in their midst and said to them, "Peace be with you." But they were startled and terrified and thought that they were seeing a ghost. Then he said to them, "Why are you troubled? And why do questions arise in your hearts?"

Jesus appeared to his disciples after the resurrection...
the ones who had abandoned him...
the ones who had turned their backs and ran away.
But Jesus didn't return with threats of reprisal and punishment.

He didn't even call them on the carpet and scold them.
No... instead Jesus said, "Peace be with you."
We've *all* been there.
We've *all* turned our backs on Jesus.

We've all chosen our own selfish interests over choices
we knew were more *caring* and *compassionate* to others.
We have all been troubled and have doubted.

But we are told that the risen Christ stood in the midst of all
who had turned their backs on him and offered "peace."
Fear and doubt *dissolve* in the presence of the risen Christ.

This is the Love that holds *all* things together...
the so-called *good* and *bad*...
and offers the peace of *acceptance*.
The peace of Christ *is with you*.

Listen to the song of the day "Radically Okay" on the *Mercy Reigns* album.

12 | LOVE WINS

Psalm 27:1

The Lord is my light and my salvation;
whom do I fear?
The Lord is my life's refuge;
of whom am I afraid?

One thing Jesus told his followers *over and over* was to *not be afraid.*

**Fear is produced by the *ego* over not wanting to lose
power, prestige, or possessions
which are all *masks* and *illusions* that will soon or later *disappear*.**

Fear *paralyzes* us from moving forward due to the *risk of loss*.
We willingly must *let go* of our ego's fears so that we can *grow*.

The *true you* is *not* your power, prestige, or possessions.
The true you is the *unique, beloved daughter or son of God* that you are.

That's it.
You are significant and infinitely loved *just as you are...*
warts, blemishes, and weaknesses included.

You do not have to earn or merit God's love or acceptance.

Jesus showed us this quite clearly. If you doubt this...
simply read the story of the "Prodigal Son" (Luke 15:11-32).
So now that you know that your Creator loves you *unconditionally...*
what is there to fear?

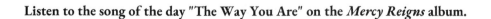

Listen to the song of the day "The Way You Are" on the *Mercy Reigns* album.

GOSPEL OF THE KINGDOM

Matthew 9:35-36

Jesus went around to all the towns and villages, teaching in their synagogues, proclaiming the gospel of the kingdom, and curing every disease and illness. At the sight of the crowds, his heart was moved with pity for them because they were troubled and abandoned, like sheep without a shepherd.

Do you ever feel like one of the people in this crowd?
Are you troubled over something or feel abandoned?
**Each of us has a wounded place inside in need of
unconditional love and compassion.**

We have an issue or a struggle that we just can't seem to deal with on our own.
It is a part of the human condition that Jesus knew well.
**Jesus did not come to these people with a message of condemnation or fear.
He came with a message of compassion and comfort.**

Jesus went everywhere "proclaiming the gospel of the kingdom,
and curing every disease and illness."
He wanted to be with the people who were suffering and in need of help.
He wanted them to know that *all* were *included* and *accepted* in the eyes of God.
In the "gospel of the kingdom", Love overcomes and prevails.

God's *grace* wins the day!
The risen Christ wants to be *your* shepherd today.
Bring your troubles to Him.

Listen to the song of the day "Love Will Always Lead You Home" on the *Mercy Reigns* album.

14 HAVE FAITH

Psalm 69:21

Insult has broken my heart, and I am weak;
I looked for compassion, but there was none,
for comforters, but found none.

I can truly empathize with the psalmist's words when I look over
the atrocities going on in the world.
There is so much cruelty and heartless behavior.
Jesus experienced the *worst* of it.
He *became the one spurned*...
the *outcast*, the *scapegoat*...
so that we could see just how *wrong* and *ugly* it is.

He knows what it's like to be *completely rejected* and *unjustly persecuted*.
So you know that Jesus can *empathize* with us and *comfort* us
when we experience being persecuted and rejected.

Jesus became the most thoroughly rejected one...
so that he could show us exactly what unconditional love *is* by
forgiving his persecutors *even when they didn't ask for forgiveness*.
Jesus became the outcast so that he could show us,
once and for all, that
Love wins.

Death leads to *life*.
God *is* Love.
Acts of love *are* overwhelming the acts of hate all over the world each day.

May the comfort of this awareness rest in your heart...
and may you *share* it with *others*.

Listen to the song of the day "Mercy Reigns" on the *Mercy Reigns* album.

RADICAL GRACE

John 6:37-39

"Everything that the Father gives me
will come to me,
and I will not reject anyone who comes to me,
because I came down from heaven
not to do my own will,
but the will of the one who sent me.
And this is the will of the one who sent me,
that I should not lose anything of what He gave me,
but that I should raise it [on] the last day."

How *comforting* are these words of Jesus!
They reflect a Love that is *unconditional*.

This does not mean that our actions don't have consequences... as they surely *do*.
It just means that our hurtful actions do *not nullify* the love that God has for us.

We will no doubt have to face any pain we caused for others when we face our Creator...
but we will face it in the light of an *Eternal Love*.
What Jesus is saying is that God loves us like any *loving parent* would love us...
***times infinity*.**

So *let go* of any *fear* or *thoughts of unworthiness*...
and *slowly re-read* the words of Jesus above.
Allow them settle in your heart.
Then live in the freedom of God's amazing grace.

**Listen to the song of the day "God's Love Is All You Need" on the *Listen to Your
Heart* album.**

16 GOD SPEAKS IN SILENCE

John 6:45

"Everyone who listens to my Father and learns from him comes to me."

It's not what we *do* that brings us closer to God,
but what we *let be done to us* by God.
Our lives are *not* an *achievement contest* or a *life-long SAT test!*

It's about simply *being in relationship* with of our Loving Creator.

Allow God to draw you closer.
Listen.
Hear that *you* are God's *beloved child.*
Bask in that *awareness.*

**Then your actions will not be to *merit* or *achieve* anything...
but will simply be your *response to being loved*.**

Come to Christ *in your brokenness...*
just as you are.
Allow God's unconditional love to *transform* you.
It's only then that you can be a channel
of that same Love and Compassion to others.

**For this to happen...
it's essential to set aside quiet time
in the presence of the *Divine Presence*.**

Just listen.

**Listen to the song of the day "Turn Off the Noise" on the *Listen to Your Heart*
album.**

LAYING DOWN YOUR LIFE

John 3:16-17

For God so loved the world that
He gave his only Son,
so that everyone who believes in him might not
perish but might have eternal life.
For God did not send his Son
into the world to condemn the world,
but that the world might be saved through him.

God taking on flesh in Jesus was not "plan B" but "plan A".
This is what many theologians believe... and so do I.
God becoming human bridges the gap of spirit and matter.

God is part of it all.
God *celebrates* with us... and *suffers* with us as well.
**God shows us that the path to *wholeness* (salvation) is the path of
letting go of power, prestige, and possessions.**

It's the path of *becoming one with all.*
Jesus said, "I am the way and the truth and the life" (John 14:6).
God did not send his Son to condemn us but to save us (*show us the way to wholeness*)...
even though God knew we would kill Jesus.
God (in Jesus) actually became one of us in the flesh.
**Matter became divine.
The earth and all creation became filled with God.**

Let us take a few moments to contemplate such self-emptying Love... and be thankful!

Listen to the song of the day "Come to Jesus" on the *Live to Love* album.

18 | GIVE PRAISE AND THANKS

Psalm 34:2

I will bless the Lord at all times; praise shall be always in my mouth.

This is a common theme in the spiritual writings throughout history.

Even in the struggles...
spiritually conscious people were thanking and praising God.

**God can take the seemingly *bad* situations...
and transform them for *good*...
if you allow your loving Creator to work through you.**

Trust that God is in the process of leading you through the darkest struggles...
to the brightest victories.

New life is *always* in the making.

Ask God for the faith to believe this.
Praise God!

Listen to the song of the day "Give Praise and Thanks" on the *Give Praise and Thanks* album.

BORN ANEW | 19

John 3:3

"Amen, amen, I say to you,
no one can see the kingdom of God
without being born from above."

The Pharisees were the religious leaders who had all the answers based on the law.
But Jesus *broke* laws sometimes when he was healing people.

One Pharisee named Nicodemus came to Jesus in the secrecy of the night,
looking for explanations.

Jesus gave him something *beyond* religious answers.

Black and *white* theological information is a nice foundation to build on,
but it does not bring about the transformative journey into the kingdom of God.

For that there must be a *rebirth from above*.

When we come to the end of our rope and see that
we are *unable to save ourselves* with our answers,
then we are open to experience the transformative
unconditional love, mercy, and forgiveness of God.

**Then it's not about *our* goodness...
but *God's*.**

The kingdom of God is truly at hand right *here and now*
for those who are willing to *die to themselves*...
so God can give birth to something new.

**Listen to the song of the day "Pour Me Out" on the *Give Praise and Thanks*
album.**

20 ALL ARE WELCOME

John 10:9

> "I am the gate.
> Whoever enters through me will be saved,
> and will come in and go out
> and find pasture."

Jesus said he was "the way and the truth and the life (John 14:6)."

He shows us the *template* of how to live so that
we can be the *full, unique* reflections of God's love that only *each* of us can be.

Following his way is like entering a gate.
This gate leads us to safety as well as freedom.

Through it we come to know God's *unconditional love* and *mercy*.
Through it we also are freed of all the worldly distractions
that divert us from being our *true selves*.

We are promised genuine freedom and inner peace.

Entering this gate is possible in *each* and *every* moment.

All are invited.

The time to do it...
is *now*.

Listen to the song of the day "All Are Welcome" on the *Give Praise and Thanks* album.

GOOD SHEPHERD | 21

John 10:27-28

"My sheep hear my voice;
I know them, and they follow me.
I give them eternal life,
and they shall never perish.
No one can take them out of my hand."

We are the sheep of the Good Shepherd who cares tenderly for each of us.

Jesus said he knows us...
which means he knows both the light and the shadow side of each of us.

**Jesus doesn't say we have to get rid of the shadow side
before he will care for us.**

This is the Love of God!

The love of God does *not* depend on our *worthiness*.

We *don't* have to *merit* it.
God's love is a *gift*.
Eternal life is a *gift*.

Jesus promises that *no one* can take us out of his hand.
Doesn't that make you want to *listen* for his voice...
and to *follow*?

I guarantee it will lead you to a place of inner peace.

Listen to the song of the day "I Will Give You Rest" on the *Live to Love* album.

22 | TRUE LIFE

John 10:10

"I came so that they might have life and have it more abundantly."

Jesus did not become human to give us an *evacuation plan to heaven*.

He came that we "might have life (*now*) and have it more abundantly (*now!*)."

Jesus showed us how to be *fully alive* as human beings.

As St. Irenaeus said,
"The glory of God is the human being fully alive."

**If we follow Jesus and allow him to shepherd us...
we will have life to the full *now*.**

It is through a daily practice of dying and rising...
dying to our false self (created by our egos) so that our true self can *rise*...
that we will become our *true selves*.

**Let's begin again...
now...
being who you are:
A child of God.**

If you are being *you* and living for the kingdom of God *now*...
then when death *does* come...
your *now* will be abundant *indeed!*

Listen to the song of the day "How Wonderful to Me" on the *Live to Love* album.

SAVING LIGHT

John 12:46

"I came into the world as light,
so that everyone who believes in me
might not remain in darkness."

It's easy to become lost in the noise of the world.
There are so many competing messages telling us *this* is the way to happiness.

So why are there so many unfulfilled and unhappy people?

Jesus said that he was "the way, the truth, and the life" (John 14:6).

If you want to find new life...
allow the Light to shine upon you.

**If you are yearning for light in your darkness...
come to Jesus.**

Read and meditate on the gospels.

You *don't* have to have your life together.

Worthiness is *not* a factor.

The Light is a *free gift*.

Jesus rejects *no one*!

Listen to the song of the day "I Stand in the Light" on the *Mercy Reigns* album.

24 | REASON TO REJOICE

Psalm 89:2-3

The promises of the Lord I will sing forever,
proclaim your loyalty through all ages.
For you said, "My love is established forever;
my loyalty will stand as long as the heavens."

God loved us from the very beginning...
before the *beginning of time* as we know it.
That's beyond our mind's ability to grasp.
God *is* Love (1 John 4:8). That *cannot change*.

What does Love *do*? Love can *only love*.
There is no *vengeance* in love.
Love is kind. It endures all things and never fails (1 Corinthians 13:4-8).

God (Love) does not change by whims and moods like we do.
God simply loves and promises to do so *forever*.

Jesus demonstrated God's love with his life.
Even when people killed him on the cross...
his response was *forgiveness*.
"Father, forgive them, they know not what they do" (Luke 23:34).
Then the resurrected Christ didn't seek retribution or reproach
against those who killed or abandoned him...
but offered peace: "Peace be with you" (John 20:19).
That is a response anchored in Infinite Love.
This is the love that *sustains* us and *partners* with us *each* moment!
This is the love our Creator has for us!
Alleluia!

Listen to the song of the day "Lift Up Our Voices" on the *Give Praise and Thanks* album.

BE STILL | 25

Cast all your worries upon him because he cares for you.

Why do we worry?

How can worry *possibly help us*?

I sometimes catch my mind as it repeats the same old "what if?" scenarios...
usually with painful outcomes!
Thankfully, I now also hear what's becoming a *more familiar* "other" voice.

It says, *"Do not fear."*

Jesus said that over and over.
"Can any of you by worrying add a single moment to your life-span?" (Matthew 6:27)
The only time that is real...
is *now*.
God is in *this* moment.

And in *this* moment God loves us *thoroughly* and *completely* just as we are.

There is *nothing* we have to do to earn that love.
We have *nothing* to prove.

How freeing that is...
if you only *believe* it!

Why not accept this Good News? It is the Gospel!
Open yourself to God's abiding Presence within you...
then feel your worries *dissolve*.

Listen to the song of the day "The Way You Are" on the *Mercy Reigns* album.

26 | PATH TO LIFE

Acts 14:22

They strengthened the spirits of the disciples
and exhorted them to persevere in the faith,
saying, "It is necessary for us to undergo many
hardships to enter the kingdom of God."

Paul and Barnabas were rallying the followers of Jesus
in the aftermath of his death and resurrection.

It was *not easy* to be a follower of Christ... and *still isn't*.

Paul had literally been *stoned* but somehow survived.
Most of the apostles would be martyred.
Jesus had warned his followers that they would be persecuted.
But following Jesus *is* a path that leads to true life.

The path requires *dying to self...*
the false *ego-centered* self...
so that the *true self* can rise.
It means *carrying your cross...*
being an agent of mercy, compassion, forgiveness, and justice
while facing the resulting repercussions.

**Jesus showed us that this path leads to
*growth, transformation, wholeness, and being our true selves.***

It's the *process* through which we begin to experience
the building of the kingdom of God in the *present*.
What could be more important?

**Listen to the song of the day "Take the Road Less Traveled" on the *Live to Love*
album.**

BE MADE WHOLE

Luke 7:20, 22

When the men came to Jesus, they said,
"John the Baptist has sent us to you to ask,
'Are you the one who is to come,
or should we look for another?'"
And he said to them in reply,
"Go and tell John what you have seen and heard:
the blind regain their sight, the lame walk,
lepers are cleansed, the deaf hear, the dead are raised,
the poor have the good news proclaimed to them."

Jesus was *not* the type of Messiah that any Jew had expected.
They wanted a military ruler to put them into power.
John the Baptist was given the grace to recognize the Promised One...
but even *he* needed *reassurance.*

Who are you looking for to save you?

Who or *what* are you *expecting* to fill the gaping hole in your heart...
to bring you satisfaction and completion?
God created that hole in your heart so that only God can fill it.

Follow Jesus...
the Wounded Healer...
who delivered the broken to wholeness.
This is what God promises for you.

**Listen to the song of the day "I Want to Follow You" on the *Listen to Your Heart*
album.**

28 TRANSFORMED BY GRACE

Acts 9:15-16

But the Lord said to him, "Go, for this man is a chosen instrument of mine to carry my name before Gentiles, kings, and Israelites, and I will show him what he will have to suffer for my name."

It seems many people wrestle with feelings of *unworthiness*...
that they're *not good enough* and that they just don't measure up to God's demands.
**From the *deepest* part of my heart I know that
God wants me to tell you that this is totally *untrue*!**
God loves us *in* our weaknesses and failings.
That is what *unconditional* love *means*!
Each of us is loved as a newborn son or daughter.
God *knows full well* of our *inability* to be perfect because that's the way God made us.

Saul was the *worst of the worst*.
He was *persecuting* Christians... even leading them to their deaths.
But God chose *him* to be an instrument to preach the name of Jesus!
Saul became St. Paul... the most influential evangelist *ever*.
**His zeal for the Lord no doubt came directly from his knowledge
that he had been forgiven and that it had
nothing to do with his worthiness, ability, or merit.**

It was *pure* Grace.
It was simply a gift from God.
God's love is *transforming*.
Accept it.
Allow it to transform *you*.

Listen to the song of the day "Changed" on the *Give Praise and Thanks* album.

GOD OF LOVE

John 14:7

"If you know me, then you will also know my Father."

Jesus reaches out in unconditional love to *all*.

He stood up to any injustice but, while doing so,
never condemned or caused any harm.

**Jesus was always reaching out to *include* those who had been rejected.
He instructed us to love our enemies and pray for those who persecute us.
(Matthew 5:44)**

Even when unjustly put to death,
he extended *mercy, compassion, and forgiveness* —
"Father, forgive them, they know not what they do" (Luke 23:34).

Jesus says that if we know *him*...
then we also know *God*.

**So...
why would we *fear* such a *God*?**

This is *Good News*!

Listen to the song of the day "God Is" on the *Give Praise and Thanks* album.

30 | ALL BELONG

Luke 15:4-6

"What man among you having a hundred sheep and losing one of them would not leave the ninety-nine in the desert and go after the lost one until he finds it? And when he does find it, he sets it on his shoulders with great joy and, upon his arrival home, he calls together his friends and neighbors and says to them, 'Rejoice with me because I have found my lost sheep.'"

If you feel *lost* in any way...
or like there is something about you that if anyone knew...
they could not possibly love you...
know that God loves you *just the way you are*.
Jesus tells us in today's scripture verses the amazing depth of God's care for *you*.

God will *never* give up on you or turn away from you...
but instead will *relentlessly pursue* you.
And wherever it is inside you that you feel no one could possibly love you...
or whatever it is that you did that you are ashamed of...
know that that is *exactly* where God wants to *embrace* you...
accept you...
and call you *beloved* "son" or "daughter."
God's love does *not* depend on *your* goodness...
but *God's*.
Rest in *that*.

Listen to the song of the day "I Will Give You Rest" on the *Live to Love* album.

BASK IN SILENCE | I

Acts 16:13-14

On the Sabbath we went outside the city gate along the river where we thought there would be a place of prayer. We sat and spoke with the women who had gathered there. One of them, a woman named Lydia... listened, and the Lord opened her heart to pay attention to what Paul was saying.

Sometimes we need to find a place of prayer...
a *tranquil* place that allows us to put aside the distractions of life.
Then, we need *let go*.
Let go of the *thoughts* that constantly *flood* our brains...
let go of our *personal agendas.*
Let go.

Be present.
Be silent.
Listen.
**As thoughts pop up... simply *observe* them...
and *allow* them to *dissolve*.**

Open your heart and pay attention to the *inner voice* there.
Set aside special silent time each day to be present to the Divine Presence and
see how your heart is opened to new insights, peace and love.
**Then... you'll find you will be able to enter this *silent place of peace*...
even amid the *clamor* and *turbulence* of any situation.**

Let this peace fill you now.

**Listen to the song of the day "Turn Off the Noise" on the *Listen to Your Heart*
album.**

125

2 BELIEVE

John 20:16

Jesus said to her, "Mary!" She turned and said to him in Hebrew, "Rabbouni," which means "Teacher".

Sometimes we feel *abandoned*.

I vividly remember a day when I was very sick in a hospital bed following a ruptured appendix. In the middle of the night... I felt scared, helpless and alone.

Then... suddenly I was enveloped by an overwhelming Compassion and I "heard" a voice in my heart that said,

"I love you. You don't have to do anything to merit my love."

I knew in that amazing moment that God loved *all* people *unconditionally* and was intimately *with* me *in* my struggle.

I was *not* alone.

I had experienced Grace.

Mary of Magdala must have felt abandoned at the tomb of Jesus, grief-stricken over his death.

She had witnessed her close friend's crucifixion and had been there at his entombment.

It seemed like *defeat*!

But how could this be?

This was her "disorienting dilemma".

She returned to the tomb to find it empty.

Mary had *never stopped* following Jesus... even when all seemed lost.

It was then in her despair and seeming abandonment that she came face to face with the resurrected Christ and experienced firsthand the ultimate victory of Love over death.

Life does *not* end... but is *transformed*!

All struggles lead to new life in the Light of Love.

Can you imagine Mary's elation to be the *first* to witness this... and the *first* commissioned to tell the Good News?

Believe and *persevere* in the knowledge that Love is victorious!

Listen to the song of the day "Mercy Reigns" on the *Mercy Reigns* album.

SOURCE OF LIFE |

Acts 17:24-25

"The God who made the world and all that is in it,
the Lord of heaven and earth,
does not dwell in sanctuaries made by human
hands, nor is he served by human hands
because he needs anything.
Rather it is he who gives to
everyone life and breath and everything."

God is *so beyond* any concept our minds can construct...
mystery within mystery within mystery.

**Just by saying the word "God" I *diminish* our Creator...
boxing up the *Infinite* in a *three-letter word*.
This Source of Life is *Love* itself!**

It needs *nothing* from us.
And yet this same Infinite Mystery loves you and me as a *beloved son or daughter*!
We **and *all of creation* are *accepted* and *belong*.**

Whatever might be your struggle today...
allow this Love to fill you and simply be with you.
God's love conquers all pain and hardships.

Death itself dissolves in the Light of Love.
It is a Love that is *unconditional* and *never-ending*.
It is all you need *now* and *forever*.

Listen to the song of the day "Breathe On Me" on the *Listen to Your Heart* album.

4 COMPASSION OF CHRIST

John 14:27

> "Peace I leave with you; my peace I give to you.
> Not as the world gives do I give it to you.
> Do not let your hearts be troubled or afraid."

Do you have inner peace?
If you're like me... sometimes you find yourself *anxious* and *worried*.
When this happens... it's good to catch it at the *first inkling*.

Contemplative prayer or meditation is an invaluable practice to help you do this.
It helps you to live in the present moment.
Many times our worries are due to fears over a *perceived lack* of something.
The truth is... you *are enough* and you *have enough*.
When anxiousness arises... simply *observe* the feeling.
Just *observe* it.
Realize that the person observing it... your *true self*...
is completely *whole* and *fine*.

Sure... there might be some things going on that you don't like...
but your *true self* is *secure*.
The feelings you are having are *feelings*... but they aren't *you!*
In the presence of the *Divine Presence*...
the true *you* is perfectly loved and embraced *as is*.

As St. Paul said, "Then the peace of God that surpasses all understanding
will guard your hearts and minds in Christ Jesus" (Philippians 4:7).
Jesus brought this message of peace to his followers and
continues to *offer it* to the *whole world*.
It is ours to *accept* or *reject*.
Why not accept it now?

Listen to the song of the day "God's Love Is All You Need" on the *Listen to Your Heart* album.

TRUST IN LOVE

John 16:20

"Amen, amen, I say to you, you will weep and mourn, while the world rejoices; you will grieve, but your grief will become joy."

We *all* go through hard times.
But be careful about labeling these times as "bad".

In today's scripture verse, Jesus was preparing his followers for his death and resurrection.
He goes on to say that when a woman gives birth,
she no longer remembers the pain of labor...
she only experiences the joy of the newborn child.

For the *joy* of the *birth* of something *new* in our lives...
we have to go through the *labor pains*.
***Change* and *paradigm shifts* are *never easy*.**

The *self-centered* ways that we sought satisfaction as a child have to be released
so we are able to experience the true joy of *giving*.
The dissolving of the illusion that
"I am the center of the universe" is usually a painful process...
but necessary in becoming who I truly am.
Take a moment to focus on your breathing.
When you do...
you will be *totally present*.
Let go into the Presence and know that God *is with you*.

You are a child of God...
wholly *loved* and *accepted*.
Let go of your judgments and *allow* Love to *transform* you.

Listen to the song of the day "Changed" on the *Give Praise and Thanks* album.

6 BE GLAD

Psalm 96:1-2

Sing to the Lord a new song;
sing to the Lord, all the earth.
Sing to the Lord, bless his name;
announce his salvation day after day.

The Maker of the universe made *you*.
The God of all creation wanted *you* to be a part of it.

As St. Paul said, "Blessed be the God and Father of our Lord Jesus Christ...
as He chose us in him, before the foundation of the world,
to be holy and without blemish before him.
In love He destined us for adoption to himself through Jesus Christ,
in accord with the favor of his will,
for the praise of the glory of his grace that He granted us in the beloved"
(Ephesians 1: 3-6).

**We know from looking at the life of Jesus that
God's love for *each* of us is *unconditional*.**

He responds to persecution with *compassion* and to crucifixion with *forgiveness*.
No matter what we do... we can't make God love us any more... or any less.

God's love for each of us is already *infinite*.
So... what is there to *fear*?
Salvation is *freely given*.

How can you keep from singing?

Listen to the song of the day "Sing a New Song" on the *Live to Love* album.

REJOICE

Psalm 138:2

I praise your name for your fidelity and love. For you have exalted over all your name and your promise.

Our Loving Creator chose to create us out of sheer *generosity* and *love*.

We are cherished as *daughters* and *sons* with a love *beyond measure*.

This same *Source of Life* is as close to each of us as the *air* we *breathe*.

The same wondrous God who made the galaxies and
continues to create in each moment...
also resides in our *innermost being* and wants nothing more than
to be with each of us *exactly as we are*.

You do *not* have to *earn* or *merit* this love.

It is *always given* and *never withdrawn*.
Allow this truth to *sink in*.

**Turn to this Love that will *never* reject you,
but will *always* embrace you and
accompany you in times of sorrow and happiness.**

Abide now in peace and joy.

Listen to the song of the day "The Way You Are" on the *Mercy Reigns* album.

8 GOOD NEWS

Luke 15:3-6

"What man among you having a hundred sheep
and losing one of them would not leave the
ninety-nine in the desert and go after the lost
one until he finds it? And when he does find it,
he sets it on his shoulders with great joy and,
upon his arrival home, he calls together his friends
and neighbors and says to them, 'Rejoice
with me because I have found my lost sheep.'"

Jesus told this parable to Pharisees (religious leaders) after they had
criticized him for eating with "sinners".

**Jesus shows us the true character of God...
who is *not* waiting to *punish* you...
but is *yearning* to *love* you.**

Jesus shows us a God who will go to *any length* to *restore* you...
heal you...
include you and *make you whole*.
That is *salvation*!

Where is the place inside you that you feel that you are the "lost sheep"
and that no one could possibly love you because of it?
That is *precisely the place* where God wants to *embrace* you and say,
*"Fear not. I will *never* let you go. I love you."*

Listen to the song of the day "God Is" on the *Give Praise and Thanks* album.

GOD IS WITH YOU

John 16:32-33

"Behold, the hour is coming and has arrived when each of you will be scattered to his own home and you will leave me alone. But I am not alone, because the Father is with me. I have told you this so that you might have peace in me.
In the world you will have trouble, but take courage, I have conquered the world."

How fickle! The same men who told Jesus that they believed that he came from God... would shortly abandon him.
Jesus knew this would happen... but did not reject them because of it or scold them or threaten any sort of reprisal.
What his followers *believed*... apparently wasn't that important.
The love of God didn't appear to depend on their belief at all.
Don't we all do the *same* thing?

We repeatedly turn away from God (or if you prefer... we turn away from doing what is good and loving) only to be forgiven and accepted *over and over again*.
In response to the disciples' impending abandonment... Jesus offered peace.

That's because the love, mercy, forgiveness, and compassion of God are unconditional.
God *is* Love and we are God's beloved daughters and sons.
So *take courage*.
Love wins!

That, my friend, is *transforming* and truly *Good News*!

Listen to the song of the day "Salvation" on the *Live to Love* album.

10 | KEEP THE FAITH

John 12:44-45

Jesus cried out and said, "Whoever believes in me believes not only in me but also in the one who sent me, and whoever sees me sees the one who sent me."

This is a very comforting thought.
Jesus basically said, "If you want to know what *God* is like... look at *me*."

Humanity's understanding of God evolved over thousands of years...
usually reflecting the way human beings behaved.
If they were *vindictive* and *vengeful*... well then... God was *vindictive* and *vengeful* as well.
But a Benevolent Consciousness was in the *process* of rising in human beings.

This Love fueling the universe was always a *constant*... but it was *we* who had to *change*.
Did you ever see Jesus squash anyone? How about threaten to destroy anyone?
No!
Jesus gave all of himself in life to show
***love, mercy, forgiveness,* and *compassion* equally to *all*.**

He spent his time with those on the margins... those who were rejected by society.
He didn't condemn *anyone*... even the woman caught in adultery.
The *only* people who *really angered* Jesus were the
self-righteous, judgmental religious leaders.
Jesus offered compassion to those who messed up...
to those who were broken and in need.
Isn't that all of us?

Jesus reflected a Creator who loves *everyone*.
Bask in that knowledge... and be thankful.

Listen to the song of the day "Radically Okay" on the *Mercy Reigns* album.

GRACE II

John 14:1-3

"Do not let your hearts be troubled. You have faith in God; have faith also in me. In my Father's house there are many dwelling places. If there were not, would I have told you that I am going to prepare a place for you? And if I go and prepare a place for you, I will come back again and take you to myself, so that where I am you also may be."

This is such a comforting message from Jesus.
And yet there are *so many* people who *fear* death.
I've met many such people in my ministry to the sick and elderly.
And *no wonder*... with so much *fear* having been preached to them throughout their lives!
And yet Jesus preached *over and over* to *not be afraid*.
He showed us that life does not *end*... but is *transformed*!
Death is *not* an *end* but a *doorway* to *new life*.

Jesus promised that he would prepare a place for us.
Remember that scripture says that God *is* love (1 John 4:8).
And it also says, "There is no fear in love, but perfect love drives out fear because fear has to do with punishment, and so one who fears is not yet perfect in love" (1 John 4:18).
So *know* that you are *eternally loved!*

Whatever you are struggling with now...
remember that the Love that created you is *with* you... *now* and *forever*.
Nothing can stop transformation and new life from happening...
if you are open to it!

Listen to the song of the day "Love Will Always Lead You Home" on the *Mercy Reigns* album.

12 | IMMERSED IN GRACE

2 Timothy 1:9-11

He saved us and called us to a holy life, not according to our works but according to his own design and the grace bestowed on us in Christ Jesus before time began, but now made manifest through the appearance of our savior Christ Jesus, who destroyed death and brought life and immortality to light through the gospel, for which I was appointed preacher and apostle and teacher.

When St. Paul speaks... he speaks a *mouthful!*
Read the scripture passage again... and allow his words to sink in.
God saved us not by *our works* but by *grace in Christ* "before time began."
This, my friend, is *original blessing.*
It's a "saving" that *accepts* us, *loves* us, and *makes us whole.*
Christ became human.
In other words, "the Word became flesh" (John 1:14) in Jesus and showed us that death is an *illusion.* It does *not* have the final say.
Jesus also showed us *the way to eternal life* in *each moment* of our lives through the way he lived each day and through the way he died.
St. Paul, who was first a persecutor of Christians and involved in their murders, was *transformed* into the greatest evangelist of all time by *grace.* This same man, who never met the historical Jesus in the flesh but in a mystical experience on the road, said he was "appointed preacher and apostle and teacher."
No matter what we've done, the same kind of transformation is promised to us today. Thank God for grace and compassion!

Listen to the song of the day "The Way You Are" on the *Mercy Reigns* album.

GRACE UPON GRACE

Psalm 103:1-2

Bless the Lord, my soul;
all my being, bless his holy name!
Bless the Lord, my soul;
do not forget all the gifts of God.

How amazing that the Creator of the universe created you and me!

From space dust our bodies are fashioned.
As Teilhard de Chardin said, "We are spiritual beings having a human experience."
We have been *graced* with eternal life.

It's a totally *free* gift from our Maker who *loved us into existence* and who could not stop
loving us any more than we could stop loving our own sons or daughters...
or any more than we could stop the sun from shining.

**The Love that shines upon us has nothing to do with what we *do* to *merit* it,
or any *achievements* or *accomplishments*...
or *mistakes* we make or *struggles* we have...
but it has *everything* to do with *who God is*: Love.**

As St. Paul says, "For I am convinced that
neither death, nor life, nor angels, nor principalities, nor present things,
nor future things, nor powers, nor height, nor depth, nor any other creature
will be able to separate us from the love of God in Christ Jesus our Lord."
(Romans 8:38-39)
Alleluia!

Amen.

**Listen to the song of the day "Give Praise and Thanks" on the *Give Praise and
Thanks* album.**

14 | INNER STRENGTH

Psalm 138:3

When I cried out, you answered; you strengthened my spirit.

How often do we instinctively cry out to God for help?
Seems to happen quite frequently... at least with me.

We have a *built-in* need for something bigger than us...
Someone who will always be *for* us...
Someone who would *never leave us*.

Isn't it interesting that this desire is "built-in"?

Could it be that God loves nothing more than to come
running to our aid in times of need?

Yes... it's true!
Even when all seems lost...
God is with us.

As a matter of fact...
God *doesn't come running*...
because God *is already here*...
in the very fabric of your being...
at your deepest core.

Find strength and comfort in that.

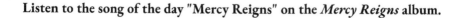

Listen to the song of the day "Mercy Reigns" on the *Mercy Reigns* album.

KENOSIS | 15

John 14:5-6

Thomas said to him,
Master, we do not know where you are going;
how can we know the way?"
Jesus said to him,
"I am the way and the truth and the life.
No one comes to the Father except through me."

True life happens through the process of *letting go*...
letting go of all the stuff that you thought defined you...
all the *labels*...
all the *masks*...
all the *possessions*...
the things that our egos try desperately to hold on to.

If you practice this process of letting go or "kenosis"
(from a Greek word meaning the self-emptying of one's own will
and becoming entirely receptive to God's will)
and follow the One who said he was *the way, the truth and the life*...
then the *final* letting go will not be difficult.

It will just be another experience of *resurrection* and *new life*.

For when we surrender our *attachments* to things that will *not* last...
God fills us with the Life that *never ends*!

Listen to the song of the day "Let It Be Done to Me" on the *Mercy Reigns* album.

16 | ALL IS ONE

John 17:22

"And I have given them the glory you gave me,
so that they may be one, as we are one,
I in them and you in me,
that they may be brought to perfection as one,
that the world may know that you sent me,
and that you loved them even as you loved me."

Read again the words Jesus spoke above and *contemplate* them in your *heart*.

**As you think about this prayer that Jesus made to God...
do you get the feeling that the meaning of life is *so much deeper*
than simply *assenting to a set of beliefs*?**

Jesus was speaking of a certain *Oneness of all things* that goes
beyond any *left-brained, intellectual* explanation.

**Jesus was attempting to put into words a mystery
that could only be approached if the *right side* of your brain was engaged...
the side that deals with *creativity, awe,* and *wonder*.**

Jesus said that God's love makes all of us one...
and that we are being brought to perfection in this Oneness.

**Is there *anything* to *fear* in this?
*No!***

Rest in that.

**Listen to the song of the day "Breathe On Me" on the *Listen to Your Heart*
album.**

INFINITE LOVE 17

All wisdom is from the Lord and
remains with him forever.
The sands of the sea,
the drops of rain,
the days of eternity –
who can count them?

〜

Did you know that a single grain of sand contains 22 quintillion atoms
(that's 22 with *18 zeroes*)?

Rob Bell in his book titled *What We Talk About When We Talk About God*
says that an "atom is in size to a golf ball as a golf ball is in size to Earth."

**He goes on to explain how science has now revealed a whole lot of other
subatomic particles that make an atom appear to be a giant.**

Meanwhile the edge of the universe is roughly ninety billion trillion miles away...
and *expanding*.
God is *still creating*.

It's *mind boggling*.

You and I are part of this *on-going* creation.

And despite how tiny each of us is in the spectrum of the universe...
we know through Jesus that each of us...
is *infinitely loved*.

〜

Listen to the song of the day "How Wonderful to Me" on the *Live to Love* album.

18 | BIG PICTURE

Psalm 138:8

The Lord is with me to the end.
Lord, your love endures forever.

As we grow older it becomes more apparent how *fragile* life really is...
and how *precious*.

**We sooner or later realize that material things
eventually lose their luster and crumble.**

Some relationships change and wither.

**How wonderful it is to know that God *never changes*.
Our Creator's love for us is *constant, deep,* and *eternal*.
It always *was* and always *will be*.**

Love "bears all things, believes all things,
hopes all things, and endures all things."
(1 Corinthians 13:7)

It's a Love that holds you *now*.

Put your faith in *that*.
Be *present* to it.

**And don't worry...
because this Love will *never let you go*.**

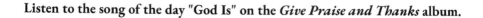

Listen to the song of the day "God Is" on the *Give Praise and Thanks* album.

LIFE GIVER | 19

Acts 17:26-28

"...he fixed the ordered seasons and the boundaries of their regions, so that people might seek God, even perhaps grope for him and find him, though indeed he is not far from any one of us. For 'In him we live and move and have our being.'"

The seasons remind us that the *budding* life of *spring*...
flourishes in *summer* but *wanes* in *autumn* and then *withers* in *winter*.
How sad if that was the end.
But it's not.
Life is *revived* again in the *spring*.
God is Present *throughout*.
Sometimes God seems so far away.
Other times, God's Presence fills us as we experience a joyful smile...
a beautiful sunset...
a selfless act of kindness or a loving hug.
God is with us through each of our cycles of dying and rising.
There is an *emptying*... and then a *refilling* and God is in the *midst of it all*.
"In him we live and move and have our being."
God is a mystery...
way beyond the grasp of our minds.
But within each of us is an intense *longing* to *know* our Creator.
Could that be because God has *first* longed for *us* and we are simply *responding*?
Be *present* to this inner longing.
Rest in the peace and quiet of each *moment*,
where God *yearns* to be *with you* and renew you.
Set aside ten or twenty minutes today to simply *be*.
You will be rejuvenated!

Listen to the song of the day "Seasons" on the *Listen to Your Heart* album.

20 FRIEND FOREVER

Sirach 6:14-15

A faithful friend is a sturdy shelter;
he who finds one finds a treasure.
A faithful friend is beyond price,
no sum can balance his worth.

**Take a moment to cherish any true friendship
you may have
or may have had.**

Such a friend is with you through all the ups *and downs* as well.

**If your heart aches to find such a friend as this...
turn to Jesus.**

He will *never abandon* you and is *always for* you.

**Allow him to walk with you in your time of need.
Allow him to help you carry your cross.**

Befriend him in your heart...
and he'll lead you to new life.

Listen to the song of the day "Come to Jesus" on the *Live to Love* album.

ABUNDANT LIFE |

Psalm 47:2

All you peoples,
clap your hands;
shout to God with joyful cries.
For the Lord, the Most High,
inspires awe...

In the midst of struggles and hardships...
there is *much* to be *thankful* for...
to be in *amazement* over.

Look at the mind-boggling expanse of the universe (which is *still expanding*).
Look at the beauty of a tiny flower.
Look at the mountains or the sun setting on the ocean.

And each of us...
each of us **is part of this awesome creation.**
Each **of us is loved** ***unconditionally*** **by our Creator.**

We are surrounded *with* and immersed *in* blessings.

Eternal life awaits us.

Take a moment to give praise and thanks for such a
magnificent, wondrous, and glorious Creator!

Listen to the song of the day "How Magnificent, Wondrous and Glorious" on the
***Mercy Reigns* album.**

22 | REDEMPTION IN PROGRESS

Mark 10:51-52

Jesus said to him in reply, "What do you want me to do for you?" The blind man replied to him, "Master, I want to see." Jesus told him, "Go your way; your faith has saved you." Immediately he received his sight and followed him on the way.

The blind man, Bartimaeus, was calling out *so loudly* as Jesus passed by
that he could be heard over the noise of the sizable crowd.
Even when people in that crowd told Bartimaeus to be quiet...
he yelled even louder, "Jesus, son of David, have pity on me."
The blind man wasn't so blind... when it came to his *faith*!
Despite his *physical* blindness... he recognized that Jesus was a great healer.
However, many sighted people were *spiritually* blind!

Jesus confirmed that Bartimaeus' faith would lead him to *wholeness* (salvation)...
before miraculously restoring his sight.
Actually...the *greater* result is that the man is *restored to his community*.
He was no longer cast-out on the fringes... but was again *included*.
Not everyone receives miraculous physical healing...
but I believe that when people in need have faith...
they will receive *restoration* in the way they
(and those around them) *most need it spiritually*.

Bartimaeus did not run off to celebrate...
but with his restored sight he joined the others
in following Jesus "on the way" to new life.
Jesus invites *us* to do the same.

Listen to the song of the day "I Want to Follow You" on the *Listen to Your Heart* album.

ALL SHALL BE WELL | 23

Psalm 91:2

Say to the Lord,
"My refuge and fortress,
my God in whom I trust."

God *never leaves us* no matter how many times we, in a sense, leave God.
Of course... we can't *really* leave God because
God is the sustenance of everything that is!

**God pervades all things,
encompasses all things,
and holds all things.**

But we do sometimes choose our own *egocentric* desires over the desires God has for us.
A person's ego is only concerned about *self-centered* interests.
God is concerned about *all creation's* interests.

However, even when we turn away from caring for all and
focus only on our own desires...
God *never turns away from us.*
Our Creator is *always* supporting us and loving us.

So... no matter what you've done...
no matter how far you drifted from the path you were meant to be on...
all you have to do is *turn around* and you will see that
the Great Love that made you has never left you...
but has been *pursuing* you the *whole* time.

**Ponder this as you deal with whatever struggles or transitions you are facing...
and trust in a Higher Power to get you through.**

**Listen to the song of the day "God's Love Is All You Need" on the *Listen to Your
Heart* album.**

24 | GREATEST COMMANDMENT

John 15:12-13

"This is my commandment:
love one another as I love you.
No one has greater love than this,
to lay down one's life for one's friends."

That's it in a nutshell.
That's *the* message.

Love one another as God loves us.

Jesus said that if we know *him* then we would know *God* (John 14:7).

So let's look at Jesus.
He lived his life by channeling love, mercy, forgiveness, and compassion to all...
even when he was *persecuted and crucified*.
This demonstrates who God is!

**What could prove God's love *more* than to be
totally and *thoroughly* rejected...
but then to respond with *forgiveness*?**

From the cross Jesus asked God to forgive "for they know not what they do."

***That* is *unconditional Love*.**

Allow the awe and wonder of it to fill you!

Listen to the song of the day "Lift Up Our Voices" on the *Give Praise and Thanks* album.

LET IT BE DONE TO ME | 25

Luke 1:46-47

"My soul proclaims the greatness of the Lord;
my spirit rejoices in God my savior."

Mary's statement *resonates* in my *heart*.
**When I am *in the flow* of the will of God...
my *innermost being exults*.**

No matter what struggles are in my life...
there seems to be an inner *calm*...
a certain "yes" that pervades my interior.
There are really no words to describe it accurately.
It is at the level of mystery.

**When I am operating in the will of God,
I am saying *yes* to this great Mystery at work in me.**

My egocentric desires are neutralized.

**When I am in this state of being...
I am my *true self*.**

It's not so much that I have done anything...
it is more like *it is being done to me!*

I wish I could say this is the case all the time, but it is *far from it*.
I must continually return to *letting go* and *being present*.

May we all surrender to God's desires for us and, like Mary, say,
"May it be done to me according to your word" (Luke 1:38).

Listen to the song of the day "Let It Be Done to Me" on the *Mercy Reigns* album.

26 | SURRENDER TO GRACE

Mark 1:23-26

In their synagogue was a man with an unclean spirit;
he cried out, "What have you to do with us,
Jesus of Nazareth? Have you come to destroy us?
I know who you are -- the Holy One of God!"
Jesus rebuked him and said,
"Quiet! Come out of him!"
The unclean spirit convulsed him and
with a loud cry came out of him.

Each of us is no doubt plagued with an "unclean spirit" of some sort.
We struggle with all kinds of addictions, obsessions, and compulsions.
As St. Paul stated, "What I do, I do not understand.
For I do not do what I want, but I do what I hate" (Romans 7:15).
Just like Paul, we struggle with a "thorn in our sides" that we just can't seem to get rid of.
But Jesus offers us *relief* and *comfort*.
He did not criticize, scold, or shame the man afflicted by the unclean spirit.
Instead, Jesus gladly *restored* him to *wholeness*.
In the Catholic Easter Vigil, sin is called a "happy fault."
It is the place where *we can't save ourselves* and *only God can!*

The place of our biggest inner struggle...
is *exactly the place* where Unconditional Love can *transform* us.
God will surely transform whatever affliction we have for
our good and even the good of *others*.
Bring your affliction to Jesus without fear!

Listen to the song of the day "Come to Jesus" on the *Live to Love* album.

LIGHT BEARER | 27

Mark 2:1-2

When Jesus returned to Capernaum after some days, it became known that he was at home. Many gathered together so that there was no longer room for them, not even around the door, and he preached the Word to them.

What was it that drew crowds to Jesus?

**No one had ever spoken the way he was speaking...
words that *inspired*, *healed,* and *touched hearts*.**

Jesus spoke words of comfort to the broken.
He brought news of God's *unconditional love*.

He was a *light of hope*.

All clamored to hear him.

The only critical words we ever heard Jesus speak were directed to the *Pharisees*...
the *rigid* religious leaders who arrogantly believed they had all the answers.
They held the people to stringent rules and guidelines without compassion.

Which spiritual leaders today remind you of the *Pharisees*
and which remind you of *Jesus*?
**I don't know about you...
but I'm listening to the ones who mirror
love, mercy, grace, forgiveness, and compassion.**

Listen to the song of the day "Salvation" on the *Live to Love* album.

28 | HAVE FAITH

Hebrews 2:18

Because he himself was tested through what he suffered, he is able to help those who are being tested.

Jesus knows what you are going through.

He experienced all the joys and sorrows of being human.

As St. Irenaeus said,
"The glory of God is the human fully alive."
All of human experience is sacred...
the joys and sorrows.

**Whatever pain and suffering you are going through...
know that Jesus went through the pain of total rejection,
extreme persecution, and what *appeared* to be *total defeat*.**

But he did so *not by resisting*...
but by *responding with love, mercy, forgiveness, and compassion.*

**Total *defeat* was *transformed* into total *victory* in the resurrection.
Your pain will either *transform* you or
you will *transmit* that pain to the world.**

Walk with Jesus in your pain and he will lead you to *transformation* and *new life*.
Go with the flow of Love.

Then *you* will be a *source of transformation* and *new life* for *others*.

Listen to the song of the day "You'll Lead Me" on the *Listen to Your Heart* album.

SAVED BY GRACE | **29**

Hebrews 13:5

Let your life be free from love of money but be
content with what you have, for he has said,
"I will never forsake you or abandon you."

Are you consumed with striving to *make more money* and *gain more material things...*
or are you *content with what you have*?
There is no harm in wanting to provide more for your family...
but where is your *heart* in the matter?
Is your heart consumed with striving for more money...
or striving to *love* more and better?

The fickle economy and death itself are good reminders that
the stuff of this world will not last.
But the risen Christ said in the last line of the gospel of Matthew:
"I am with you always, until the end of the age" (Matthew 28:20).
God is with you *now*... in *this moment*...
drawing you forward to a greater love and *fullness of being*.

Jesus said, "I came that they might have life and have it more abundantly" (John 10:10).
Jesus meant for you to have an abundant life *now*.
This *abundance* or *wholeness* in *this present moment*
does not depend on *money*...
but on *Unconditional Love*.

Jesus modeled for us the way to have life to the full...
and as Hebrews 13:8 states:
"Jesus Christ is the same yesterday, today and forever."

Seems like the *perfect model* to follow... right *now*.

**Listen to the song of the day "I Want to Follow You" on the *Listen to Your Heart*
album.**

30 | BLESSINGS ABOUND

Mark 8:11-12

The Pharisees came forward and began
to argue with him,
seeking from him a sign from heaven to test him.
He sighed from the depth of his spirit and said,
"Why does this generation seek a sign?"

God surrounds us with many divine signs.
Creation is teeming with signs of God's love...
and we are immersed in it all.
Stop for a moment and take stock of all the blessings you have received.
If you are struggling... think of the people who have come into your life to help you.
Look at the beauty of creation that surrounds you.

The Pharisees were eye-witnesses of "signs from heaven."
They witnessed many of Jesus' miraculous healings.
But they had preconceived agendas.
Their hearts and minds were closed.

They were blind to God working in their very midst...
so they were incapable of witnessing more signs from Jesus.
Our faith is tested many times in the storms of life.
***Cling* to your faith.**

Jesus promises to *never* let you go.
Look back over your experiences...
and you will see the thread of God's Presence and wondrous signs of
Unconditional Love all along the way.

Listen to the song of the day "How Magnificent, Wondrous and Glorious" on the
Mercy Reigns album.

NEW LIFE AHEAD | 31

Psalm 23:4

Even when I walk through a dark valley, I fear no harm for you are at my side.

Life is filled with *ups* and *downs*.
Jesus showed us the *pattern* of salvation throughout his ministry.

Struggles and **brokenness** would be **transformed** into
new life and **wholeness**
by the **grace** and **unconditional love** of God.

The blind would *see*, the deaf would *hear,* and the dead would be *raised*.
What *appeared* to be the *end* when Jesus was crucified was followed by
a glorious *new beginning* at the resurrection.

Death could **not** defeat Jesus...
and so it cannot defeat **us** either.
This is also true for all the **small deaths** we encounter along life's journey.

What *appears* to be an *obstacle* is *actually* an *opportunity*.
What on the surface *appears* to be *tragic* can be *transformed* into *triumph*...
if we have faith in the God of Love.
Cling to this Hope in the dark valleys of life and
you will be led *again* and *again* to shining and glorious mountaintops.

New life is on the way.

Hold on...
and *trust*.

Listen to the song of the day "Love Will Always Lead You Home" on the *Mercy Reigns* album.

I GLORY BE

John 17:22-23

"And I have given them the glory you gave me,
so that they may be one, as we are one,
I in them and you in me,
that they may be brought to perfection as one,
that the world may know that you sent me,
and that you loved them even as you loved me."

Jesus is attempting to put into words something that is
beyond our ability to mentally grasp.
He wants us... *ALL* of us... including the people we *don't like...*
including the people we *disagree with...* including the people of *every nation...*
to be *ONE...* as Jesus is *ONE* with God.
Jesus wants all of us to know we are included *in* him... as ONE body of Christ.
The mystical truth is... we are *already ONE.*

To *not* see this... to create *artificial divisions...* is to live in a *delusion.*
God loves us *unconditionally...*
such that Jesus was willing to lay down his life
to show what *that kind of love looks like.*

It's a Love that would die for the beloved...
even when the beloved has completely rejected that Love.
Jesus also showed us that such a Love totally poured out...
does *not end* but is *transformed* into *new life.*
This is what "saves" you.
This is the *glory* given by God to Jesus and shared with *each* of us.

Listen to the song of the day "All Are One" on the *Mercy Reigns* album.

BODY OF CHRIST

John 16:32-33

"But I am not alone, because the Father is with me.
I have told you this so that
you might have peace in me.
In the world you will have trouble,
but take courage, I have conquered the world."

Jesus knew that he would be abandoned and crucified alone...
with only a few of his followers remaining throughout his ordeal.
Jesus also knew that God would *never* abandon him...
even though that was how it *felt* when he hung on the cross.

**Jesus felt every *rejection* and unjust *persecution* imaginable...
but he knew that the cross was *not* the end.**

Though it *appears* to be a dead-end to the world... in reality...
it was the *gateway* to the *ultimate* New Life.
You may recall that Jesus cried out from the cross,
"My God, my God, why have you forsaken me?"
Did you know that he was quoting the beginning of Psalm 22?
While the psalm starts out in *lament*...
it ends in *praise* of God's *faithfulness*.

**Know that whatever you are struggling with...
God is there *with* you.**

The power, prestige, and possessions of this world will disintegrate...
but the love modeled by Jesus and the New Life God promises...
will last *forever*!

Listen to the song of the day "Mercy Reigns" on the *Mercy Reigns* album.

3 RELAX

Ezekiel 34:15

I myself will pasture my sheep; I myself will give them rest, says the Lord God.

God is not a tyrant waiting to punish us.
So many people have such toxic images of our Creator.

**However, the prophet Ezekiel had a completely *opposite* image.
He was inspired to write the words of comfort above...
six hundred years before the birth of Jesus.**

As a prophet speaking on behalf of God...
he wrote of a Loving Creator
who will go to *any length* to protect and look after us.
Jesus said if you knew *him*...
then you would also know *God* (John 14:7).
He also said, "I am the good shepherd.
A good shepherd lays down his life for the sheep," (John 10:11).

We (*all of humanity*) are the sheep.

Jesus showed us that he would die to demonstrate God's tender love.
In return for unjust persecution and then being nailed to a cross...
he responded with *love* and *truth*.
His resurrection showed us that death and hate have *no hold on us*...
no matter what we have done.
The love God has for each of us is *unconditional* and *eternal*.

Rest in *that*.

Listen to the song of the day "God Is" on the *Give Praise and Thanks* album.

GOOD SHEPHERD

Matthew 11:28

"Come to me,
all you who labor and are burdened,
and I will give you rest."

Life is not easy.
There is suffering.

**Are you burdened with something...
or struggling with something?**

Try sitting in silence and invite Jesus to be with you.

**He is the Good Shepherd...
the one who *pursues* and *comforts* all the lost sheep.
Jesus shows us who God is...
not a God of harsh judgment and punishment...
but one of *compassion, forgiveness, and mercy*.**

Bring your burden or struggle to Jesus.

He promises to bring you *rest*.

This is *unconditional love* that disperses all fear.

Listen to the song of the day "I Will Give You Rest" on the *Live to Love* album.

5 OUR SOURCE IS LOVE

Psalm 146:6-7

The maker of heaven and earth,
the seas and all that is in them,
who keeps faith forever,
secures justice for the oppressed,
gives food to the hungry.
The Lord sets prisoners free.

God wants to set you free from whatever is oppressing you...
whatever is holding you in bondage...
whatever is blocking you from God's *free-flowing*, *unconditional* love.

God wants to *feed* you where you are *hungry* and *set you free*.

It has *nothing* to do with your *worthiness*.

God loves you not because *you* are good but because *God* is good.

God *is* love (1 John 4:8).

**So whatever it is that is holding you captive...
turn it over to your loving Creator.**

Let go.
Fall into the arms of Grace.
Rejoice!

Listen to the song of the day "My Lord and My God" on the *Live to Love* album.

REASON TO REJOICE

Psalm 103:2-4

Bless the Lord, my soul;
and do not forget all his gifts,
Who pardons all your sins,
and heals all your ills,
Who redeems your life from the pit,
and crowns you with mercy and compassion.

God indeed *is* Love (1 John 4:8).
This is *not* the mushy, sentimental, *Hollywood-movie kind of love.*

This is *agape kind of love*...
the kind that is *gratuitous* and given abundantly
even when the beloved is unresponsive and does not merit it.

It's the kind of Love that would pour itself out to you
even if you rejected it or responded to it with hate.

Jesus demonstrated this to us quite clearly
when he forgave his killers from the cross,
"Father, forgive them, they know not what they do" (Luke 23:34).

Knowing this... and knowing, as St. Paul put it, that
in God "we live and move and have our being" (Acts 17:28)...
then we have MUCH to be *thankful for* and *joyful about!*

Receive God's forgiveness...
and let your soul rejoice.

Listen to the song of the day "Give Praise and Thanks" on the *Give Praise and Thanks* album.

7 | BE NOT AFRAID

Ephesians 3:17-19

> That you, rooted and grounded in love,
> may have strength to comprehend with all
> the holy ones what is the breadth and length
> and height and depth, and to know the love
> of Christ that surpasses knowledge, so that you
> may be filled with all the fullness of God.

God's love is *so* immense.
It is *boundless.*
Infinite.
And St. Paul says that *each* of us is "grounded" in that Love.
It is beyond anything we can grasp with our finite minds ("surpasses knowledge").
The question is: Are we *aware* of our rootedness in Love?

This takes *surrendering* our ego's insatiable desires... a 'self-emptying' if you will.
We must follow Jesus' example:
"Who, though he was in the form of God,
did not regard equality with God something to be grasped.
Rather, he emptied himself, taking the form of a slave,
coming in human likeness, and found human in appearance,
he humbled himself, becoming obedient to death,
even death on a cross" (Philippians 2:6-7).

When I empty myself of "my" desires (ego)...
only then can I be "filled with all the fullness of God."
Paradoxically, it is then that I am born to new life and I discover my *true self*...
love grounded in Love.

Listen to the song of the day "Pour Me Out" on the *Give Praise and Thanks* album.

LIFE GIVING GRACE

2 Corinthians 3:5-6

Our qualification comes from God,
who has indeed qualified us as
ministers of a new covenant,
not of letter but of spirit;
for the letter brings death,
but the Spirit gives life.

We are all called to be ministers of God in whatever state of life we are in.

**The new covenant made with us by Jesus is
God's *unconditional, unmerited love*.**

It is *freely given* to us by God.
It is based in *grace*.

**It is not based on what we *do* or how well we follow the rules
(the "letter" or the "letter of the law" or "law"),
but simply *accepting God's grace*.**

That is the path to true life!

Do you accept it?

Listen to the song of the day "God's Love Is All You Need" on the *Listen to Your Heart* album.

9 | GOD'S LOVE NEVER FAILS

2 Corinthians 3:4

Such confidence we have through Christ toward God.

St. Paul knew the love of God through the risen Christ.
The God of *legalism* and *punishment* was the God Paul *used* to believe in
when he was known as *Saul*...
a man who *persecuted* Christians in the name of God.
**But *everything changed* after his mystical encounter with
the risen Christ on the road to Damascus when he was *transformed*.**

Over time... *Saul* became known as *Paul*...
a man who believed in a God of *grace* and *forgiveness*.
His encounter with Christ came when he was *least worthy*...
when he was persecuting Christians.
Forgiveness and Unconditional Love changed him.

Jesus showed each of us how to *live*...
responding to persecution with *love*...
even while hanging on the cross when he forgave those who had crucified him.

This is the reality of who God *is*.

God *is love* (1 John 4:8) and love *drives out fear*.
"There is no fear in love, but perfect love drives out fear
because fear has to do with punishment,
and so one who fears is not yet perfect in love" (1 John 4:18).

It is the risen Christ who gives us this confidence!
This is reason to *rejoice*!

Listen to the song of the day "Lift Up Our Voices" on the *Give Praise and Thanks* album.

KEY TO GOD'S KINGDOM | 10

Matthew 5:43-45

"You have heard that it was said,
'You shall love your neighbor and hate your enemy.'
But I say to you, love your enemies,
and pray for those who persecute you,
that you may be children of your heavenly Father,
for he makes his sun rise on the bad and the good,
and causes rain to fall on the just and the unjust. "

This is one of the teachings of Jesus that most people simply *ignore*.

**We make many Church teachings non-negotiable but for some reason
a *direct* teaching from Jesus like this one is hardly *ever* quoted.**

That's because it's *hard*.
**But is *this* not what saves us...
the unconditional love and forgiveness of God?**

Christ gladly comes to *be with us in our* failings to *lift* us so that we know
it's *not about our own doing* that saves us.
It's about *Who* God *Is*—Love.

To love an enemy, we must see that person as God *does*...
as a beloved son or daughter.

**Let us ask God for help...
because forgiveness is the *only way* to the kingdom of God.**

Listen to the song of the day "Mercy Reigns" on the *Mercy Reigns* album.

II | SANCTUARY

Matthew 6:6

> "But when you pray, go to your inner room,
> close the door, and pray to your Father in secret.
> And your Father who sees in secret will repay you."

Jesus seemed to be instructing his followers to pray with few words.
Instead, we've been instructed to recite written prayers to God.

But Jesus himself told his followers to spend time with God in "your inner room."

In the next verse he tells his followers to "not babble like the pagans,
who think that they will be heard because of their many words."
Jesus goes on to say that God "knows what you need before you ask him."

**Jesus seems to be telling us to spend quiet time with God...
and simply be present to the Divine Presence.**

Following Jesus is about *experiencing* the *Paschal Mystery*.

**It is about experiencing Christ's "dying and rising"...
death leading to new life...
in our *daily lives*.**

One way to "die to yourself" is to practice contemplative prayer.
Sit in silence.
Let go of your ego.
***Let go* of your incessant thoughts... and simply *be*.**

Allow God to commune with you...
and you will most assuredly begin to experience new life... *right now*.

**Listen to the song of the day "Turn Off the Noise" on the *Listen to Your Heart*
album.**

PRAYERFUL PATIENCE

Psalm 5:3-4

To you I pray, O Lord;
at dawn you will hear my cry;
at dawn I will plead before you and wait.

I know what *I* want... but what does *God* want?
What if God wants something *different* than what my *ego* wants?

**Am I able to distinguish between what my *ego* wants and
what my *deepest, truest self* really *needs?***

One thing for sure...
what God wants will be just what my true self needs to flourish and
experience God's love in an amazing way!

**Could the circumstances in our lives be ways
through which God might be asking us to reconsider
what we *think* we want so that something
even more amazing could happen?**

Set aside some quiet time with God and pray,
"Thy will be done... not *mine."*

Make your plea to God...
and then *wait* and *listen.*

Our Loving Creator wants what's best for us.
Trust the process.

Listen to the song of the day "Let It Be Done to Me" on the *Mercy Reigns* album.

13 | DIVINE PRESENCE

2 Corinthians 6:2

Behold, now is a very acceptable time; behold, now is the day of salvation.

We are *surrounded* by God's blueprint for life...
plants, creatures, and the very seasons themselves.

It's a *continuous cycle* of *dying* and rising.

Our lives are made up of a *series* of little deaths to self...
and then *rising* again...
when we're made new *through the experience* of the struggle.
Jesus showed us that even the *final* death...
is *not* the end at all...
but the *ultimate* new beginning.
So when will it be time for *your* new beginning?

Now... of course.

It's the only time that is *real*.
It's the time and place where God is *"present"*.

**It's the time for your healing and
the *beginning* of your road to *wholeness* (salvation).**

The time is *now*.
Are you ready to start?

"A clean heart create for me, God;
renew in me a steadfast spirit" (Psalm 51:12).

Listen to the song of the day "Seasons" on the *Listen to Your Heart* album.

BREATHE 14

Psalm 33:20

Our soul waits for the Lord, who is our help and shield.

Waiting is not something human beings are very good at
in these days of *instant gratification.*
Someone once said that *patience* is a *virtue*... but *not so much now.*
Many people tend to want what they want... *right now.*
Our egos hate to *wait* because they always want to be in *control.*

When we're *waiting,* we *feel* like we are *out of control.*
But remember that Jesus said we need to *die to self*...
meaning our egos need to *let go*...
so that *new life can emerge.*

This takes *practice.*
It takes saying *yes* to the moment... instead of *no.*
It takes *listening to our hearts* for God's *soft whisper.*

It takes *turning off the noise of the world* and
allowing our *runaway thoughts* to *slow* and then *cease.*
When we *stop* and *listen*...
we are truly *present* which allows all illusions to *dissolve.*
Then our *false identities* and *attachments* can *fall away.*
We *surrender* to *God's care.*

And then... in our poverty...
each of us will know in our hearts that we are a *precious child of God.*
So *wait – breathe slowly* – and *know* with *each breath*
that you are *infinitely loved* simply because you...
are *you.*

Listen to the song of the day "Breathe On Me" on the *Listen to Your Heart* album.

15 | GOD ALONE

Psalm 97:7

All who serve idols are put to shame, who glory in worthless things.

It's easy to look at others and be critical of how they
are idolizing sports, celebrities, wealth, material possessions, sex, etc.

**But instead of judging *others*, why not ask:
Is there anything that *I* am putting before *my* relationship with God?**

Am I trying to satisfy that *deep yearning* inside of me with
some *pursuit, activity, person, or object*...
when the only source that will *truly satisfy* such a yearning...
is *God*?

The deep yearning each of us experiences is on the *spiritual* level...
not the *physical*.

How does God want to satisfy the deepest desires of your *soul*?

Set aside some quiet time with your Loving Creator.
Let go...
and *listen*.

Hear the voice in your heart that says, "I love you."

Listen to the song of the day "Listen to Your Heart" on the *Listen to Your Heart* album.

LOVE UNITES | 16

Matthew 7:1-2

"Stop judging, that you may not be judged.
For as you judge, so will you be judged,
and the measure with which you measure
will be measured out to you."

Jesus tells us that before we notice the "splinter" in our neighbor's eye...
we should attend to the "wooden beam" in our own.
While I have to laugh at the humor in that statement...
I am also amazed at the keen insight.
**How often do I look at everything in my line of vision and simply
judge what's *good* and what's *bad*, what's *in* and what's *out*...
with *me* as the *all-knowing judge*?**
How tainted is my vision by *misperceptions* and *lack of information and wisdom*?
**Jesus says each of us has more than enough obstacles in our eyes
to cloud our vision... so we'd best focus our attention
on our *own* improvement before focusing on someone *else's*.**
Instead of rejecting people we disagree with... what if we tried to figure out how to
remain in relationship with them and attempt to *dialogue* about our *differences*?
The fact is... there are *no divisions* in God's eyes.
Everything is *included*.
Jesus *commanded* us to *love our enemies*... for God "makes his sun rise on the bad
and the good, and causes rain to fall on the just and the unjust" (Matthew 5:45).
Our Creator loves each person *exactly the same*... faults *included*!
God made each of us flawed... with areas of brokenness.
That isn't so God can then judge us as unworthy...
but so we can come to know God's love and mercy.
**Our broken places are where we truly encounter God's *unconditional love*.
Those places then become sacred places of transformation and growth.**

Listen to the song of the day "The Way You Are" on the *Mercy Reigns* album.

17 TRUE WEALTH

Matthew 6:20-21

"Store up treasures in heaven,
where neither moth nor decay destroys,
nor thieves break in and steal.
For where your treasure is,
there also will your heart be."

Are your treasures *material* or *spiritual*?

We know that anything material will eventually
turn to *dust* or end up in a *garbage dump*.

**Jesus tells us that *true wealth* comes from the *Holy Spirit*
in the form of *faith, hope, love, forgiveness, and compassion*.**

Our Loving God has *freely given* all these to us...
so that we might *pass them on to others*.

**Giving your heart to material things leads to *emptiness*,
but giving your heart to *God* leads you to experience
the *endless wealth* of *inner peace, contentment, and joy*.**

It's never too early or too late to give your heart to God.

Why not *now*?

**Listen to the song of the day "You'll Lead Me" on the *Listen to Your Heart*
album.**

THE HEART OF THE MATTER | 18

Matthew 12:7

If you knew what this meant, 'I desire mercy, not sacrifice,' you would not have condemned these innocent men.

Jesus' followers were picking heads of grain and eating them on the Sabbath.
Such "reaping" on the Sabbath was forbidden by religious law.
But the scripture says they were "hungry."
The religious leaders called Jesus to task for allowing his followers to break the law.
For Jesus...
love **is the deciding factor in all that we do.**

His followers were hungry...
therefore the *loving* thing was to allow them to eat.

**Laws are good foundations...
but love is *always* the *top priority*.**

Following rules and laws is necessary to avoid chaos and to give us a good foundation...
but following them does *not* win you favor with God.

You *already have favor* by being God's *beloved daughter or son*.

Notice how quickly Jesus chucked the law in favor of mercy
in regard to his hungry followers.

God also looks upon you with the eyes of mercy.

Listen to the song of the day "Salvation" on the *Live to Love* album.

19 LET YOUR HEART LEAD YOU

Matthew 7:21

"Not everyone who says to me, 'Lord, Lord,' will enter the kingdom of heaven, but only the one who does the will of my Father in heaven."

Jesus would alternately use the phrases 'kingdom of heaven' and 'kingdom of God.'
He would sometimes say that the kingdom of God "is at hand."
He also said to someone else who understood that the greatest Commandment was to
love both God and neighbor that he was "not far from the kingdom of God."

**The kingdom of God could break into the present moment
whenever someone loved God and neighbor...
whenever someone did the will of God.**

A person can go to church, do rituals, say prayers
and utter words like 'Lord, Lord' all they want...
but if that person isn't also living the gospel...
being Jesus' hands and feet in the world...
doing the will of God...
then he or she is not entering...
or experiencing...
the kingdom.
**This requires both faith and action...
which many times will only happen by way of a transformed heart.**

And that may only happen through a painful struggle...
when you can truly experience God's unconditional love.

**Open your heart...
and receive it.**

Listen to the song of the day "Changed" on the *Give Praise and Thanks* album.

EVERYTHING BELONGS

Matthew 8:1-3

When Jesus came down from the mountain,
great crowds followed him. And then a leper
approached, did him homage, and said,
"Lord, if you wish, you can make me clean."
He stretched out his hand, touched him, and said,
"I will do it. Be made clean."
His leprosy was cleansed immediately.

The leper is an outcast due to his disease.
The religious community of the time would have expelled him as "unclean."
His disease would have been seen as a punishment from God for some kind of sinfulness.

In reality...
expelling the leper was the *religious community's sin*.

Jesus heals him so he would be included again.
How do we expel others due to their differences or something we find "distasteful"?

Jesus became the ultimate outcast on the cross so that
through his forgiveness and his resurrection...
all would know:
Throw *no one* out.

All are included in God's kingdom...
and that includes *you*...
as well as the person who irritates you!

Listen to the song of the day "All Are Welcome" on the *Give Praise and Thanks*
album.

21 | GO WITH THE FLOW

2 Timothy 4:6

For I am already being poured out like a libation, and the time of my departure is at hand.

When St. Paul spoke these words... he realized his martyrdom was imminent.
At the time of *physical* death...
it will be the final "pouring out" of our lives here.
But our faith tells us that it is *not* the end.
It is the *beginning* of eternal life.

Jesus showed us this truth.
Our lives are made up of many *little deaths*...
transitions that lead to *transformations* to *new life*...
when we go with the flow of the Spirit.
It means we have to *let go* when life dictates a *transition-in-progress*.

It will feel like being "poured out like a libation."
But that's only so your Source of Life can then *fill you again with new life*.

It is *taking part* in the very life of God... the *Trinitarian flow* of life.
God *pours out* all to Christ...
who in turn *empties* himself and *returns all* to God (Philippians 2:6-8).

Life and death are part of *one continuous Flow*.
We see it in the seasons.
We see it each day as night is followed by a new dawn.
You are in this Flow *now* and *always*.

Nothing can keep you from the Love of God (Romans 8:38-39).
Nothing!

Listen to the song of the day "Pour Me Out" on the *Give Praise and Thanks* album.

POWER OF PRAYER | 22

Acts 12:5

Peter thus was being kept in prison,
but prayer by the church was fervently
being made to God on his behalf.

Sometimes we go through trials and painful struggles...
like Peter did when he was imprisoned.
Sometimes painful things happen to us and there seems to be no answer.
We feel like we are imprisoned.
But how many times has prayer made a difference?

A community (such as the church) gathers and
is paradoxically pulled together by the struggle.
Then wondrous manifestations of God's love pour forth.
While God didn't cause the struggle...
God struggled with us...
was in pain with us...
mourned with us...
cried with us...
and loved with us.

"I sought the Lord, who answered me, delivered me from all my fears" (Psalm 34:5).
We somehow emerge from the struggle wounded...
but strengthened and more compassionate because of the experience
and more willing to help others in their struggles.

As St. Paul said,
"The Lord will rescue me from every evil threat and
will bring me safe to his heavenly kingdom.
To God be glory forever and ever. Amen" (2 Timothy 4:18).

Listen to the song of the day "Love Will Always Lead You Home" on the *Mercy Reigns* album.

23 | BE COMPASSION

Matthew 5:20

"I tell you, unless your righteousness surpasses that of the scribes and Pharisees, you will not enter into the kingdom of heaven."

The scribes and Pharisees believed they were *doing everything right*.
They held people strictly to the *letter of the law...*
and they believed as religious leaders *they* were *beyond reproach*.
Everything was black or white.
You were either *in* or *out*.
They, of course, were *in*.
They didn't need forgiveness.
Of course... this is *false*.
Everyone needs forgiveness because *everyone messes up*.
We are *all* flawed and imperfect.
The *so-called* sinners... the likes of the tax collectors and prostitutes...
allowed Jesus to reach out to them.
They knew they needed forgiveness.
Life is not about *being right*... but it is about
being in right relationship with each other and with God.
God wants to be with us *in our brokenness*.
God *wants* to forgive us.
Didn't Jesus show this *quite plainly*?
When we allow God to forgive us and when we freely
pass on this forgiveness to others...
the ***kingdom of God*** **breaks into the *present*.**
You can start entering right *now*!
Loving God, forgive us as we forgive others...
and may your kingdom come on earth as it is in heaven.
Amen.

Listen to the song of the day "Let It Be Done to Me" on the *Mercy Reigns* album.

OPEN TO CHANGE | 24

Psalm 51:10

Create in me a clean heart, O God, and put a new and right spirit within me.

Now is a perfect time to *repent*.

**That means *change directions*...
turn back to God.**

Allow God to change our hearts.
How is my heart in need of change?

**Where does it need to be *cleansed* of a *wrong spirit*...
a spirit *not* of God but of my own *self-centered desires*?**

Generally, we are blind to the answers to these questions.

Take some time to go into the *desert* with Jesus.

Find some *quiet time*...
and allow the Holy Spirit to open your eyes
to the places in your heart that need
God's love, mercy, grace, forgiveness, and compassion.

For this to happen...
we need to *be open* to *receiving* this healing Grace.

Listen to the song of the day "Heal Me" on the *Live to Love* album.

25 SAVED BY GRACE

Psalm 31:6

Into your hands I commend my spirit;
you will redeem me, Lord, faithful God.

It seems it is only when we experience the *unmerited, unearned* redemption of God
that *we* are able to extend that same redemption
to others through our words and actions.

Until then... we will likely be harsh critics of sinners...
***not* instruments of God's redemption.**

However, sooner or later... *each* of us *fails*.
We *each* have some (or *many*) flaws.

These are not places of shame, but rather the *entry points* of God's grace.

Allow yourself to contemplate the unconditional love demonstrated
by Jesus when he responded with compassion after his brutal crucifixion...
forgiving his persecutors from the cross...
even when they had not asked for forgiveness!
Allow that amazing truth to sink into your soul.

How can you do *anything else* but fall into the loving embrace of such a God?
It is not through *our strength* or *actions* that we are redeemed...
but *only* through the *Grace of God*.

In the words of St. Paul,
"For when I am weak, then I am strong (2 Corinthians 12:10)."
God loves us because *God* is good...
not because *we* are.

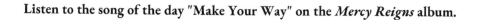

Listen to the song of the day "Make Your Way" on the *Mercy Reigns* album.

LOVE CASTS OUT FEAR | 26

Luke 12:6-7

Are not five sparrows sold for two small coins?
Yet not one of them has escaped the notice of God.
Even the hairs of your head have all been counted.
Do not be afraid.
You are worth more than many sparrows.

Fear.

How often does it stop us in our tracks...
or push us to do what we *don't want* to do or not do what we *want* to?

And yet Jesus said many times: "Do not be afraid."

Do we fear that God really doesn't love us?
Jesus says that we are loved *beyond what words can express...*
no matter what we do!

We are *free* from the bondage of having to *earn* God's love.

It has already forever been given.

As St. Paul stated,
"In him we were also chosen, destined in accord with the purpose of
the One who accomplishes all things according to the intention of his will,
so that we might exist for the praise of his glory..."(Ephesians 1:11-12).

Fear *not*...
for *you* are God's beloved!

Listen to the song of the day "The Way You Are" on the *Mercy Reigns* album.

27 THANKFUL

Psalm 118:1

Give thanks to the Lord, for He is good, his mercy endures forever.

Pause for a moment to give thanks.

God's love is *unconditional*.

Nothing we can do can make God love us more...
or less.

**God's mercy and forgiveness are freely given...
if we accept it.**

No matter how many times we slip and stumble...
God graciously picks us up and embraces us.
All we need to do...
is allow it.

It's an endless cycle of love.

We are invited to take part in this never-ending flow of Trinitarian Love.

Let us give thanks!

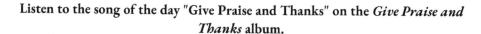

Listen to the song of the day "Give Praise and Thanks" on the *Give Praise and Thanks* album.

LET THE JOY RISE | 28

"Everything that the Father gives me will come to me, and I will not reject anyone who comes to me, because I came down from heaven not to do my own will but the will of the one who sent me. And this is the will of the one who sent me, that I should not lose anything of what he gave me, but that I should raise it on the last day."

This is one of the most *profound* and *amazing* statements made by Jesus.

For those who mistakenly believe in some fear-based religion
in which you are constantly trying to do things to make God somehow love you
or so that you can appease God enough to let you into some distant heaven...
please re-read today's scripture verses.

Read them slowly...
and then *re-read* and then *re-read* them again.

**What seems too good to be true...
is *so*.**

Jesus said it.
***Believe* it!**

This is the *Good News* of Jesus the Christ!

Listen to the song of the day "Let the Joy Rise" on the *Give Praise and Thanks* album.

29 | THE FACE OF LOVE

John 14:7

> "If you know me,
> then you will also know my Father.
> From now on,
> you do know him and have seen him."

God has *not* changed...
but human *understanding* of God *has* changed and evolved over time
until the definitive revelation came in Jesus.

**He told us that if we *knew him*...
we also would *know* God.**

Jesus loved and forgave *freely* and *unconditionally*.

**The only people he had difficulty with were those
who held others unbendingly to rules and were self-righteous.**

Jesus hung out with sinners and others who had been *thrown-out* and rejected.
He showed love to those who showed *no* love to him and
forgave those who unjustly killed him...
when they *hadn't even asked for forgiveness*!

***How could you help but fall in love with such a* God?**

Allow that knowledge to *sink* into your heart and soul.

Listen to the song of the day "Radically Okay" on the *Mercy Reigns* album.

NEW LIFE AHEAD | **30**

"Amen, amen I say to you,
you will weep and mourn,
while the world rejoices;
you will grieve,
but your grief will become joy."

Jesus knew that his followers would grieve when he was killed...
but he also knew that they would rejoice after his resurrection.

**Such it is in life when we lose something or someone...
or even as we slowly lose the false image of ourselves.**

As we grow...
the egocentric version of ourselves must die so that our true selves can emerge...
the self that reflects the unique image of God that we were meant to reflect.

Change **and** ***transformation*** **are never easy and always painful...
but as Jesus showed us...
for something new and beautiful to start...
something old must end.**

Dying leads to resurrection!

**Listen to the song of the day "Take the Road Less Traveled" on the *Live to Love*
album.**

I HAPPY FAULT

Matthew 9:11-13

The Pharisees saw this and said to his disciples,
"Why does your teacher eat with tax collectors and
sinners?" He heard this and said, "Those who are
well do not need a physician, but the sick do.
Go and learn the meaning of the words,
'I desire mercy, not sacrifice.'
I did not come to call the righteous, but sinners."

Jesus was always hanging out with the "wrong" crowd.
He was often sharing meals with so-called "sinners."
He seemed to have harsh words for only *one* group... the Pharisees...
the *religious leaders* who were constantly trying to enforce the letter of the law.
The Pharisees, of course, were sinners as well... but they acted as if they were not.
No one is perfect.
Everyone misses the mark on occasion and sometimes on *many* occasions.
Jesus knew that.
God made us imperfect so that we could experience what unconditional love is.
(*Think about it. Why would God make us imperfect and then
punish us for being imperfect? That makes no sense!*)
Jesus demonstrated for us that God is a God of mercy who wants nothing more
than to be *with us in our struggles and short-comings.*
For when we experience God's unmerited
love, forgiveness, compassion, and mercy, our hearts are *transformed*.
Then we can't help but want to pass that same unconditional love
and mercy on to others.
Are you aware that God loves you eternally just as you are?

Listen to the song of the day "The Way You Are" on the *Mercy Reigns* album.

INNER PEACE | 2

Matthew 8:24-26

Suddenly a violent storm came up on the sea,
so that the boat was being swamped by waves;
but he was asleep. They came and woke him,
saying, "Lord, save us! We are perishing!"
He said to them, "Why are you terrified,
O you of little faith?" Then he got up,
rebuked the winds and the sea,
and there was great calm.

Most of us are *control freaks*.
That's why we *freak out* so much when we encounter storms in our lives.
But Jesus' message to his followers is to *trust* him when those storms pop up.

This is when our faith can be nurtured as we admit that *we* are *not* in control.
Jesus constantly told his followers: "Do not be afraid."
God's unconditional love for us *never* changes.

It is only *in those times of turmoil* that we can truly *experience*
what *faith* is and how it can *transform* us.
Practice turning to Jesus by setting aside times of
quiet meditation or *silent time* with him.
Then even when storms surround us...
inner calm will *remain*.

What are the *storms* that are raging in *your* life?
Are you turning to Jesus for *inner calm*?

Listen to the song of the day "Come to Jesus" on the *Live to Love* album.

3 | LOVE HEALS

Matthew 8:8

> The centurion said in reply,
> "Lord, I am not worthy to have you
> enter under my roof;
> only say the word and my servant will be healed."

A Roman military officer came to Jesus to ask that he heal his servant who was paralyzed.

**The centurion, who had great military power,
was under no duty to do anything to help his servant...
but he apparently was a man of compassion.**

He was also humble... knowing he needed to turn to a Higher Power.
A centurion would not have shared *any* of Jesus' beliefs.
Notice how Jesus did not test the centurion about his *beliefs*
nor did he try to change him in any way.

**The centurion's beliefs were not a *criterion* to determine
whether or not Jesus would associate with him.**

The one thing that the centurion did exhibit was a simple *faith* that
a mere word from Jesus would be sufficient to heal his servant.
For Jesus...
that sufficed.
How would you like the Living Christ to heal *you*?

**Ask...
and trust that God will bring you the healing
that will lead you to wholeness.**

Listen to the song of the day "God's Love Is All You Need" on the *Listen to Your Heart* album.

REST | 4

Matthew 9:36

At the sight of the crowds, his heart was moved with pity for them because they were troubled and abandoned, like sheep without a shepherd.

It takes being at the *bottom* before you realize how much you need a *Higher Power*.
When you are at the top it is difficult to be aware that you truly *need* God.

Why *would* you... if you are wealthy, healthy, and powerful?
Those at the top are more likely to want to protect and accumulate what they have.
They have little motivation to help someone poor and struggling.
Many times... they don't even see such people.
Remember Jesus saying how hard it was for a rich person to enter the kingdom of God?
That's because many times they become attached to
their power, possessions, and prestige.
Thankfully, there are some very generous people of wealth willing to put their money,
power, and influence at work for good.
Jesus modeled the way for us to follow.

He moved *down* the so-called *ladder of success*... and joined those at the *bottom*.
Jesus *reached out* to those who were *cast out* by society.
Many were sick and in need of healing.
They were "troubled and abandoned, like sheep without a shepherd."

Jesus showed us that God has a deep love for those who are poor and suffering.

Sometimes it takes being troubled and abandoned before we are able
to let go of our attachments to things that can't save us (as in *make us whole*)...
so that we can turn to the Shepherd who will rescue us *every time*.
Why not do it *now*?

Listen to the song of the day "Let It Be Done to Me" on the *Mercy Reigns* album.

5 TRUST IN A HIGHER POWER

Matthew 9:20-22

A woman suffering hemorrhages
for twelve years came up behind him and
touched the tassel on his cloak. She said to herself,
"If only I can touch his cloak, I shall be cured."
Jesus turned around and saw her, and said,
"Courage, daughter! Your faith has saved you."
And from that hour the woman was cured.

Is there something you are struggling with?
Is there a problem, hurt, or issue that you can't seem to shake?
The woman in today's scripture suffered a horrible medical problem for twelve years...
one that would have made her "unclean" in the eyes of her community.
According to the religious rules at the time...
this woman would have been *cast out* by her church community.
She not only was suffering physically, but emotionally and spiritually.
But she *persevered* and put her hope in Jesus.
Her hope was in a *Higher Power*... a Love that would *not* forsake her.
This was an *Unconditional Love*... one that has *no* boundaries...
a Love that *includes* and shows *mercy and compassion* to *all*.

What wound(s) do *you* carry?

It may take time...
it may not happen the way *we* want it to...
but if we persevere and reach out to Jesus (God, Divine Source) in faith...
healing, wholeness, and new life are *assured*.

Listen to the song of the day "Heal Me" on the *Live to Love* album.

THE GREAT COMPASSION

Psalm 145:8-9

The Lord is gracious and merciful,
slow to anger and abounding in love.
The Lord is good to all,
compassionate to every creature.

Jesus says if you know *him* then you know *God* (John 14:7).

Who do we see in Jesus?

We see a man who reaches out to those in pain, suffering, and need.

We see a man who does not condemn a woman caught in adultery,
but instead *forgives* her in love and thereby *transforms* her.

We see a man who likens himself to a "Good Shepherd" who refuses
to let *one* sheep go astray.

We see a man who personifies *love, mercy, forgiveness, and compassion.*

We see a man who would permit others to kill him so that he could show
that God responds with love even when rejected in the most extreme fashion.

So *this* is Who God Is.

And our Creator feels the same about not only each of us but about *all* of creation:
"God looked at everything he had made, and found it very good" (Genesis 1:31).

Allow this experience of God to settle in your soul.

Listen to the song of the day "Salvation" on the *Live to Love* album.

7 STAND IN THE LIGHT

Psalm 18:3-4

I love you, Lord, my strength,
Lord, my rock, my fortress, my deliverer,
my God, my rock of refuge, my shield,
my saving horn, my stronghold!
Praised be the Lord, I exclaim!
I have been delivered from my enemies.

Sometimes we are persecuted in life.

**But if we rely on God...
we *will be rescued*.**

When you are unable to save yourself...
allow God to take care of it.

God is really *good* at it!

Jesus showed us the extent God was willing to go to show us unconditional Love.

If you are in the middle of a storm...
allow God to hold you like a father or mother would cradle a child,
while whispering into your ear,
*"I love you...
we're going to make it...
together!"*

Listen to the song of the day "I Stand in the Light" on the *Mercy Reigns* album.

ALL ARE FORGIVEN | **8**

Psalm 51:3

Have mercy on me, God, in your goodness;
in your abundant compassion,
blot out my offense.

We are all wounded.

We have all done things we are not proud of.

We are not perfect. We were made that way. Why would God do that?
Perhaps so that we would allow God to forgive us...
heal us...
console us...
comfort us...
and love us back into wholeness!
That's what God yearns to do.

How else would be experience compassion?

God wants to love you exactly in the place that you feel nobody could!

Is this *your* understanding of God?

Jesus showed us the abundant compassion of God:
"Come to me, all you who labor and are burdened, and I will give you rest"
(Matthew 11:28).

Come to him just as you are!
Allow Mercy to heal you.

Listen to the song of the day "Radically Okay" on the *Mercy Reigns* album.

9 | TURN TO LOVE

Matthew 11:20

Then Jesus began to reproach the towns where most of his mighty deeds had been done, since they had not repented.

To *repent* is to *change the direction* in which you are seeking *happiness* or *fulfillment*.
**Jesus went about curing people *not* to get *rave reviews* of his miracles and become a *celebrity,* but so people could see that God wants *everyone* to be "whole".
God wants us all to know that we *belong*... we are *included*.**

Jesus cured the sick (who would have been *cast-out* of their communities as "unclean")
and were therefore *restored*.
**Most people are looking for *wholeness, meaning,* and *fulfillment*
in the *wrong* places.**

They are trying to find something that is missing...
trying to satisfy an inner yearning for wholeness through
power, prestige, and possessions or physical pleasure.
But the space that needs filling... can only be filled by God who *is* Love.
Only *God* can satisfy that deep, spiritual yearning for *wholeness.*
A deeper connection with God... the Loving Source of all life... is the *only* answer.

A stronger relationship with Jesus is a great way to strengthen your bond with God.
He showed us how to *live* and how to *die.*
He showed us how to *love.*
**All it takes is a decision that can be made with *each new moment*...
to *turn away* from the things that cannot provide our wholeness and
to *turn toward* the only *One* who *can*.**

Why not *now?*

**Listen to the song of the day "You'll Lead Me" on the *Listen to Your Heart*
album.**

YOU ARE CHERISHED |

Psalm 94:14

You, Lord, will not forsake your people, nor abandon your very own.

Perhaps you are struggling with something.
Perhaps it's a health issue, money issue, or relationship issue.
Perhaps it's an addiction.
It may be that proverbial thorn in your side that you *can't seem to shake*.

**Know that God is there in the *midst* of it... not *against* you...
but *with* you... not *judging* or *condemning* you...
but *accepting* and *comforting* you.**

It is the place where you *need* God...
the place where God wants to *commune* with you and *lift* you...
to *heal* you and *bring you to wholeness*.
But it will happen in God's way and God's time.

**If you *trust* and *let go*... your *scar* will be *transformed* into a *star*.
Jesus showed us that death is *always transformed into new life* and *wholeness*.**

Some of my greatest struggles led to me writing songs that in turn
I now share with those who are suffering, as well as in jail ministry.

**The very things that tormented me
were transformed into healing balm for others.**

This is what Love *does*.
Cling to this hope!
Where would we be... where would we turn... without it?
Loving God, I trust in You!

Listen to the song of the day "Changed" on the *Give Praise and Thanks* album.

II ETERNAL COMFORT

Matthew 11:28

"Come to me,
all you who labor and are burdened,
and I will give you rest."

Jesus was speaking to the people burdened
by being held to the *letter of the law* by their religious leaders.
**Sometimes life hands us situations that do not fit
so easily into "black and white" categories.**

Jesus simply invited people to bring their struggles to him.
There was no *judgment*...
no *condemnation*...
only *acceptance* and *mercy*.

**Jesus invites us to follow *his* ways with the assurance that
this path will bring us *inner peace*.**

Are *you* struggling with issues in your life or your faith?
Let Jesus' words be a *comfort* to you.

God looks at you through the lens of unconditional love and compassion.
Allow that *gaze* to settle upon you.
Share that gaze with others who struggle in the "gray" areas of life's issues.

And while you're at it...
let your loving gaze...
fall upon *yourself*...
and find *rest*.

Listen to the song of the day "I Will Give You Rest" on the *Live to Love* album.

GOD IS LOVE | 12

Psalm 69:3, 34

I have sunk into the mire of the deep,
where there is no foothold.
I have gone down to the watery depths;
the flood overwhelms me.
The Lord hears the poor,
does not spurn those in bondage.

Sometimes it takes sinking to the *deepest depths*
before our pride is weakened enough
to allow our egos to *surrender*
so that we can *fall into the loving arms of God.*

**God has *no* intention of *letting go* of us because
we are God's *beloved daughters and sons.***

This is why the depths of your deepest fall,
the place of your most painful wound,
becomes the place of your most wondrous *redemption and healing.*

**It's the *only place* where you can truly experience
the transforming *unconditional love* of God.**

Why sink any further...
when you can turn to your loving Creator *now...*
right where you are?

Listen to the song of the day "God Is" on the *Give Praise and Thanks* album.

197

13 LOVE EMBRACES EVERYTHING

Exodus 3:2-3

As Moses looked on, he was surprised to see that the bush, though on fire, was not consumed. So Moses decided, "I must go over to look at this remarkable sight, and see why the bush is not burned."

God comes to Moses in *both* the *ordinary* (the bush) *and*
the *extraordinary* (a flaming bush not being consumed) at the *same time.*
First off, God is present in the *ordinary*.
But are *we* being present enough to experience the Divine Presence?
Are we paying attention?
**Secondly, God comes... not in a clear "black and white" concept...
but in a *contradiction*: a *burning* bush that at the same time is *not burned*.**
We can take comfort in knowing that God is present amidst
the contradictions of life and amidst our struggles with them...
all the while holding them together as one.
God seems perfectly comfortable with paradoxes like,
"Whoever finds his life will lose it, and whoever loses his life for my sake will find
it" (Matthew 10:39) or "virgin mother."
**It would seem that we are being invited into the
contradictions and paradoxes of life where there are no easy answers.**
As Rainer Maria Rilke stated: "Do not seek answers which cannot be given you because
you would not be able to live them. Live the questions now. Perhaps you will then,
gradually, without noticing it, live along some distant day into answer"
(*Letters to a Young Poet*, New York: Norton, 1954, pp. 34-5).
**So perhaps we are being taught to get beyond our "*either-or*" judgmental
thinking... so we can experience a "*both-and*"... all-loving God.**
God is holding *our* contradictions... and responding with acceptance and love.
Thank God!

Listen to the song of the day "How Magnificent, Wondrous and Glorious" on the
Mercy Reigns album.

UNCONDITIONALLY LOVED

Isaiah 7:9

Unless your faith is firm, you shall not be firm!

How many times do we think that we have to have our lives *totally together* before we'll be ready to take a stand in faith?

"Totally together" will never happen.

It's a set up for *constant striving* and *constant failure* and *guilt*.

If God *is* Love as it says in scripture (1 John 4:8),

then God is *not* some ogre looking to punish you for not being perfect.

What a cruel God that would be!

God *is* Love.

I hope that you have experienced being unconditionally loved by someone in your lifetime.

If you have, then know that God is *infinitely more loving* than that person.

And if you *haven't* experienced such love...

I hope that you will hear my voice as I say to you here and now:

God loves you with no strings attached!

We are not here to prove ourselves *worthy* of God's love.

God does not love us because *we* are good...

but because *God* is good.

God loves each of us infinitely *just as we are!*

Allow that to sink in.

It's a foundation that you can *stand on* and have *faith in*...

no matter how *badly broken* you are.

God wants to love you *in* your brokenness!

Read about all the broken people Jesus reached out to in the Gospels.

Look at all the broken people that he still picked to follow him.

The Living Christ is reaching out to *you*...

and wants to *be with you* and give you *new life*.

Have faith in *that!*

Listen to the song of the day "The Way You Are" on the *Mercy Reigns* album.

Matthew 12:1-2, 7

His disciples were hungry and began to pick the heads of grain and eat them. When the Pharisees saw this, they said to him, "See, your disciples are doing what is unlawful to do on the Sabbath." Jesus said to them, "If you knew what this meant, 'I desire mercy, not sacrifice,' you would not have condemned these innocent men."

Rules are all well and good to keep us from running wild...
giving us healthy boundaries so that we can truly become what God intended.
For the young and immature... clear rules are necessary.
But as we grow in *age* and *consciousness*... we need a *bigger picture*.
Rules remain important... but Jesus clearly says that mercy and love *trump* the rules.
The disciples were hungry...
so it was okay for them to eat even though they were breaking Sabbath rules.
When your mind is looking through an "either-or" lens (like the Pharisees) you can only
see *black and white*. You *either* follow the rule and you are good...
or break it and you are bad.
Jesus looks through a "both-and" lens seeing the *grays* of life.
You can *both* keep the rules *and* break them when it's in the name of love and mercy...
and still be *good*.
Your mind may be rebelling against this concept. Perhaps you need a *new lens*!

As St. Paul says, "be renewed in the spirit of your minds and
put on the new self" (Ephesians 4:23-24).

Listen to the song of the day "Mercy Reigns" on the *Mercy Reigns* album.

GOD IS FOR YOU | 16

Exodus 14:12

"Did we not tell you this in Egypt, when we said, 'Leave us alone. Let us serve the Egyptians'? Far better for us to be the slaves of the Egyptians than to die in the desert."

How many times in our lives does it seem that just when things go *well...* something happens to pull the proverbial rug *out* from under us?

It's then when we many times *rail against* God for supposedly *leaving* us. The Israelites were jubilant in following Moses out of Egypt after *hundreds of years of captivity* until Pharaoh changed his mind about releasing them and sent hundreds of Egyptian soldiers after them in the desert. So the Israelites *turned on* Moses and on God in *despair.*

There are peaks and valleys in our lives. *Hard times* come due to the free-will choices *we* make or *others* make... or just by *chance.* The story of salvation history shows us that *despite the people turning against* God... **God *never left them.***

Over and over and over God *remained* loyal. Jesus showed us the *extreme lengths* God will go in the face of total *rejection* to say, "I love you. I forgive you. I will never let you go... *never.*"

If you're struggling... **God *is most assuredly still with you!***

Listen to the song of the day "How Wonderful to Me" on the *Live to Love* album.

17 | OCEAN OF LOVE

Micah 7:19

You will cast into the depths of the sea all our sins.

There is a grand plan for all of creation to reach its fullness.
We are *part* of that plan.

**All we need to do is *awaken* to *who we are* as a
beloved son or daughter of God...
to *awaken* to our wholeness in God.**

Each of us is flawed in our humanness.
Each of us is imperfect.
That is *totally okay.*

It is *in our imperfection* that we *meet God.*

It is *not* the place where God is unhappy with us or wants to punish us.
It *is* the place where God *yearns to be with us* and *transform us*
with *unconditional love* and *acceptance.*
Why would God make us *imperfect* and then punish us for being *imperfect*?

God's love for us does not change.

It is our very *imperfections* that lead us to discover
the *love, mercy, forgiveness, and compassion* of God.
Jesus showed us that God *always* responds with *love and forgiveness*
("Father, forgive them, they know not what they do" – Luke 23:34).

It is the only way to transformation and wholeness...
or in a word, "salvation."

Listen to the song of the day "Salvation" on the *Live to Love* album.

LISTEN TO YOUR HEART | 18

Matthew 13:2

Such large crowds gathered around him that he got into a boat and sat down, and the whole crowd stood along the shore.

Jesus was quite the attraction.
But he did not want to be a celebrity.
While our culture flocks to worship celebrities who identify with their power, prestige, and wealth... Jesus identified with no *thing*.
His identity was not attached to the stuff of this world.
He spoke of equality, justice for the poor, compassion, humility, and detachment from possessions... not renouncing them, just not identifying with them.

While our culture promotes and esteems competition as the
pinnacle principle to success (as in climbing to the top)...
Jesus promoted service and reaching out to help
those who were left behind or cast out (as in joining those at the bottom).
Jesus never preached *winning*... but rather helping the one who is *losing*.

While our culture clamors to attain more... more and more...
Jesus calls us to aspire to attain less.
Power, prestige, and possessions will never satisfy on the soul level.

If you are looking for soul satisfaction... why not turn to the man who said he was
"the way, the truth, and the life" (John 14:6)?
Crowds came to hear Jesus speak.
Do we make the same effort to listen to him speak
through scripture and quiet meditation?
Set aside some time to simply sit and listen.
It just might change your life... and set you free.

Listen to the song of the day "Listen to Your Heart" on the *Listen to Your Heart* album.

19 | GOD IS CARRYING YOU

Psalm 18:2-3

I love you, Lord, my strength, Lord, my rock,
my fortress, my deliverer, my God,
my rock of refuge, my shield,
my saving horn, my stronghold!

Whatever you are going through now...
know that you *will get through it*.
You *will*!
You are an *eternal*, *spiritual* being having a *human* experience.

God is *with* you.
**It is in the *process* of getting through your struggles
that you will be *transformed*.**
You will find *new life*.
**This is your Loving Creator's desire...
to *deliver* you to a better place... to *wholeness*.**

This is your *salvation*.
One day you will look back on this struggle and see it differently.
If you want encouragement...
just look at Jesus on the cross and see how what appeared to be
the ultimate, humiliating *defeat*...
turned into the ultimate, glorious *victory*!

**When you walk the path of *self-emptying love*...
you will find *life everlasting*.**

Love will *always* lead you home.

Listen to the song of the day "Love Will Always Lead You Home" on the *Mercy Reigns* album.

BOUNDLESS LOVE

Psalm 36:6

Lord, your love reaches to heaven; your fidelity, to the clouds.

God's extreme, extravagant love is so *immense*...
so *amazing*...
so *beyond what we can fathom*...
it *boggles* our minds.
It's beyond reason.

Love with *NO* conditions!
Throw out rational logic.
Just *accept* it.

Laws and rules are needed...
but with Jesus...
love always had the final say.

And *so it is* with our Creator.
Jesus repeatedly forgave sinners *even when they didn't ask for forgiveness*.
A legalistic mind cannot handle that!

You are loved *just because you are God's beloved*.
It has *nothing* to do with what you *do*...
but *who God is*.

Allow that to settle in your heart.
It will *transform* you...
which is *exactly what God wants*...
so you can share it with others.

Listen to the song of the day "Pour Me Out" on the *Give Praise and Thanks* album.

21 | GIFT OF GRACE

Micah 6:8

You have been told...
what is good, and what the Lord requires of you:
Only to do the right
and to love goodness,
and to walk humbly with your God.

The prophet Micah says that God is not interested in your sacrifices
to *prove* yourself *more worthy* of God's love.

God is only interested in your *heart*.

God *already loves you infinitely*...
and that love is *unconditional*!

**We would do well to simply *awaken* to that fact and
allow it to *sink in* and *fill* us.**

Doesn't *that* kind of love make you *fall in love* with such a God?
Doesn't *that* kind of love make you want to
"do the right and to love goodness,
and to walk humbly with your God"?

**Listen to the song of the day "You'll Lead Me" on the *Listen to Your Heart*
album.**

ALL ARE ONE IN GOD

Jeremiah 14:22

Among the nations' idols,
is there any that gives rain?
O, can the mere heavens send showers?
Is it not you alone, O Lord,
our God, to whom we look?
You alone have done all these things.

God causes the rain to fall on *all* people... the *just* and the *unjust* alike.
Some say, "Unfair!"
Our egos don't like this unconditional love of God!

Have you heard that "ego" stands for "Edge God Out"?
God is generous *beyond our understanding*... even to those we *dislike*.
Jesus told us that we *must* love our enemies.
This is a hard saying when we are operating from a mind that is
constantly dividing people into those who are "in" and those who are "out."
What we need is a *transformed* mind.

In the words of St. Paul: "Do not conform yourself to this age,
but be transformed by the renewal of your mind,
that you may discern what is the will of God,
what is good and pleasing and perfect" (Romans 12:2).
**This is not by our *own* doing...
but totally by the *grace of God*.**
Our minds need to be changed by the unconditional love of God...
who sends the rains on all people as one body of Christ.
And may we all respond as *one*, "Amen!"

Listen to the song of the day "All Are One" on the *Mercy Reigns* album.

23 | LIFE GIVING WORDS

Matthew 13:22

"The seed sown among thorns
is the one who hears the word,
but then worldly anxiety and the lure of riches
choke the word and it bears no fruit."

Sometimes people think Jesus is irrelevant to their lives.
But have they truly listened to his words and followed them?

**Could it be that they have bought into the ways of the world
and so any alternative message is not welcome?**

For the words of Jesus to truly take root we must cultivate
the soil of our hearts so the seeds can grow.
What are some of the things we do that allow thorns to pollute our soil?

**To nourish the soil of our hearts will require setting aside
some special time of silence to sit and read the words of Jesus.**

Allow the words to settle deep in your heart.
This practice led to some drastic and difficult changes in my life...
but ones that have led to great peace, inner joy, and freedom.

Why not set aside a few minutes for silent reflection today?

**Listen to the song of the day "Turn Off the Noise" on the *Listen to Your Heart*
album.**

YOU ARE A MASTERPIECE

24

Jeremiah 18:6

Indeed, like clay in the hand of the potter,
so are you in my hand, house of Israel.

Just as God's words came to the prophet Jeremiah...
they are still true for each of us *today*.

**No matter what you've done in the past...
no matter how badly you have *messed up* your life...
God can mold you again.**

You are a work of art... *in progress*.
You are actually *already a masterpiece* in the eyes of God...
but perhaps are *unaware* of your beauty due to life's circumstances.

**Like clay in the hand of the potter...
God wants to re-fashion you *again* and *again* and *again*
to carry on the *on-going love story of creation*.**

This story is like a *cosmic dance* with God...
accompanied by the most amazing music!
You are part of the story.
You are *included*.

God *never* turns away from you.

The invitation to the dance is *never* withdrawn and is
always being offered as long as you have breath.
Will you accept the invitation?
The time to do so... is *now*.

Listen to the song of the day "Shall We Sing" on the *Listen to Your Heart* album.

25 | AWAKEN

Psalm 84:3

My heart and flesh cry out for the living God.

We are all *yearning* at a soul-level
to be filled and *embraced* by our Loving Creator.
Unfortunately, many do not realize this *yearning* is for
oneness with God
and try to satisfy this deep *thirst*
with a physical or material solution.

Instead of *reaching out* to grasp or cling to something...
the true *objective* is to *let go* of things...
releasing attachments so we can have open hands.

Then we are awakened to the Divine Presence.

It is only through *emptying* ourselves of our egos' desires
that God can *give* us what we *truly need* and are *yearning* for.

**As St. Augustine said,
"Our hearts are restless until they rest in You."**

Listen to the song of the day "I Surrender" on the *Live to Love* album.

ALL IS WELL | **26**

Psalm 103:12

As far as the east is from the west, so far has he removed our sins from us.

Are you refusing to let go of your baggage?
Are you still clinging to old hurts...
old resentments...
old wrong-doings (whether committed by you or against you)?

God forgives you *freely* and *completely*.

We see this repeatedly in the scriptures...
whether it be the story of the Prodigal Son,
the woman caught in adultery...
or most magnificently when Jesus said while hanging on the cross,
"Father forgive them,
they know not what they do" (Luke 23:34).

**You see...
that is what grace *is*.**

Grace is unearned, unconditional love and forgiveness...
freely given to us.

**It doesn't seem fair...
because it's *not*.**

It's *Grace!*
Allow yourself to feel it now...
and be free!

Listen to the song of the day "Radically Okay" on the *Mercy Reigns* album.

27 | LET GO AND BELIEVE

Psalm 31:6

Into your hands I commend my spirit;
you will redeem me,
Lord, faithful God.

Sometimes there are no answers.
**There are times in life when we come to the jarring conclusion
that we are clueless as to what to do...
that we are clearly unable to handle the situation alone.**

Easy answers are very convenient...
but they rob us of the necessary tough journeys of
living out the answers to the questions.
These journeys are critical to deepening our spiritual development
and are necessary in finding out who we are
and in discovering that a loving God
is always embracing us along the path of discovery...
a God who wants each of us to be whole and happy.

**Sometimes when faced with a difficult situation...
I simply place it in the hands of a Loving Providence.**

Jesus seldom gave answers but mostly taught with parables
that invited his followers into paradoxical situations.

**As I grow older I realize more and more that wrestling
with harder questions is far more enlightening
than being given easy answers.**

Trust in the process.

Listen to the song of the day "Make Your Way" on the *Mercy Reigns* album.

SWEET SURRENDER | **28**

Luke 11:38-39

The Pharisee was amazed to see that Jesus did not observe the prescribed washing before the meal. The Lord said to him, "Oh you Pharisees! Although you cleanse the outside of the cup and the dish, inside you are filled with plunder and evil."

How many times do we wear a mask...
putting on a false, outer appearance...
pretending we have it all together when we are quite messed up inside?
Jesus knew that what really mattered was what was in a person's heart.
Doing all the rituals and following all the rules doesn't mean anything
if the inner motivation isn't love.
**If you don't undergo an *inner transformation* through which
you become more *loving* and *compassionate*...
then *what good is it*?**
It's interesting to see that Jesus had nothing but compassion for those
who struggled and failed...
who humbly admitted it.
His contempt was for the self-righteous...
those who judged and looked down on others...
putting the law ahead of Love.
**Our imperfection isn't scorned by God...
it is rather the very means by which we experience God's
unconditional love and acceptance.**
It's the place where we *need* God.
If you are struggling with something...
you are the type of person that Jesus *wants* to be with.
Bring your struggles to him and *be free*.

Listen to the song of the day "Come to Jesus" on the *Live to Love* album.

29 TRANSFORMATION IN PROGRESS

Psalm 91:15

He will call upon me
and I will answer;
I will be with him in distress.

No one of us wants to go through the valley of the shadow of death.
We don't enjoy trials and tribulations.

But...
I know that those are the times in my life
when I *most* felt the *presence of God*.

There was *Something larger than myself...*
a *Divine Presence...*
carrying me through the turmoil.

And on the *other side* of the struggle...
came *transformation* and *new life*.

Always.
God is in the *transformation business*.

That's what Love does...
when you hang in the struggle and cling to hope...
trusting that there is a Great Compassion drawing us forward...
leading us to a *deeper experience* of Love.

Listen to the song of the day "Love Will Always Lead You Home" on the *Mercy Reigns* album.

THE ETERNAL PROMISE |

John 6:37-39

"Everything that the Father gives me
will come to me, and
I will not reject anyone who comes to me,
because I came down from heaven not to do my
own will but the will of the one who sent me.
And this is the will of the one who sent me,
that I should not lose anything of what he gave me,
but that I should raise it on the last day."

For all who have lost a loved one...
or who struggle with a fear of death in *any way*...
take comfort in these words of Jesus.

**The One who told us *over and over* not to be afraid of *anything*...
pledges in today's scripture reading that he will *never let go of you*!**

All of us are welcomed by God.

**If you accept the invitation...
Jesus will *not* reject you!**

The communion of saints must be quite the array of characters!
You and *I* are included.

Amen.

Listen to the song of the day "All Are Welcome" on the *Give Praise and Thanks* album.

31 LET GO

Matthew 6:6-8

"When you pray, go to your inner room,
close the door, and pray to your Father in secret.
And your Father who sees in secret will repay you.
In praying, do not babble like the pagans,
who think that they will be heard because of their
many words. Do not be like them.
Your Father knows what you need
before you ask him."

Could Jesus have been any clearer in his instruction on how to pray?
Prayer is a very intimate encounter with your Loving Creator
where you spend time in the *Presence of Love*.

God knows what you truly need...
so why not go to the quiet place inside yourself,
allow your ego's cravings to be exposed.
Allow them to *fade*.

Then... turn to the Divine Presence for satisfaction.
As the saying goes, "Let go... and let God."
Jesus taught us to pray that *God's* will be done.
What God wants for us is *infinitely* better
than anything we could possibly imagine!

What would it take to create a space for some quiet prayer or "*letting go time*" today?

Listen to the song of the day "Turn Off the Noise" on the *Listen to Your Heart*
album.

HAVE FAITH | I

Matthew 14:29-31

Jesus said, "Come." Peter got out of the boat and began to walk on the water toward Jesus. But when he saw how strong the wind was he became frightened; and, beginning to sink, he cried out, "Lord, save me!" Immediately Jesus stretched out his hand and caught him, and said to him, "O, you of little faith, why did you doubt?"

Are you distressed about something that has come up?
Have you become *anxious* and *fearful* over life's circumstances?
**What if the *seemingly* frightful turn of events is *actually* a *new door opening*...
an *invitation* to *new life*?**
Situations *in and of themselves are what they are.*
Your *reaction* to them is *another matter.*
What thoughts are being produced by your mind?
Be still.
In the storm, Jesus walked on the water to his fearful followers. He was the *calm* in the center of the storm. Just as he invited Peter to step out of the boat, he invites *you* to step out of your *comfort zone* — where you might *feel* safe, but are *paralyzed* to any *real growth.* Step out into the waves, but make sure you keep your eyes on Jesus.
In his calmness, he invites you to "come."
Know that the Source of Life is drawing you forward.
The experience will lead you to *growth* and a *deeper discovery* of your *true self.*
Should you falter and begin to sink... your Loving Creator will *always* catch you.
That's what *Love* does... *time after time after time.*
Have faith! A Great Love is leading you to *new life* and *wholeness*!

Listen to the song of the day "Heal Me" on the *Live to Love* album.

2 LOVE IS OUR SOURCE & DESTINATION

Jeremiah 31:3-4

> With age-old love I have loved you;
> so I have kept my mercy toward you.
> Again I will restore you,
> and you shall be rebuilt.

God did not make us *imperfect* in order to *punish and condemn us for our imperfection.*
Besides not making sense...
a God who did such a thing would be a *cruel tyrant.*

**God made us imperfect so God could be *with us in our imperfection*...
so that we could then *experience* and come to *know*
true *unconditional love, mercy, forgiveness, and compassion*...
and be *transformed* in the process.**

If you look at the story of God's people throughout the Bible,
it is *one example after another* of the people *rejecting* God...
and God *relentlessly pursuing* and *calling them back*...
over and over and over.
Sound familiar?

Do *we* not do the *same* thing?

**Jesus showed us that God will go to *any lengths*
to show us *love* in the face of rejection...
and that *love will win in the end.***

Our Loving Source will *never* stop working to *restore* and *redeem* us.
This is the *Good News* of *salvation*!

Listen to the song of the day "Salvation" on the *Live to Love* album.

FEAR NO MORE

Luke 24:36-39

While they were still speaking about this,
he stood in their midst and said to them,
"Peace be with you."
But they were startled and terrified and
thought that they were seeing a ghost.
Then he said to them, "Why are you troubled?
And why do questions arise in your hearts?
Look at my hands and my feet, that it is I myself."

After suffering the greatest injustice in *history*...
the resurrected Jesus returns to his followers...
well... his *deserters* at this point...
and he wishes them "peace."

There were *no* condemnations... *no* reprimands.
He tells them not to be afraid or troubled.
Why fear *anything* anymore?
Jesus has showed them (and us) the path to wholeness and peace.

Death does *not* win. New Life is *assured*.

But notice that the scars *remain* on Jesus' body.
While they are no longer bleeding...
the marks are *still there*.
**The struggles, pains, and sufferings of life are a necessary part
of the journey that leads to wholeness and your *true self*.**

**Listen to the song of the day "Take the Road Less Traveled" on the *Live to Love*
album.**

4 TRANSFIGURED BY LOVE

2 Peter 1:18-19

We ourselves heard this voice come
from heaven while we were with him
on the holy mountain.
Moreover, we possess the prophetic
message that is altogether reliable.
You will do well to be attentive to it,
as to a lamp shining in a dark place,
until day dawns and the morning star
rises in your hearts.

Peter was with James and John when Jesus was transfigured
into dazzling white on a mountain.
They heard the voice of God announce to them that
Jesus was His chosen Son and to listen to him.

Jesus was the *perfect reflection* of God.

We are called to follow Jesus and his ways
by using our unique gifts and talents
so that we are unique yet *imperfect reflections* of God as well.

**Are you being attentive to the *Divine Voice* that names *you*
the *beloved son or daughter*?**

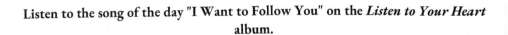

**Listen to the song of the day "I Want to Follow You" on the *Listen to Your Heart*
album.**

LOST AND FOUND | 5

Matthew 18:12-14

"If a man has a hundred sheep and one of them goes astray, will he not leave the ninety-nine in the hills and go in search of the stray? And if he finds it, amen, I say to you, he rejoices more over it than over the ninety-nine that did not stray. In just the same way, it is not the will of your heavenly Father that one of these little ones be lost."

Have *you* ever *strayed* from God?
I'm sure you have. Me, too.
We *all* have.

Perhaps you are *off track* now?
Perhaps you have done things that you think could
never be forgiven or disqualify you from God's love?
Not so!

Jesus says that there is *nothing* you can do to stop God
from *seeking you out* and *returning you* to the fold.
Nothing!

God loves you because you are a son or daughter...
and *nothing* can *change* that!
**All you need to do is to forgive *others and* yourself...
then *return* into God's open arms.**

Listen to the song of the day "Love Will Always Lead You Home" on the *Mercy Reigns* album.

6 DEATH LEADS TO LIFE

Matthew 17:22-23

As they were gathering in Galilee,
Jesus said to them,
"The Son of Man is to be handed over to men,
and they will kill him,
and he will be raised on the third day."
And they were overwhelmed with grief.

Sometimes life is hard.

Things happen that cause us to *suffer*.
There are all kinds of theories as to why...
but it remains a *mystery*.

However, we know *this*: *Jesus suffered*.

He also said that if you knew him then you would know God (John 8:19).
That means God *suffered with* him.
God *suffers with* us.

Jesus *poured out* his life in acts of love, mercy, forgiveness, and compassion
without condition or lines of division.
He showed us that ultimately...
death leads to New Life!

So does *each episode* of *suffering* we experience...
if we *cling* to Jesus who is *more than willing to help us.*
That is Good News!

Listen to the song of the day "Make Your Way" on the *Mercy Reigns* album.

RELEASE THE PAST | 7

Matthew 18:21-22

Then Peter came to Jesus and asked, "Lord,
how many times shall I forgive my brother
or sister who sins against me?
As many as seven times?"
Jesus answered, "I say to you,
not seven times but seventy-seven times."

In effect... Jesus tells us that the number of times we must forgive others is *limitless*.
It is truly the *key* to our *salvation*...
and by *salvation* I mean *completion* and *wholeness*.
**You cannot be freely engaged in the Flow of God's Love in the *present moment*...
if you are *fixated* on a *past grievance*.
You cannot move freely into the freedom of the kingdom of God
while shackled in the chains of grudges and resentments.**

Jesus showed us the importance of forgiveness in
the prayer that he taught us when he instructed us to pray,
"Forgive us as we forgive those who trespass against us."

In his book, *The Four Things that Matter Most*, author Ira Byock writes,
"It is wrong to think that people need to feel forgiveness in order to give forgiveness.
Forgiveness is actually about emotional economics.
It's about a one-time cost that you pay to clear up years of compounded emotional pain."
"Refusing to forgive is a decision to remain in debt."
God's forgiveness is freely given to you.
Accept it... then *pay it forward*.
Forgive... and *be free*!

**Listen to the song of the day "God's Love Is All You Need" on the *Listen to Your
Heart* album.**

8 BE GRATEFUL

Psalm 148:11-13

You kings of the earth and all peoples,
princes, and all who govern on earth;
Young men and women too, old and young alike.
Let them all praise the Lord's name,
for his name alone is exalted,
majestic above earth and heaven.

Stop for a moment and consider all your blessings.
Look back at your life and all the amazing, wonderful people who made a difference.
Without them...
you would not be the person you are today.
Look at the blessings that surround you now.

Your senses are immersed in gifts from God.
Each *breath* is a gift.

Yes... each of us has struggles.
But at the same time...
God *never* stops showering us with free gifts of
love, mercy, grace, forgiveness, and compassion.

**It is only *through the struggles* that we can truly experience
God's *unconditional* love.**

God is *so close* to each of us. At our *deepest* core... our deepest *essence*... is God.
Our Creator has *loved each of us into existence* and will *never* abandon us.
How amazing is the One who made us!

Listen to the song of the day "Give Praise and Thanks" on the *Give Praise and Thanks* album.

FORGIVENESS IS FREE 9

Ezekiel 16:62-63

For I will re-establish my covenant with you,
that you may remember and be covered with
confusion, and that you may be utterly
silenced for shame when I pardon you for
all you have done, says the Lord God.

God's people *constantly* broke their covenant with God... *time after time after time.*
We *continue* to do so.
But God offers us *unconditional* love.
God *IS* Unconditional Love!

Yet each of us has turned away... *many* times...
choosing to serve our egos instead.
Despite this... God *did* not and *does* not reject us.
Instead of *condemning*... God *forgives*!

I believe that it is *precisely the fact that God forgives when we don't deserve it*...
that makes all the difference.
We are *not punished* but *loved* by a Creator who *can only love.*
And when we receive this Unconditional Love in response to our sinfulness...
we are "covered with confusion" and "utterly silenced for shame."
We weep in the face of such unmerited Love.
Our hearts are *changed*.

This is the *transformation* we undergo as we gaze upon Jesus on the cross as he looks
down upon those who have rejected him in the most *extreme* manner and says,
"Father, forgive them, they know not what they do" (Luke 23:34).
This is a Love that *transforms* us... and *sets us free*.

Listen to the song of the day "Changed" on the *Give Praise and Thanks* album.

10 DIVINE RELATIONSHIP

Matthew 18:19-20

Again, (amen,) I say to you, if two of you agree on earth about anything for which they are to pray, it shall be granted to them by my heavenly Father. For where two or three are gathered together in my name, there am I in the midst of them."

God clearly wants us to be in *communal relationships* and not just on a *personal salvation project*.
While Jesus *did* want his followers to pray in *solitude* at times
("When you pray, go to your inner room, close the door, and pray to your Father in secret." Matthew 6:6),
he also made it clear to his followers in today's scripture verse that he wanted them to *gather together* to pray as well.
And when they did... he would be truly *present* and that God would answer their prayers.
God's answer, however, might *not* be exactly what *we* want.

We must remember that God sees the BIG picture.
God is not Santa Claus or a genie ready to grant our every whim and wish.
It seems to me that God wants nothing more than for each of us to become our *true self*... to be *whole*... the person we were created to be.

God wants us to *know* Love, be *transformed* by Love, and to *transmit* that Love on to others.
While we sometimes don't understand why God doesn't answer our prayers the way we want... Jesus says we must be like "children"... trusting that God has our *best interests* at heart and is giving us exactly what we *need*.

Listen to the song of the day "Let It Be Done to Me" on the *Mercy Reigns* album.

G∞D NEWS | II

Praise the Lord, who is so good;
God's love endures forever.

We all get caught up in a false premise that we need to *earn* God's love.
We get caught up in a *worthiness contest*...
a game we play to win God's favor.

This is an *illusion*.
Or should I say *delusion*.
God loved you *before you were born*, loves you *now*, and *will* love you *forever*.

In each moment, God's love is being poured out *in* and *through* all things.
It cannot be withheld because *that's* what God *does*...
fills all things with love...
even when it's hard to see and feel it.
Our "sinfulness"... our *imperfection*... does not diminish God's ability to love us.

That's exactly how we come to know what *unconditional* Love *is!*
(God *made* us imperfect, *right?*)
It is *through* our *imperfection* that we come to know Love.

It happens *over and over and over* throughout the Bible.
Despite the sinful people...
God *relentlessly pursues* them.
Then to make it quite clear...
Jesus *forgives* and *loves* those who have nailed him to the cross.
What more *proof* do you need that God's love *never ends!*

That is *Good News* and reason to *give thanks*!

Listen to the song of the day "Lift Up Our Voices" on the *Give Praise and Thanks* album.

12 GOD RESTORES AND RENEWS

Ezekiel 36:25-26

I will sprinkle clean water upon you
to cleanse you from all your impurities,
and from all your idols I will cleanse you.
I will give you a new heart and place
a new spirit within you, taking from your bodies
your stony hearts and giving you natural hearts.

Prophets like Ezekiel had some harsh predictions for God's people
after they had turned to idols and to *self-centered* and *non-life-giving* pursuits.
But he also had comforting words when they returned to God.
In reality... it wasn't *God* who made bad things happen to them.
They were responsible since they had *turned away* from their *Loving Source.*
God had *never* left them. That would be *impossible*!
God is *always reaching out in love* to each of us because *that's what Love does*.
But we always have the option of whether we want to *cooperate.*
It's about *relationship*.
When the people turned back to God... there was *no chastisement.*
God immediately began the process of cleansing them
from their impurities and giving them a new heart and spirit.
Is there some area of *your* life where you have *turned from God*
and have instead pursued some kind of *idol* such as *power, prestige,*
***possessions, wealth, physical appearance, sports, or even religion itself*?**
What is standing in the way of your relationship with God?
What is standing in the way of you being able to love all people and all creation?
Whatever it is... lay it down before your loving Creator.
God is always ready to "sprinkle clean water upon you" and restore you...
again and again and again.

Listen to the song of the day "Singing My Song" on the *Live to Love* album.

GOD IS GENEROSITY 13

Matthew 20:1

"The kingdom of heaven is like
a landowner who went out at dawn
to hire laborers for his vineyard."

The parable of the landowner and his workers
completely subverts our concept of fairness.

The workers hired at nine in the morning to work in the landowner's vineyard
get the *same pay* as those hired at noon, three o'clock and five.
The ones hired at nine grumble about the *unfairness*.

The truth is...
they need a new way of seeing to understand God's generosity!

Jesus says God is willing to give full benefits of the kingdom of God
whenever a person is ready to receive it!

Why would we begrudge anyone who comes into the kingdom?

We should be extremely happy for that person!
There is no "*first*" or "*last*" in the kingdom of God!
It's all gift!

God wants nothing more than to overwhelm you with generosity!

Listen to the song of the day "Pour Me Out" on the *Give Praise and Thanks*
album.

14 THE DIVINE DELIVERER

Psalm 107:5-6

Hungry and thirsty, their life was wasting away
within them. They cried to the Lord in their
distress; from their straits he rescued them.

Jesus said that he is the vine and we are the branches.
When we sever our connection to the Giver of Life... we wither.
**Of course... we can never *actually* sever our connection with God...
but we can *choose to ignore it*. It's a matter of *consciousness*.**
We can *choose to live apart from this conscious union* with our Loving Creator...
or simply be *unconscious* of it...
perhaps deluded by the attractions of power, prestige, and possessions.
**We can *nurture* a *conscious connection* with our Loving Source
by practicing *being present* to the *Divine Presence*.**

Try contemplative practices such as:
Centering prayer and *meditation*.
Lectio Divina: Read scripture in silence while listening in your heart
for a word or phrase that moves you.
Walk or sit in nature and nurture a sense of awe and wonder.
Lose yourself in anything creative... like music, poetry, or art.

**If we do this we will begin to be aware of
promptings from God on decisions in life.**
At one time, I was "hungry and thirsty" with my life seemingly "wasting away" within me.
I did cry out to the God in my distress... and it was in the silence of my surrender
that I heard a gentle whisper that redirected my life.
Looking back... I clearly see how God rescued me (and *many times since*!).
Have faith and trust that God will lead you *through* your struggles to *wholeness*.
God is *always good* even when we or life's happenings are *seemingly not*!

Listen to the song of the day "God Is" on the *Give Praise and Thanks* album.

YOU ARE INVITED | 15

Matthew 22:9-10

"Go out, therefore, into the main roads and
invite to the feast whomever you find."
The servants went out into the streets
and gathered all they found,
bad and good alike,
and the hall was filled with guests.

Jesus likened the kingdom of God to a *wedding feast*.
Most of the people the king invited were too busy or simply didn't care to come.
The king (God) then invited all people "bad and good alike."
**Notice that the so-called "bad" people were not tested or rebuked in any way...
they were simply welcomed to the feast.**

The only one who is escorted out is the one who refuses to wear a wedding garment...
which, by the way, would have been provided.

**While he wanted the free party...
he simply did not want to be with such a diverse bunch of...
you know...
all *those* people.**

The kingdom of God is *not* an *exclusive country club*...
but a place where *all* people are *welcomed* through
the *unconditional love* and *mercy* of God.

**Are *you* ready to join such a table?
Are *you* ready to be *one* with *all*?**

**Listen to the song of the day "All Are Welcome" on the *Give Praise and Thanks*
album.**

16 GOD SAVES

Psalm 51:12

A clean heart create for me, O God, and a steadfast spirit renew within me.

Sometimes we can be on a spiritual high when everything is going our way and we seem to be in that "zone" where it just couldn't get any better.

It's also during these times when it seems so easy to slip and fall... when we get cocky and believe we are somehow spiritually ahead of others.

**When this happens...
don't beat yourself up over it.**

Allow the Holy Spirit to lead you back to God.

**Jesus said that he came for *sinners*...
not the *self-righteous*.**

Jesus still wants to be with you!

***You* don't save *you*...
Jesus does...
and he *loves* doing it!**

Your life is not about *your* goodness...
but about *God's*.

This is really Good News!

Listen to the song of the day "Come to Jesus" on the *Live to Love* album.

LOVE NEVER LETS GO | 17

2 Thessalonians 2:16-17

May our Lord Jesus Christ himself and God our Father, who has loved us and given us everlasting encouragement and good hope through his grace, encourage your hearts and strengthen them in every good deed and word.

Here is some more really, *really good* news:
The Creator of all things...is love (1 John 4:8).

Love is *carrying* us...
inspiring us...
consoling us...
grieving with us...
laughing with us...
and *celebrating* with us.

Love is giving us "everlasting encouragement and good hope" through *grace*.

Allow today's scripture reading to *settle in your soul*.

Meditate on it.
Rest in it.

Feel the *peace* this brings.

Amen... and alleluia!
Share it with someone you meet today.

Listen to the song of the day "How Wonderful to Me" on the *Live to Love* album.

18 | AMAZING GRACE

Psalm 139:4-5

Even before a word is on my tongue,
Lord, you know it all.
Behind and before you encircle me and
rest your hand upon me.

Who is God?

Whatever concept comes into our minds...
it is *grossly* limiting to the identity of God.

The Maker of all things...
the One who crafted the vastness of the universe
and the intricacy of all living things...
also crafted *you*.

This same Loving Creator also is *present* in the deepest depths of your being.
The Bible says that we are made in God's image.
Our femaleness and maleness *mirror* the grandeur of God.

No matter what struggles you may be dealing with...
rest in the comfort of knowing that God is holding you
and will *never let you go*.

Listen to the song of the day "I Stand in the Light" on the *Mercy Reigns* album.

GOD IS WITH YOU | **19**

Psalm 139:1-2

Lord, you have probed me, you know me:
you know when I sit and stand;
you understand my thoughts from afar.

There is no fooling God.
Our Creator knows *everything* about each of us...
our thoughts...
our desires...
our struggles...
our failings...
our joys and our sorrows.

When God made you...
God placed a stamp of approval on you.

From the *first* moment...
God *loved* you...
loved you into existence...
so that God could *share* love with you.
You can turn from that love...
but God can *never* turn from you.

There is nothing you can do that can make God love you *less*...
or *more*.
God is as close as the air you breathe.
You are God's *beloved*...
not because of anything you believe, do or achieve...
but simply for *being you*.
Allow that knowledge to *sink* in... and *fill* you.

Listen to the song of the day "The Way You Are" on the *Mercy Reigns* album.

20 | LOVE OVER LAW

Matthew 23:27-28

"Woe to you,
scribes and Pharisees,
you hypocrites...
on the outside you appear righteous,
but inside you are filled with
hypocrisy and evildoing."

Jesus showed compassion to all the "sinners" of his day...
but he had sharp criticism for the religious leaders.

They were the ones who held all people to the letter of the law
without any filter of love, compassion or forgiveness.
They looked down on others and held themselves in high-esteem.

The law without compassion is *not Christianity*.
***None* of us can *save ourselves*!**
***None* of us can keep the law perfectly because we are *im*perfect!**

If we didn't have that certain *shortcoming* that we *just can't seem to shake*...
we *wouldn't need* God...
would we?

It's precisely in *that place* where you are struggling...
that Jesus *wants to embrace you and save you*!

That is Good News!

Listen to the song of the day "Mercy Reigns" on the *Mercy Reigns* album.

GOD IS PRESENT | 21

Matthew 25:13

"Therefore, stay awake, for you know neither the day nor the hour."

Many times this statement by Jesus is taken to mean some sort of *warning* about when death will come... and that *you better have your act together or else!* That is a very *fearful* interpretation.
Does *that* interpretation sound like something the same guy who preached *love and forgiveness* would say?

It seems a *far cry* from the guy who commanded us to "love your enemies" (Matthew 5:44).
Jesus *always reached out* to those who were struggling in their *imperfection* and *unworthiness*. That's because *God's love does not depend on our worthiness.*

God's love is given *continuously*... in *each moment*.
True love is *never* withheld.
But are we ready to receive it?
Are we "awake" to the Grace that God is ready to give us?
Or are we *asleep*... distracted by other worldly things with no lasting importance?

God wants to lift us in the places where we are unable to do so...
with a Love that will *heal* us and make us *whole*.
For this to happen... our egos have to get out of the way.
Stop. Be silent.
Awaken to the *Divine Presence*.

As Jesus said: "This is the time of fulfillment.
The kingdom of God is at hand" (Mark 1:15).
The time of salvation and freedom... is *now*!

Listen to the song of the day "Breathe On Me" on the *Listen to Your Heart* album.

22 | KINGDOM OF GOD

Matthew 23:13

"Woe to you, scribes and Pharisees, you hypocrites. You lock the kingdom of heaven before human beings. You do not enter yourselves, nor do you allow entrance to those trying to enter."

When it comes to some of the things many "religious" people consider morally offensive behavior... Jesus said almost *nothing*.

He always seemed to extend compassion to people who had been cast out or seen as "unclean", meeting them with unconditional love.
This is what *transformed* and *healed* them.

But this was *not* the way of the Pharisees.
The religious leaders of the time held people to strict rules *without* compassion.
These are the only people Jesus sharply criticized.
Compassion opens the doors to the kingdom of heaven (kingdom of God).

Notice that in today's scripture verse Jesus was again talking about the kingdom of heaven in the *present* tense...
as something to enter *now*.
The Pharisees not only blocked *others* from entering but *themselves* as well.
Rules are meant to be used as *guidelines*... not as *clubs* to *punish* people.

Harsh rules without compassion create harsh people.
Compassion changes hearts and leads to *transformation*.

Open your heart to God's unconditional love and forgiveness.
It's totally *free* and available *now*.

Listen to the song of the day "There Is Three" on the *Mercy Reigns* album.

DIVINE PRESENCE |

Psalm 145:13

Your kingdom is a kingdom for all ages,
and your dominion endures
through all generations.

The *kingdom of God* or the *reign of God* is eternally *present*
when we are totally *present* to God...
our Source.

God rejects *no one*!

When we are "in tune" with God's presence and unconditional love
we will naturally want to cooperate in God's *on-going* creative process.
We will be taking part in "building the kingdom of God."

**However, usually our minds are so busy mulling over *past* events
and pondering *future* possibilities that we are almost never
present to the *moment*...
the only time that is actually *real* and where God wants to engage us.**

No wonder we are flustered and uneasy because we are
out of touch with our Loving Source!

The Eternal Now...
the kingdom of God...
will break into our lives if we *stop*...
focus on the *stillness* and *listen* for
God's *gentle voice* that will always say,
"I love you and accept you!"

**Listen to the song of the day "Turn Off the Noise" on the *Listen to Your Heart*
album.**

24 | NOW IS THE TIME

Matthew 24:42

"Stay awake!
For you do not know on
which day your Lord will come."

Jesus wants to *jar* his audience awake.
He wants them to go from spiritual *unconsciousness* to *consciousness*.
The truth is... many people are wandering around completely *unconscious*...
unaware of their true identities as beloved *daughters* and *sons* of God.

They are not living in that reality.
They are instead immersed in the *delusion* and *madness* of the world.
They are not awake to God's Presence and Love.
They are preoccupied and busy with schedules packed with endless activities.
Their minds are rattling off a constant barrage of thoughts and comments
so that they never truly enter fully into the *present moment*...
open and empty...
so God's Presence can fill them.
Days and nights are filled with a *steady stream* of stimuli...
numbing the senses.
Stop!

Be *silent*.
***Let go* of your thoughts.**

Be at peace.
Be present.
Be.
God is yearning to be Present to *you*.

Listen to the song of the day "Slow Me Down" on the *Mercy Reigns* album.

YOU ARE LOVED | 25

Psalm 145:9

The Lord is good to all
and compassionate
toward all his works.

~

While we tend to treat others only as well as *they treat us*...
God *pours out* grace and compassion on all things
no matter how *"good"* they are.

That's because in God's eyes...
all is good.
Life is precious and *all* life is created with Love.

Without God's *constant cooperation* in *willing* us to *be*...
we would *cease to exist*.

So... in times of darkness and pain...
know that God is *hanging in there* and enduring it *with you*...
just as Jesus *hung with us on the cross*.

Nothing can keep us from the loving *embrace* of God!

~

Listen to the song of the day "Make Your Way" on the *Mercy Reigns* album.

26 | OPEN YOUR HEART

Matthew 6:19-21

"Do not store up for yourselves treasures on earth,
where moth and decay destroy,
and thieves break in and steal.
But store up treasures in heaven,
where neither moth nor decay destroys,
nor thieves break in and steal.
For where your treasure is,
there also will your heart be."

What are your *treasures*?
Are they *material things* of this world...
or are they *spiritual things* like "love of God" and "love of your neighbor"?

**If your heart is in the grip of material things that will *not* last...
Jesus says the momentary happiness that they bring is destined for "decay."**

But if your heart is dedicated to *love*...
you will find an *everlasting joy* even in troubled times.
What do you need to let go of?

It's never to late or too early to enter into the kingdom of God.
It's available *now*.

Let Love lead you.

**Listen to the song of the day "You'll Lead Me" on the *Listen to Your Heart*
album.**

LIFE-CHANGING GRACE

Matthew 11:20

Then he began to reproach the towns
where most of his mighty deeds had been done,
since they had not repented.

How many times have we seen God work in our lives
where something magical happens and we feel so blessed
through no merit of our own...
only to find ourselves relapsing to our old cynical ways
and forgetting what had happened?

**It was no different when Jesus himself performed amazing feats
only to see the people of various towns dismiss him.**

Jesus never called attention to *himself* in the healings he performed.

**That's because he knew that it *wasn't about him*...
but about the *wholeness* of the people he healed.**

Remember one of the times your heart was touched by
an *unexplainable* Unconditional Love.
Allow it to slowly transform your heart again.

Listen to the song of the day "Changed" on the *Give Praise and Thanks* album.

28 | BE RENEWED

Matthew 11:28

"Come to me, all you who labor and are burdened, and I will give you rest."

Jesus counters the heavy rules and regulations of the scribes and Pharisees (religious leaders) with his *unconditional* love.

There were no prerequisites or conditions you had to fulfill for you to come to Jesus.

His message was to *'come as you are.'*

Life is not about you and I *passing some test* in order for God to like us.

God *already loves us infinitely.*
Jesus showed us this by the way he *lived* and by the way he *died...*
responding throughout the journey with
love, mercy, forgiveness, and compassion...
even when that response *wasn't merited.*

Do you know that *you* are the *beloved son or daughter* of God?

Allow this fact to *sink* into your heart.
There is *nothing* you *have done* or *can do* to change this!
Find rest in the Presence of your Loving Creator.

Listen to the song of the day "I Will Give You Rest" on the *Live to Love* album.

CONTEMPLATION | 29

Matthew 6:6

"But when you pray, go to your inner room,
close the door, and pray to your Father in secret.
And your Father who sees in secret will repay you."

Let's once again consider these words of Jesus closely.
"Go to your inner room."

What is your "inner room"?
It's that place at the center of your being...
where your *true self* and *God* meet.

It's the place of *pure Presence*.

The Creator of the universe is there to commune with you and to speak with you.

**But to hear the voice of your Creator you must be willing
to *turn off the noise* of the world...
be still...
and simply *be* with God.**

Jesus said that we should not be like the ones
who believe they will be heard because of their many words.
"Your Father knows what you need before you ask him" (Matthew 6:8).

God wants to give you what you *truly need*.

Listen.
God *speaks* in *silence*.

**Listen to the song of the day "Turn Off the Noise" on the *Listen to Your Heart*
album.**

30 | LOVE RESTORES

Matthew 20:4

"You, too, go into my vineyard, and I will give you what is just."

Jesus told the parable of the landowner who hired laborers to work in his vineyard at the start of the day... during the middle of the day... and at the end of the day.
But they were all paid the *same* wage which resulted in the ones
who worked the *longest* to grumble in anger.
It's just seems *unfair!*
Jesus likened the vineyard to the "kingdom of heaven."
This is the kind of world God wants...
a place where we all work together for peace and justice...
and all receive the same amount of God's endless love.
The landowner in this parable is God.
The people invited to do God's work in the vineyard are each of us.
At the end of the parable the landowner asked the grumbling workers,
"Are you envious because I am generous?"
God's love is free and abundant. There is *no end*.

And it has nothing to do with our *earning* it or being *worthy* of it.
We only are asked to *accept* it.
This is Good News!

We are all asked to rejoice for anyone who turns and accepts God's love
at any time in their life's journey.
God's justice is restorative... not *punitive*.
In the kingdom of God... *all* are loved *equally* and *extravagantly*.
It has nothing to do with *our* goodness... but everything to do with *God's*.

You are being invited into the vineyard.
Will you accept the invitation?

Listen to the song of the day "All Are Welcome" on the *Give Praise and Thanks* album.

RADICAL TRUST | 31

Matthew 8:5-8

When Jesus entered Capernaum, a centurion approached him and appealed to him, saying, "Lord, my servant is lying at home paralyzed, suffering dreadfully." He said to him, "I will come and cure him." The centurion said in reply, "Lord, I am not worthy to have you enter under my roof; only say the word and my servant will be healed."

Jesus goes on to say that "in no one in Israel have I found such faith."
This was a centurion...
a *professional officer in the Roman army.*

To call this encounter *unexpected* would be a *dramatic understatement.*

God would later choose a *persecutor* of Christians named Saul to be
one of the greatest *promoters* of Christ...
a man who would go on to be known as St. Paul.

**Perhaps one lesson is that we should not prejudge anyone.
God sees the core goodness in all!**

God loves each person no matter what they've done and works relentlessly
for everyone's conversion and wholeness ("holiness").

As long as you are breathing... *God isn't through with you!*

Listen to the song of the day "God's Love Is All You Need" on the *Listen to Your Heart* album.

I | ONE BODY

Colossians 1:16-17

All things were created
through Him and for Him.
He is before all things,
and in Him all things hold together.

We all start our lives believing we are at the center of the universe.
Unfortunately, some people never come to realize it's a delusion.

**Each person's ego lobbies for the position that
everything revolves around it and its satisfaction.**

Dying to this...
letting go of this stance...
is the *process* through which we *follow* Christ and *find our* true selves.
This path involves the *letting go of all things...*
even our lives...
by being forgiving and compassionate in the service of others.
For Christ is at the center of all things and *holds* all things together as one...
the broken,
the sinners,
the saints,
and all creation.

That includes *you* and *me*.

Amen.
Alleluia!

Listen to the song of the day "All Are One" on the *Mercy Reigns* album.

JESUS REDEEMS | 2

Luke 4:36

They were all amazed and said to one another,
"What is there about his word?
For with authority and power
he commands the unclean spirits,
and they come out."

We may not see people who are definitely *possessed* by a *legion of evil spirits*.
**But we may see people *obsessed* with things that lead them from God...
and thereby *are possessed* by them.**

Who has not on occasion (*or many occasions*) been led astray
by selfishness... greed... or lust?
It's not an easy task to break free of the allure of satisfying
our physical desires or our ego's insatiable appetite.
**But with the help of Jesus...
*all things are possible.***

It's only when we admit that we are *not* perfect and *do* have weaknesses...
that we can experience the saving power of unconditional Love.
That's what Grace *is*.

Being a Christian does *not* mean being *perfect* but being *perfectly loved*.

It means *admitting to our weaknesses* and *accepting* the *free gift* of
God's forgiveness and unconditional love.
Bring your brokenness to Jesus...
and be *free*.

Listen to the song of the day "Come to Jesus" on the *Live to Love* album.

3 BLESSED INTO BEING

Luke 5:36

"No one tears a piece from a new cloak to patch an old one. Otherwise, he will tear the new and the piece from it will not match the old cloak."

The Pharisees thought that strict adherence to all their religion's rules and regulations determined whether someone was "clean" or "worthy" of God's love.
Jesus said God's love did not *depend* on *anything*.
It was *unconditional*.

God loves us no matter how "dirty" we are.
No amount of hard work on our part can make us *worthy*.

God loves you because you are God's beloved child... *period!*

Jesus gave unconditional love to all.
He offers a completely new cloak to us.
Why do we tear bits and pieces from it to try and patch up
the old cloak we've been wearing?
Why not *let go* of our old ways that we thought would bring us happiness...
but will never truly *satisfy* us?
**That kind of satisfaction can only come through
surrendering to God's desires for us.**

Jesus is ready to be your guide.
It won't be an easy path...
but we are *guaranteed*
unconditional love, mercy, forgiveness, and compassion
every step of the way.

Listen to the song of the day "Changed" on the *Give Praise and Thanks* album.

RADICALLY OKAY

Psalm 27:1

The Lord is my light and my salvation; whom do I fear?

Jesus lived in the Presence of the awareness of God's unconditional Love.
He knew there was no lasting happiness to be found in
the power, prestige, and possessions offered by this world.

The Light that will lead you in life... is *Love*.

A sure way to allow this Light to lead you is by following Jesus.
As it says in the Gospel of John:
"What came to be through him was life,
and this life was the light of the human race;
the light shines in the darkness,
and the darkness has not overcome it" (John 1:3-5).
Is there something weighing heavily on your heart?
Is there some *apparent* obstacle in your path?

Rest in Jesus.
Allow his peace to fill you.

Jesus said in John 8:12, "I am the light of the world.
Whoever follows me will not walk in darkness,
but will have the light of life."
He is the light of the world!

That Light will lead you through the darkness of any situation
to new life and true growth.

So... *what is there to fear*?

Listen to the song of the day "Radically Okay" on the *Mercy Reigns* album.

5 STOP... LISTEN

Luke 6:12-13

In those days he departed to the mountain to pray,
and he spent the night in prayer to God.
When day came, he called his disciples to himself,
and from them he chose twelve,
whom he also named apostles.

Notice how Jesus went off to a quiet place and spent an *entire night*
in prayer to God before making a big decision about picking apostles.
Given that he also instructed his followers to pray by going to their *inner room*
and then to *not babble using many words* (Matthew 6:6-7),
it would seem that Jesus spent most of his prayer in *silent listening*.
He needed to remove all *distractions* so he could *listen* to the voice of God.

Are *you* following Jesus' example?

**When it comes to making big decisions...
or in times of struggles when you aren't sure what to do...
are *you* finding a *quiet place* to *commune* with your Maker?**

Try setting aside ten to twenty minutes regularly for quiet meditation.
Simply *let go* of your thoughts.
Allow your mind to rest from its constant judgments and commentaries.

**It may be *difficult, frustrating,* and *seemingly pointless* at first...
but with practice you will be amazed
at how your life will change for the better...
and how your *inner peace* will *grow*.**

**Listen to the song of the day "Turn Off the Noise" on the *Listen to Your Heart*
album.**

HAVE FAITH 6

Romans 8:28

We know that all things work for good for those who love God, who are called according to his purpose.

God can transform any *negative* to a *positive*...
when we open our hearts to Love.
It happens *over and over* as we see *tragedies* turned into *triumphs*.
Look at what Jesus did on the cross?
He turned what appeared to be the greatest *tragedy* in history...
to the greatest *victory*.
Love does indeed *win*!

When disaster strikes...
a *Great Compassion* rises within people
whose response then overwhelms the bad with good.

**God's plan of creation is beyond our imaginations...
but *each* of us was created to be a part of that
amazing plan of self-giving, creative love.**

For me... a ruptured appendix appeared to be a horrendous disaster...
but the spiritual transformation that came *through* it made it
one of the most *treasured, positive experiences* of my life.

**Whatever you are dealing with now...
turn it over to God.**

Let it go, trust...
and see what happens!

Listen to the song of the day "Love Will Always Lead You Home" on the *Mercy Reigns* album.

7 WHOLENESS IN PROGRESS

Psalm 13:6

> I trust in your faithfulness. Grant my heart joy in your help, that I may sing of the Lord, "How good our God has been to me!"

It's *easy* to praise God when things are going *our* way and we are filled with wonderful feelings.
But what about when we are *heartbroken* and in *pain*?

If God *is* Love (1 John 4:8) then we know that God is *not rejoicing* when we are *suffering*.

What would *Love's* response be to our pain?
I'm thinking that Love would *hold* us and *comfort* us.

Jesus showed us that God is faithful even in dark times and feelings of abandonment.

Remember that *resurrection* followed the *crucifixion*.
New Life awaits us at the other side of any pain or suffering.

Cling to Jesus. Cling to the Love that could *never let you go.*
Open yourself to this unconditional Love that *celebrates* our joys and *mourns* our sorrows.
Let go of *control.*
Trust that God is leading you *through your struggles* to *new life* and *wholeness*.

Have faith.

Listen to the song of the day "You'll Lead Me" on the *Listen to Your Heart* album.

BE FREE | 8

Luke 6:27-28

Jesus said to his disciples: "To you who hear I say, love your enemies, do good to those who hate you, bless those who curse you, pray for those who mistreat you."

Following Jesus means living a *radical* life.
He says things that contradict our natural human response.
It takes a new *transformed* mind to be able to *love your enemies...*
a "non-dualistic" mind that is able to see *all* things as *one.*
The fact is... there are *no* boundaries in the Kingdom of God.
Jesus was saying that all people are one in the Body of Christ.
God loves everyone *equally* as daughters and sons.
There are countless true stories of people who forgave others
who were guilty of horrible crimes.
That forgiveness in turn helped transform the people who perpetrated
the crimes into changed people who ended up doing great things.
**There is a saying that refusing to forgive is like
drinking poison and hoping it hurts the person who wronged you.**

Anger and vengeance wrap themselves around you like chains.
**By forgiving and loving those who hate you... you end up freeing *yourself*
and allowing God's love to transform the world.**

It's really a matter of perspective.
Are you living your life as though *you* are the center of the universe...
or are you living as though *God* is at the center?
Oh... one more thing.
While you're at it... forgive *yourself. God does.*

Listen to the song of the day "Salvation" on the *Live to Love* album.

255

9 REST

Psalm 62:6

My soul, be at rest in God alone, from whom comes my hope.

What if each day when we awaken from sleep...
we would take a deep breath and simply *rest* in the *Presence* of God?

What if, as we sat down to breakfast, before we took that first sip of coffee...
we would take a deep breath and simply *rest* in the *Presence* of God?

What if, after we got in the car, before we started the engine...
we would take a deep breath and simply *rest* in the *Presence* of God?

What if, as we found ourselves in the frenzy of angry drivers on the road...
we would mentally pause, take a deep breath, and simply *rest* in the *Presence* of God?

What if, when someone says something offensive to us, before we responded...
we would take a deep breath and simply *rest* in the *Presence* of God?

What if, when things don't go our way, before we made a *knee-jerk* reaction...
we would take a deep breath and simply *rest* in the Presence of God?

I'm thinking if we made a *practice* of this...
we would find more *peace* in our *lives* and in our *relationships*.

God's Presence is *always here*, *always with you*, and *always for you*.

Allow that *Presence* to give you hope *now*...
and *now*...
and *now*...
with each *breath*.

Listen to the song of the day "I Will Give You Rest" on the *Live to Love* album.

LOVE IS WINNING | 10

Luke 6:17-18

A great crowd of his disciples and a large number
of the people from all Judea and Jerusalem
and the coastal region of Tyre and Sidon came
to hear him and to be healed of their diseases;
and even those who were tormented
by unclean spirits were cured.

When you watch Jesus, you see that his mission was always about *healing*.
He wanted to *free* people who were being *oppressed* in *body, mind,* or *spirit*.

The oppression was sometimes inflicted by illness...
but sometimes it was inflicted by the rulers in *government* or *religion*.
This required Jesus to speak truth to power *without* resorting to *violence*.
It also required him to *reach out* to those on the *fringes of society*...
those who needed help.
Jesus wanted to *restore* all those who were suffering to *wholeness*.

He wanted to *dissolve* the *illusion* of *separation*.
**He wanted *all* to know that they were *included* and *loved* by God...
just as they are.**

This is what Jesus wants for *you*.
We are all *broken* in some way.

Jesus said that he came to be a physician for the sick (Mark 2:17).
Bring your pain and brokenness to the Divine Healer.

Listen to the song of the day "Heal Me" on the *Live to Love* album.

II | DO NOT JUDGE

Luke 6:42

"How can you say to your brother, 'Brother, let me remove that splinter in your eye,' when you do not even notice the wooden beam in your own eye? You hypocrite! Remove the wooden beam from your eye first; then you will see clearly to remove the splinter in your brother's eye."

Jesus also tells us not to judge others...
but that doesn't mean we have to "turn our brains off".
We do have to "judge" what is in our best interest.
We also can't help but to "judge" as in *determining in our own minds*
whether we think what someone else is doing is a good idea or not.
**What Jesus doesn't want us to do is to make any judgments
about another person's salvation or inner goodness.**

After all, we don't know all the reasons why that person may be doing what they are doing or what experiences might have influenced that person's actions.

**A "wooden beam" in my eye might be obstructing
a clear view of that other person...
and I might be completely clueless about that "beam"
that is clouding my understanding.**

*Loving God, remove anything that may be blocking me
from seeing the goodness in all people...
even the ones that give me a hard time.*
And... Loving God... help me to be compassionate with myself.

Listen to the song of the day "Mercy Reigns" on the *Mercy Reigns* album.

DYING AND RISING | 12

Have among yourselves the same attitude that is also yours in Christ Jesus, who, though he was in the form of God, did not regard equality with God something to be grasped. Rather, he emptied himself, taking the form of a slave, coming in human likeness; and found human in appearance, he humbled himself, becoming obedient to death, even death on a cross.

Jesus gives us the model... the *blueprint*...
for taking part in God's great, *on-going love story*.
It's all about *dying* to our ego's *self-centered desires* for power, prestige, and possessions...
emptying ourselves... so that in return we can be *filled* with the *fullness of life*.
In letting my "false self" *die*... paradoxically... my "true self" starts to *live*.
***Dying and rising* is the *pattern* of *all life*.**
Love *gives itself away* completely and freely... then *resurrection* and *new life* follow.
Our way to *wholeness* and *completion* (salvation) is through our
human experience of dying and rising. **Jesus "saves" us by showing us this.**
He demonstrates the pattern that leads you to being your true self and enjoying
abundant life *now*... as well as eternal life in the *future*. **So *be present*.**
Empty yourself of self-centered desires. *Serve* others humbly without looking for gain.
Accept whatever losses you are faced with in the journey. Then when life's ending
comes... the transition to eternal life will be *seamless*, *smooth*, and *peaceful*...
because the process has already been *well-practiced*.
If you are *not* well-versed in *letting go*...
you can always start practicing right *now*.

Listen to the song of the day "Make Your Way" on the *Mercy Reigns* album.

13 | THE GOSPEL

1 Corinthians 15:1-2

Now I am reminding you, brothers and sisters,
of the gospel I preached to you,
which you indeed received and in which you also
stand. Through it you are also being saved,
if you hold fast to the word I preached to you,
unless you believed in vain.

God is *always* ready to save us because God *is* love... and God *IS*.
**God *is present* in *each moment* of our lives and is therefore
always loving us and *saving us*.**

All you have to do is *accept* it.
***It's a free gift*.**

That's the *gospel* that St. Paul was preaching to the Corinthians and
it's the *same gospel* he's preaching to *us* today.
Are we "holding fast to the word" that he is preaching...
or have we turned the Gospel into some *burdensome exercise* of trying to *earn God's love*...
trying to convince *Love* to *love* us?

**If we *receive* the Gospel (the *Good News* of God's *unconditional love*)
and *believe* it...
we are *being saved now*...
and in *every moment*.**

Allow that to *sink into your soul*.
This is truly *Good News*!

Listen to the song of the day "God Is" on the *Give Praise and Thanks* album.

THE KEY | 14

1 Corinthians 13:1-3

If I speak in human and angelic tongues but do not have love, I am a resounding gong or a clashing cymbal. And if I have the gift of prophecy and comprehend all mysteries and all knowledge; if I have all faith so as to move mountains but do not have love, I am nothing. If I give away everything I own, and if I hand my body over so that I may boast but do not have love, I gain nothing.

St. Paul's words are amazing.
Love is the bottom line.

It's what life is all about.
But how *difficult* it is!

Jesus said the two greatest commandments are to *love* God with *all your heart, soul and strength* and to love your *neighbor as yourself.*

Love God, everyone...
***and* yourself.**

God already loves *you* with *no strings attached.*
You don't have to *earn it.*
Accept it and allow it to settle in your soul.
It's *all that matters.*

Listen to the song of the day "Love God" on the *Live to Love* album.

15 | ETERNAL WORTH

Luke 8:1-2

Afterward he journeyed from one town and village to another, preaching and proclaiming the good news of the kingdom of God. Accompanying him were the Twelve and some women who had been cured of evil spirits and infirmities.

Are we still preaching the "good news of the kingdom of God"...
or are we preaching some "merit system of holiness"?

Jesus spread a message that *God loved everyone unconditionally* and that the way of God was *mercy, forgiveness, and compassion*.

It was all *gift... unearned... grace*.

And look at the *ragtag group* Jesus brought along with him:
A bunch of uneducated fishermen, a tax collector, one a traitor — some of them boastful, some vengeful — and all of them without a *clue* as to what Jesus was all about!
And with them... some women "who had been cured of evil spirits and infirmities."

**Jesus apparently wanted to hang with *both* men *and* women
who didn't have it all together.
*Thank God!***

Do you see yourself among those followers?
Welcome! Jesus wants to be with *you*, too!
This is Who God Is.
This is *Good News!*

Listen to the song of the day "Come to Jesus" on the *Live to Love* album.

FORGIVE ALWAYS | **16**

Luke 7:47

"But the one to whom little is forgiven, loves little."

Jesus is *always* ready to *forgive*.
But some people are not ready to *receive* it.

To receive it...
you must be willing to forgive *yourself*...
and to forgive *others*.

Some want to hold on to grudges and past hurts...
to "get even" with those who did them harm.
This will keep you *shackled* in chains.
God wants to *free* you.

God loves to *forgive* and to *restore*.

That's why we have a savior in Jesus.

The name "Jesus" means "God saves".
Forgiveness is the *key* to freedom.
When you forgive, you remove the obstacle to God's love...
allowing it to pour *through* you and into the world!
It opens you to love and it opens the one forgiven to love as well.

The *more* you've been forgiven...
the *more* you want to love.
Who do you need to forgive?
Why not do it *today*?

Listen to the song of the day "Salvation" on the *Live to Love* album.

263

17   THROUGH THE LENS OF LOVE

1 Corinthians 13:4-6

Love is patient, love is kind.
It is not jealous, love is not pompous,
it is not inflated, it is not rude,
it does not seek its own interests,
it is not quick-tempered,
it does not brood over injury,
it does not rejoice over wrongdoing
but rejoices with the truth.

This is a great standard to measure our conduct in everyday life.

**Are we operating under the motivation of *love* in *all* that we do...
or is our motivation *self-interest*?**

None of us meets this standard perfectly.
Jesus gave us the *blueprint* of *how to love*...
even when faced with persecution and execution.

**Could it be that God wants us to *learn* to love...
in *living* our lives?**

And isn't it refreshing to know that God *is* love...
and therefore *always* acts according to that standard in dealing with each of us?

Listen to the song of the day "Radically Okay" on the *Mercy Reigns* album.

GOD IS WITH YOU

Ecclesiastes 3:1-2, 4

There is an appointed time for everything,
and a time for every affair under the heavens.
A time to be born, a time to die;
a time to plant, a time to uproot the plant.
A time to weep, and a time to laugh;
a time to mourn, and a time to dance.

Life is a gift with a broad spectrum of experiences that will all lead us to wholeness...
if we allow ourselves to be *present* to *each experience*.
For when we are *present* to *each moment*...
we are *already whole*!

Be open to how God is at work in these experiences.
Life is a journey of ups and downs.
You can't have the mountaintops without the valleys.

What is the main struggle that you are dealing with now?
If it is death or hardship...
bring it to the foot of the cross where Jesus is waiting to suffer with you.
If it is a time of joy...
bring it to the resurrected Christ to celebrate.
Pray with him in the Garden of Gethsemane and
dance with him at the wedding at Cana.

The One who said he was "the way, the truth and the life"
will lead you to the fullness of life *here and now*...
and for *eternity*.

Listen to the song of the day "There Is Three" on the *Mercy Reigns* album.

19 | HEALING PRESENCE

Luke 9:2

Jesus sent them to proclaim the kingdom of God and to heal the sick.

Jesus wanted all to know that when you follow his ways and love others...
you are cooperating in bringing about the kingdom of God.

The "kingdom" starts *here*.

You and I are being called to do this.

We have to ask ourselves whether we are proclaiming
this "kingdom" of unconditional love that reaches out
to those in need of healing...
whether it be emotional, physical, or spiritual healing.

Do others know of God's amazing, unconditional love...
just by witnessing our lives?

Perhaps *you* are the one in need of healing.

If so, ask God to send healers into your life.

**Be *present* to the Divine Presence...
and allow your healing to begin.**

The healing may not be what you *want*...
but it will be what you *need*.

Listen to the song of the day "Heal Me" on the *Live to Love* album.

DEATH TO LIFE | 20

Psalm 90:3-5

A thousand years in your eyes are merely a yesterday,
but humans you return to dust, saying,
"Return, you mortals!"
Before a watch passes in the night,
you have brought them to their end.

Life can seem meaningless when viewed in a "worldly" perspective.
Without a belief in something more when this life ends,
"dust" would be our final destination.

But thanks to Jesus...
we believe that God loves us and that there is life after death.

Many witnessed the resurrected Jesus.
This gives us hope.
Jesus instructed us to start building God's Kingdom now
by spreading this good news (Gospel) of God's unconditional love
and by living a life of love, mercy, forgiveness, and compassion.

Our bodies will end this life in dust...
but our spiritual lives will continue in a way that is a mystery to us.

Jesus promised that God would transform this world into a new creation.

We are called to consciously take part in that on-going transformation!

Listen to the song of the day "God Is the Goal" on the *Live to Love* album.

21 BE STILL

Luke 9:61-62

Another said, "I will follow you, Lord, but first let me say farewell to my family at home." Jesus answered him, "No one who sets a hand to the plow and looks to what was left behind is fit for the kingdom of God."

Jesus was referring to a farmer directing his plow.
If the farmer turned to look back at what was left behind...
he would not be focused on the matter at hand and the plow would drift off course.
The same would happen if he was looking a mile in the distance.
Then the farmer would miss any obstacle right in front of him.

It's a great lesson for living our lives. *Stay present!*

Sometimes we get *lost* in our mind's *chatter*.
Observe its *barrage of thoughts* and *constant commentary*.
We get so caught up in *grievances* from the *past*, *worries* about the *future*,
and *endless judging* that we are unconscious of the *now*.
The only place we will find the living God is in the present... right *now*.
If you're not present... how can you ever experience *God's Presence*?
This takes constant awareness and practice. **It's a *letting go*.**
Try contemplative prayer. Let go of your thoughts and simply observe the moment.
"You" are *not* your *thoughts*!

You are *not* your *mind*! It's a useful *tool*... but it is *not you*.
Your true self is the *silent observer* of your mind.
Your *soul-self* cannot be harmed. It is eternal.

Listen to the song of the day "Breathe On Me" on the *Listen to Your Heart* album.

LET IT BE DONE | 22

Psalm 88:2

Lord, my God, I call out by day; at night I cry aloud in your presence.

Are you *enduring* some form of inner *turmoil* or *suffering* of any kind?
Sometimes we have no answers and feel like God is *not there*.

We've all had times like these.

We also know that many holy people who have gone before us like
Mother Teresa or John of the Cross *suffered* through
their "dark nights of the soul."
We know *deep inside* that God *is there*.

God cannot *not* be there. God is always present.

Could it be that this desolation could actually be what is necessary
to lead us to healing from whatever has caused us physical or mental *pain*?

First... *accept* what the situation is. Simply *observe* it.

You don't have to like it.
Take action to obtain a result you may hope for...
but observe what *is* and *let it be*.

**Suffering is the refusal to accept the moment *as is*.
When you've had enough of it... *let it go*.**

Bring your situation to Christ who will lead you through your struggle to new life.
He died and rose to assure us that we would as well.

Listen to the song of the day "Let It Be Done to Me" on the *Mercy Reigns* album.

23 | TRANSFORMING PRESENCE

Psalm 138:1, 3

I thank you, Lord,
with all my heart.
When I cried out,
you answered;
you strengthened my spirit.

God's love for us does *not* waver.
It is not *withheld* based on our behavior.
God has given us life and will *not allow us to perish*.

**Do not base your worth on what *others* say about you,
how the world *judges* you, or how you feel about yourself.**

Look into the face of *Unconditional* Love...
and know that you are perfect in the eyes of your Maker.

**Wherever that place is where you feel you *don't*
measure up or where you feel *no one* would *want to be with you*...
that is *exactly where God wants to embrace you* and *lift you*.**

Others may leave us or let us down... but not God!
Open your heart to this life-changing peace.
"Then the peace of God that surpasses all understanding
will guard your hearts and minds in Christ Jesus." (Philippians 4:7).

May you *live in that peace*!

Listen to the song of the day "Changed" on the *Give Praise and Thanks* album.

ALL SHALL BE WELL

Psalm 27:1

The Lord is my light and my salvation;
whom do I fear?
The Lord is my life's refuge;
of whom am I afraid?

God is in the loving energy that holds everything together.
God *is* Love.

God holds all and loves all *without condition*.
That includes *you*.
You do not have to *do* anything... *achieve* anything... or *prove* anything for this to be so.
As St. Paul said in Romans 8:31, "If God is for us, who can be against us?"
So... why do we fear?

Simply open yourself to God's loving gaze. It is a Light that is always shining upon you.
It is quite simply... *Grace*!

When times are tough...
God is *not* absent; you are *not* being punished.
God is still intimately with you...
and is getting you ready for a wondrous turnaround.
Something old is dying... and new life is germinating.

"Love never fails" (1 Corinthians 13:8).
"I am confident of this, that the one who began a good work in you
will continue to complete it until the day of Christ Jesus" (Philippians 1:6).
**God is working unceasingly that you become the fullness of who you are:
A beloved son or daughter of God.**

Listen to the song of the day "God's Love Is All You Need" on the *Listen to Your
Heart* album.

25 GOT FAITH?

Matthew 9:28-30

When he entered the house, the blind men
approached him and Jesus said to them,
"Do you believe that I can do this?"
"Yes, Lord," they said to him.
Then he touched their eyes and said,
"Let it be done for you according to your faith."
And their eyes were opened.
Jesus warned them sternly,
"See that no one knows about this."

Jesus wants to bring healing to *everyone* in ways that will bring
"wholeness" to *each* person.
It's all about *redemption*...
not punishment!

God has an *unending* supply of grace to *pour out* on each of us.
The goal for each of us is transformation!

Jesus wants *no attention* from the healing of the two blind men.
The *focus* is not on his healing ability...
but on the *personal inner-transformation* of the two men.

Where in *your life* do you need Christ's healing *touch*?
That is *precisely the place* where he wants to *embrace* you... and transform you!

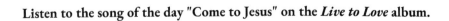

Listen to the song of the day "Come to Jesus" on the *Live to Love* album.

UNMERITED RESTORATION |

Mark 5:5-7

Night and day among the tombs and on the hillsides he was always crying out and bruising himself with stones. Catching sight of Jesus from a distance, he ran up and prostrated himself before him, crying out in a loud voice, "What have you to do with me, Jesus, Son of the Most High God?"

Have you ever felt like a *reject*...
like you were *completely unlovable*?
**Have you ever felt like God could never care for you
because of things you've done?**

In today's scripture we see a man possessed by demons...
completely wild and mentally unstable...
who has been *cast out* of his community to roam about tombs and hillsides.
He seems quite astounded that Jesus would have anything to do with him...
because apparently *no one else will*.
**When others reject you...
indeed when *you* reject *yourself*...
Jesus will *not*... nor will he ever.**

He healed this man and sent him home to be restored to his community.
Jesus rejects *no one*!

Turn to him.
Expect total *acceptance and restoration*.

Listen to the song of the day "I Will Give You Rest" on the *Live to Love* album.

27 | SAVING THE LOST

Matthew 18:12-13

"What is your opinion? If a man has a hundred sheep and one of them goes astray, will he not leave the ninety-nine in the hills and go in search of the stray? And if he finds it, amen, I say to you, he rejoices more over it than over the ninety-nine that did not stray."

We are all imperfect.
We all make mistakes.

I think God *knows this*...
since God is the One who made us!

This being the case... I think there is something very important in the fact that Jesus *isn't saying* that the owner of the sheep will chastise or punish the sheep who has run off.
No!

He says that the man (God) will *relentlessly pursue*
the wayward sheep (*you and me*) until he *finds* that sheep.

This is how we will experience the transforming love of our Creator.
Redemption is not *our* doing... but *God's!*

Allow this to sink into your soul.
This is very Good News!

Listen to the song of the day "Radically Okay" on the *Mercy Reigns* album.

BE AT PEACE | 28

"Come to me, all you who labor and are burdened, and I will give you rest."

Life brings with it its share of challenges.
Those challenges can become burdens unless we turn to a Higher Power.

We can "tap into" this Source of Life at any moment.

God... who *is* Love (1 John 4:8)... is *always present* to you
when *you are present* to God.

Jesus *personified* this Presence of love, mercy, grace, and compassion.
He *sought out* those who were rejected,
those who were suffering,
and those in need.

This same Love is pursuing *you*.

Invite this Love into your life.
One way to do this is through a relationship with Christ.
Allow him to be with you in your challenges.

Let go of your ego's demands which will *never* bring you peace...
and follow the "Prince of Peace."

Allow the Presence of this peace to enfold you and to fill you.

And *rest*.

Listen to the song of the day "Make Me a Channel" on the *Listen to Your Heart* album.

29 | HOLY LONGING

Psalm 42:2-3

As the deer longs for streams of water,
so my soul longs for you, O God.
My being thirsts for God, the living God.

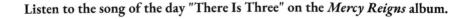

**All of us are *yearning* for God...
but I think most people are *unaware*.**

What they *think* is a *physical* craving is *actually* a *spiritual* one.
So they try to *satisfy* this insatiable *desire* by obtaining
wealth, power, prestige, or perhaps the perfect *relationship*.

While all these things might bring *happiness*...
it will only be temporary and the inner craving will return.

**I believe God created us with that inner emptiness that
only our Loving Creator can fill...
and wants to fill with love.**

But... God won't force this love on us.
That *wouldn't be* love... *would it*?

**What are you trying to *obtain* to *satisfy* your *soul craving*?
Let go of your *attachments* so that the Living God can fill you.
Spend some *quiet* time with the One who has loved you for *all time*.**

Listen to the song of the day "There Is Three" on the *Mercy Reigns* album.

GOD ALONE

Psalm 71:5

You are my hope, Lord; my trust, God, from my youth.

When things are going well...
let's face it...
we *aren't* relying on God or even *thinking* much about God.
We pretty much think we can do it all on our own.

It's only when things go awry...
not according to our plans...
when we slip and fall...
when we get hit with *pain* and *suffering*...
that we *turn* to God.

And when those times have come in my life...
a Higher Power has *always carried me through*.

A Deeper Mystery has *always held me and carried me*.

Why not open yourself to this Loving God?

Why not *empty yourself* of your ego's *endless* desires...
so that there is an open space for God to *enter* and fill?

More of God's Presence in our hearts...
would be the *best* Present we could *possibly receive*.
You are precious in God's sight.

Listen to the song of the day "The Way You Are" on the *Mercy Reigns* album.

I TRANSFORMING GRACE

Luke 10:8-9

"Whatever town you enter and
they welcome you, eat what is set before you,
cure the sick in it and say to them,
'The kingdom of God is at hand for you.'"

In today's scripture the "kingdom of God" is once again the *key message*.
Jesus sent out his messengers to tell everyone the
Good News that would free them and heal them:
God's love for all people is unconditional and does not have to be earned.

Jesus demonstrated this love by responding to persecution with love.

He demonstrated this love in the most extreme way...
forgiving his killers from the cross:
"Father, forgive them, they know not what they do" (Luke 23:34).
That is the *infinite* extent of God's love for *you*.

Accept it.

Allow it to sink into the depths of your heart and soul.

**Let go of *your* kingdom and
allow *God's* kingdom to break into the *present*.**

It's the key to your *wholeness* and *happiness*.

Listen to the song of the day "Changed" on the *Give Praise and Thanks* album.

GOD'S LOVE IS ALWAYS AVAILABLE

Matthew 18:3

"Amen, I say to you, unless you turn and become like children, you will not enter the kingdom of heaven."

Jesus tells us that child-like (*not childish*) awe and wonder
are what it takes to enter into the "kingdom of heaven"...
not just *one day in the future*... but *right now*.
When you are open to the Presence of God...
you find it *everywhere*:
in the sunrise, in the laughter of a child, in music, in art,
in flowers, in trees, in a loving relationship.

When you are *open* to *God's Presence*... you *enter into it*.

Jesus gave himself in love to all...
even allowing himself to be crucified...
to show us that true Love *pours itself out for the beloved*.
He loved *unconditionally*...
even while undergoing the most unjust persecution possible.

**Jesus put his total dependence and trust in God...
like *children* do with their parents...
because he *trusted* that *new life* was *promised*.**

May we humbly put aside our egos, die to ourselves...
and allow Unconditional Love to motivate us.
Because as St. Paul said,
nothing "will be able to separate us from the love of God
in Christ Jesus our Lord" (Romans 8:39).

Listen to the song of the day "Pour Me Out" on the *Give Praise and Thanks* album.

3 WONDERFULLY MADE

Psalm 139:13

You formed my inmost being;
you knit me in my mother's womb.
I praise you,
so wonderfully you made me;
wonderful are your works!

Do you *believe* that?
You are *wonderful* in the eyes of God!

Your intricate design is a unique and amazing *miracle*.

The creation story in the book of Genesis says
God created man and woman in "the divine image"
and then determined *everything* God made to be "very good."

We are made in the "divine image" of God!
Why do we doubt this?
Could it be that someone's hurtful words, or lies promoted by our culture
gave us some *false* belief about ourselves?

God made you *just the way you are...*
then looked at that "divine" creation and judged you to be "very good."

There is *nothing* you can do to make God stop loving you or
looking at you as "wonderful."
This is *Good News*!

Listen to the song of the day "The Way You Are" on the *Mercy Reigns* album.

LOVE NEVER FAILS

Baruch 1:21-22

For we did not heed the voice of the Lord, our God,
in all the words of the prophets whom he sent us,
but each of us went off after the devices
of our own wicked hearts, served other gods,
and did evil in the sight of the Lord, our God.

Some things *never* change. Centuries and centuries after today's scripture was written...
we are *still* doing the *same* thing. We must admit that this *still applies to us today.*
But ever notice how God's love is *not* conditional like *ours* many times is?
God *kept* loving... *keeps* loving... *despite* being rejected *over and over and over.*
If you are struggling and are not proud of some of the things you've done...
take comfort in the fact that God is *not giving up on you.*
God gave us *free will*... knowing that we would make mistakes.
Is that so we could then be *punished* for making those *inevitable* errors?
That would seem *extremely cruel*...
and since God *is* love (1 John 4:8), that just *cannot* be true.
I'm thinking that God knew that the only way we could experience
***unconditional* love was if we could experience**
being loved when we *least merited it.*
That kind of love would be *transforming.*
How else would we learn to love in the *same* way?
God is *not* looking to *punish* you... but to *love* you and *forgive* you.
God is *for* you.
God wants to see you *grow.*
What else would Love do?
Whatever your "shadow side" might be... it will likely be the *key* to your *transformation.*
So... bring your brokenness, shame and pain to God...
and experience what Unconditional Love is!

Listen to the song of the day "God Is" on the *Give Praise and Thanks* album.

5 STOP AND LISTEN

Luke 10:40-42

> Martha, burdened with much serving, came to him and said, "Lord, do you not care that my sister has left me by myself to do the serving? Tell her to help me." The Lord said to her in reply, "Martha, Martha, you are anxious and worried about many things. There is need of only one thing. Mary has chosen the better part and it will not be taken from her."

If Martha had been serving out of the joy of following the *calling in her heart...*
she would not have been "burdened."
She also would not have been concerned about what her sister Mary was doing.
Besides that, it's no great revelation to realize that
we *all* get caught up in too much *busyness* at times.

And sometimes *busyness* can even be doing too many *good* and *positive* things like Martha.
Sometimes our egos are at the helm...
and they are simply looking for attention and accolades.
We can get so caught up in the rat race that we don't take time to simply *be*...
to simply enjoy the *moment* and the blessings that surround us.

We can miss the opportunity to be silent and to *listen at the feet of Jesus.*
Perhaps if we took more time to rest in the presence of the Divine Presence...
we just might hear in our hearts the message that would bring us peace...
and set us free.

Listen to the song of the day "Listen to Your Heart" on the *Listen to Your Heart* album.

GIVE AND KNOW MERCY

Luke 10:36-37

Jesus asked, "Which of these three,
in your opinion,
was neighbor to the robbers' victim?"
He answered,
The one who treated him with mercy."
Jesus said to him, "Go and do likewise."

Today's Gospel reading is about the "Good Samaritan."
At that time Jews didn't associate with Samaritans.

So when Jesus was making a point to a Jewish scholar about
the greatest commandment being to love God and to love your neighbor as yourself,
he chose a Samaritan as his example of someone who loved his neighbor.
Others passed by the robbery victim while the Samaritan stopped to help.
This would have *infuriated* Jesus' audience!
How could the despised *Samaritan* be the *good guy*?

No one is all *good* or all *bad*.
We are all mixtures...
and works in progress.

**We are all capable of making the loving response to the one
we regard as the "other" once we recognize that
we are all God's *beloved children*.**

Be merciful...
and mercy will come back to you.

Listen to the song of the day "Mercy Reigns" on the *Mercy Reigns* album.

7 HAVE FAITH

Jonah 2:3

Out of my distress I called to the Lord,
and he answered me;
From the midst of the nether world I cried for help,
and you heard my voice.

We've all been in a situation that was dark...
where it *appeared* to be *hopeless*.
It's part of our human experience.

**But take heart that the God who created the galaxies
also created *you* and *loves you* as a *daughter* or *son*.**

Jesus said if you know *him*... then you know *God* (John 14:7).
Jesus showed us God's *unconditional* love by allowing himself to be unjustly persecuted
and then put to death on a cross so that he could respond with *love* and *forgiveness*.
This is the face of God!

Jesus showed us that God would go to *any extreme* to *save* us from distress.

He showed us that death was *not* the *end*.
There was *resurrection* and *new life*.

Love has the final say because *Love is who God is* (1 John 4:8).

Since you are made in God's image (Genesis 1:27),
Love is also at *your* very *core*.
So know that in your distress...
God is *with* you and *for* you.

Listen to the song of the day "Come to Jesus" on the *Live to Love* album.

ALLELUIA

Psalm 9:2

I will praise you, Lord, with all my heart.

Stop for a moment.

Stop.

Slowly breathe in. *Slowly* exhale.

Slowly breathe in. *Slowly* exhale.

Breathe.

Listen.

With *each breath* you proclaim your oneness with God.

Breathe in, "*Yah*"...
Breathe out, "*Weh*"...
"*Yah-weh... Yah-weh... Yah-weh...*"

A Great Love is sustaining you.

You are present to the great "I Am."

God is with you *now*... and *forever*.

Give *praise* and *thanks*!

Amen.

Listen to the song of the day "Give Praise and Thanks" on the *Give Praise and Thanks* album.

9 GRACE IS FREE

Galatians 3:10

All who depend on works of the law are under a curse.

This sounds confusing.
We are told to follow the rules... but then St. Paul tells us that if we depend on "works of the law" (in other words, the *rules*) that we "are under a curse."
Following the rules does indeed keep us in line.
We know that is especially true with children.
They need rules to make sure they don't get into trouble.

But when we grow up... while the rules are still good and with purpose... we soon come to realize that we cannot possibly keep them all perfectly.

And there is a *good reason* for that.

We can't depend on the rules to make us *whole* (or "holy").

We can't depend on following rules to lead us to the fullness of who we are as sons and daughters of God.

We can only depend on *God* to do that.

By building a relationship with Jesus... we are well on our way.
He shows us that the goal is always to *love*... not to *follow rules*.

God loves to love us *in our brokenness*.
That's what we call "grace". It is *always* freely given.

And *that's* what makes *all the difference*!

Listen to the song of the day "How Wonderful to Me" on the *Live to Love* album.

LOVE IS OUR SOURCE | 10

Luke 11:13

"If you then, who are wicked,
know how to give good gifts to your children,
how much more will the Father in heaven give the
Holy Spirit to those who ask him?"

Jesus speaks of God as being like a *loving, doting* father.
You and I are children of that God.

Do you believe that?
YOU are a *child of God.*
***Each* of us has been spawned by the Love that created the universe.**

Just before saying the scripture line above,
Jesus had said that "everyone who asks, receives."
But note that he says that those who ask will be given the "Holy Spirit."
Jesus *doesn't* say you'll be given *whatever you want.*

What *loving parent* would give their child whatever their *whim*?
A parent would give their children what they truly *need.*
**When we die to our egos and are in tune with
the groanings of the Spirit at our core...
we will receive even more of that Spirit because it is
already yearning for exactly what we need.**

The *question* is...
are we spending quiet time getting in touch with the Spirit's yearning in our hearts?
God wants intimacy with you.
What do *you* want?

Listen to the song of the day "Breathe On Me" on the *Listen to Your Heart* album.

GOOD NEWS

Psalm 86:5

Lord, you are kind and forgiving, most loving to all who call on you.

When you or I turn from God and choose to make ourselves
the center of the universe...
God does *not* get *angry* but continues to *love* us.

**Sometimes it takes hitting rock bottom for us to realize
the emptiness and dead-end of our ego's
incessant pursuit of *self-centered satisfaction*...
before our *true self* is able to *emerge* from the ego's grip and
turn back to God who *is* Love itself (1 John 4:8).**

And in return for our egregious behavior...
wonder of wonders...
we are met by the open arms of *Unconditional Love* and *Total Forgiveness*.

This is hard for many minds to grasp since we were poisoned with the
toxic myth of a *tyrannical, punishing* God.

**But the *truth* is...
God *only wants to love you*.**

And that, my friend, *is* the *Good News!*

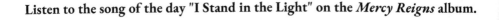

Listen to the song of the day "I Stand in the Light" on the *Mercy Reigns* album.

GLORY ABOUNDS

Romans 1:20-21, 25

Ever since the creation of the world, his invisible attributes of eternal power and divinity have been able to be understood and perceived in what he has made. As a result, they have no excuse; for although they knew God they did not accord him glory as God or give him thanks. They exchanged the truth of God for a lie and revered and worshipped the creature rather than the creator, who is blessed forever.

Paul spoke these words nearly *2000 years ago*... and humans are *still doing the same thing*!
God's glory is *all around* but many times we aren't *aware*.
Back when I was a Youth Minister, there was a time after a meeting
when we were all talking in the parking lot when one of the teens
pointed to the sky overhead and said, "A God-spot!"
We looked up and saw one of the most *incredible* night skies I have ever seen.
The moon was glowing amidst an expansive pattern of small round patches of clouds...
as if the clouds had been set there by a massive, galactic cookie-cutter.
It was quite *spectacular*... but we all might have missed this *wonder*
of God's creativity if not for one observant young lady.
While God's glory is *all around us*... our culture reveres and worships celebrities, athletes
and youthfulness... all which will fade away.
How much time and energy do we put into giving thanks and praise
for the wonders God gives us each day?
Look around you now... and *give thanks*.

Listen to the song of the day "God Is the Goal" on the *Live to Love* album.

13 THERE IS HOPE

Psalm 113:7

The Lord raises the needy from the dust, lifts the poor from the ash heap.

What do we *truly need*?

If we examine our desires,
we may find that many of the things
we *think* we "need" are actually things we "want."

God knows what we *truly* need.

Take a survey of the things you are wanting and
simply *observe* them.

Will *any* of those things
actually fill the deep need in your heart?

If you allowed those things to diminish in importance...
God could address your *true* needs.

God wants to *hold you*,
console you,
and love you
just as you are.

Listen to the song of the day "The Way You Are" on the *Mercy Reigns* album.

SAVED BY GRACE

Luke 11:38-39

The Pharisee was amazed to see that Jesus did not observe the prescribed washing before meal. The Lord said to him, "Oh you Pharisees! Although you cleanse the outside of the cup and the dish, inside you are filled with plunder and evil."

Rituals and guidelines are all well and good if they are pointing us
to God and making us more *humble* and *compassionate*.
But when they are used to *judge* others as inferior, to cast-out others as somehow not
worthy, or used to *achieve* "worthiness"... they are quite *worthless*.

**Jesus seemed to have no problem violating the religious rules because
he knew the motives of the Pharisees were to use the rules to hold themselves
above others as more worthy of God's love.**

"Look how good I am as I follow these rules to the letter!"
What *good* is *that* when at the same time you treat others with *disdain and arrogance*?
Besides... it's *not about worthiness*! God's love is a *free gift*.

The truth is...
we *all* have more than enough crud inside of each of us that needs cleansing.
Where is that place where you just keep messing up?

**That is *not* the place where God wants to *condemn* you...
but it is *precisely the place* where God wants *to be with you*...
and to *love* you.**

This is *Good News*!

Listen to the song of the day "Come to Jesus" on the *Live to Love* album.

15 | GRACE UPON GRACE

Ephesians 1:3-5

Blessed be the God and Father of
our Lord Jesus Christ...
as he chose us in him,
before the foundation of the world,
to be holy and without blemish before him.
In love he destined us for adoption
to himself through Jesus Christ,
in accord with the favor of his will.

St. Paul never met the historical Jesus in the flesh...
but he did have a mystical, life-changing experience of the resurrected Christ.

**Before that experience, Paul was a brutal persecutor of Christians.
After... he was a fervent *follower* of Christ.**

The *inner* knowledge that St. Paul received was that *you and I* had been chosen
before the foundation of the world
to be without blemish before God.

**In love, *you and I* were *destined for adoption* to God *through* Jesus!
This is Grace *beyond anything we can imagine*!**

Is this *your* image of God?
If it's not... *re-read today's passage*... again and again and again.

Listen to the song of the day "Mercy Reigns" on the *Mercy Reigns* album.

LENS OF LOVE | 16

Galatians 5:19, 22-23

Now the works of the flesh are obvious.
In contrast, the fruit of the Spirit is
love, joy, peace, patience, kindness, generosity,
faithfulness, gentleness, self-control.
Against such there is no law.

As Jesus rails against the Pharisees for their narrow focus
on following the law without regard to love,
St. Paul writes on the same topic to the Galatians.
Rules and laws are necessary to keep us all in check.
But what is *most* important is that all the rules are *tempered* by *love*.

Otherwise they are *rigid* and *heartless*.
Being *right*... is not as important as being in *right relationship*.

We first need to form a relationship with God.
We can do this through contemplative prayer,
reading and meditating on the words of Jesus as well as following him,
and simply by being present.

For then the Holy Spirit will begin to *transform our hearts*.

The fruit...
or results of that...
will be "love, joy, peace, kindness, generosity, faithfulness, gentleness, self-control."
Who doesn't want *more* of *that* in their lives?

Listen to the song of the day "How Wonderful to Me" on the *Live to Love* album.

17 INFINITE COMPASSION

Song of Songs 2:13-14

Arise, my beloved,
my beautiful one, and come!
Let me see you,
let me hear your voice,
for your voice is sweet,
and you are lovely.

For those who have experienced loving another person...
the desire to *pour yourself out* for that person...
to *lay down your life* for that person...
be grateful.

It is just a tiny fleck of the immense Love God has for *you*!

If for some reason you feel no one could love you... know that this is *not true!*

As one of my favorite authors, Richard Rohr, says,
"One of the major problems in the spiritual life is
our attachments to our own self-image—
either positively or negatively created.
We confuse the *idea* of ourselves with who we actually *are* in God.
Ideas about things are not the things themselves."
Since God *is* love and *we come from* this Love...
we are indeed *lovely* in God's eyes.

God is the Lover... and *you* are the beloved.

Listen to the song of the day "Take Me Now Forever" on the *Live to Love* album.

LISTEN | 18

I wait with longing for the Lord, my soul waits for his word.

The act... or should I say *non*-act... of "waiting" is *not* appreciated by our culture.
We are *compulsive doers*.
Patience is clearly not highly regarded.
**Most modern religion has utterly failed to teach contemplation...
the ability to *wait* in *open attentiveness*.**

It's a "*non-doing*".
**To simply be *silent* and *let our thoughts disperse*...
is a practice of *waiting in longing for God's word*.**

The *word* could actually be a word or two... or possibly be a *state of inner peace and joy*.
**In the practice of contemplation we *experience God's presence*...
because God *is present*.**

If you are never actually *present*...
but instead are *mulling over the past* or *fretting about the future*...
then how can you experience the *True Presence*?
**I think many people are so afraid of experiencing that inner longing
calling us to the *Intimate Presence* that they
busy themselves with many activities...
as if that would cause the longing to subside.**

It doesn't!
There is a longing inside of you... a *deep yearning*.
What will satisfy this craving?
There is a "hole in your heart" that can't be filled in by anything of this world.
Could it be that God *yearns deeply to fill that void*? Are you giving God a chance?

**Listen to the song of the day "Turn Off the Noise" on the *Listen to Your Heart*
album.**

19 | AMAZING GRACE

Luke 12:6-7

"Are not five sparrows sold for two small coins?
Yet not one of them has escaped the notice of God.
Even the hairs of your head have all been counted.
Do not be afraid.
You are worth more than many sparrows."

"I'm not good enough."
If you've ever felt that way... you are *not* alone.
This is a common feeling that stems from a culture that espouses perfection
and being "number one" as the goal.
It is also a *lie*... because you *are good enough*.

You are *more* than good enough.
You are *eternally loved just as you are*.

Trying to prove you are *worthy of attention* or *love* is a *human game*.
God showers you with love *no matter what you do*.
There are *no conditions*.

Look at the beauty of creation.
It is one of the many *unmerited* gifts to each of us.
Jesus says that five sparrows might not be given much value by human beings...
but they are treasured by God.
And we are treasured *many times more*.
So... *what is there to fear*?

Rejoice and *be glad!*

Listen to the song of the day "Let the Joy Rise" on the *Give Praise and Thanks* album.

BE PRESENT | 20

Luke 12:37

"Blessed are those servants whom the master finds vigilant on his arrival."

WAKE UP!
That is what Jesus meant by being "vigilant" for the master's arrival.

His statement is *not* meant as a *threat* from a God who just can't wait
to punish us if we don't have our acts together.
Jesus said that if we know *him*... then we also know *God* (John 8:19 and John 14:7).
Did you *ever* see Jesus inflicting pain and suffering on *anyone*?
Did you *ever* see Jesus threatening sinners with punishment?
If this was what God had in mind for such sinners...
don't you think Jesus would have been warning them *every chance he could*?

Instead... Jesus spent most of his time *reaching out in love*
to those who don't have their acts together.
The *only* ones Jesus verbally reprimands are the self-righteous *religious leaders*!

God loves us *right now... unconditionally...*
which means God will love us *just the same in the future.*

The question is... are you *present* to that Love?
Are you mindful of the Love of God in *this* moment?
This moment is the *only one that is real...*
the only time you can actually encounter Love beyond love.

***Wake up!* Be *present* to God in *each* moment.**

Then you will surely find that God is *always arriving* and *always loving* you.
Then... "blessed" or *happy* you would be!

Listen to the song of the day "Changed" on the *Give Praise and Thanks* album.

21 | YOU BELONG

Ephesians 3:4-6

When you read this you can understand my insight into the mystery of Christ, which was not made known to human beings in other generations as it has now been revealed to his holy apostles and prophets by the Spirit, that the Gentiles are coheirs, members of the same body, and copartners in the promise in Christ Jesus through the gospel.

God was *always* revealing Himself to humanity... but Christ was the *ultimate* revelation.

Through *dying and rising* we are *all* promised *new life*... *now* and *always*.

That saving Love of Christ is promised not to just a *few*... but to *everyone*.
St. Paul wrote that *all* are included in the Body of Christ.
He said that each of us is a "copartner in the promise in Christ Jesus."
There are *no* boundaries.

***No one* is left out.**

Jesus described Himself as the "Good Shepherd"
who would not let even one sheep get lost.
That's Good News for *you, me,* and *everyone else*!

Listen to the song of the day "Lift Up Our Voices" on the *Give Praise and Thanks* album.

BE KIND TO YOURSELF

Romans 7:24

Miserable one that I am!
Who will deliver me from this mortal body?

How often do we have the best of intentions but seem to get sidetracked?
We feel the inner urge to call a friend or send an uplifting email,
but instead we find ourselves wasting time watching a meaningless show on TV
or mindlessly surfing the internet.
Sometimes it seems our flesh is at war with our souls.

**Take comfort in knowing that the great St. Paul
also struggled with fleshly temptations and fell.**

Jesus also knew the pain of temptation.
In his humanity he experienced a wide array of enticements
during his forty days in the desert.

**Now the resurrected Christ is willing to walk with us and
pick us up when we fall, not kick us when we are down.**

On the occasion of a particularly painful personal failure,
I began to berate myself over it.
But then I heard the gentle voice of God in my heart telling me that
Christ does *not reject me in my sinfulness*...
but instead *embraces me there*!

Such unconditional love is *transforming*.

Allow Christ to do the same for you!
Forgive yourself.
God does!

Listen to the song of the day "Come to Jesus" on the *Live to Love* album.

23 ROOTED IN GOD

Ephesians 3:17-19

...that you, rooted and grounded in love,
may have strength to comprehend with all
the holy ones what is the breadth and length and
height and depth, and to know the love of Christ
that surpasses knowledge, so that you
may be filled with all the fullness of God.

St. Paul is trying to describe the love of Christ...
a love that is *so vast* that it is beyond human understanding.

That's the love Christ has for *you*.

It's a love that would do *anything* for you...
even die on a cross.

**For even when he had done nothing to deserve death...
he continued to respond with *love* and *forgiveness*.**

"Father, forgive them, they know not what they do" (Luke 23:34).
This is the kind of love that frees us to live in the joy of our *belovedness* in God.

It is a *boundless, unconditional* Love that embraces you.

It's as close to you as the very *air* you breathe.
Allow that Love to fill you...
so that it can, in turn, be *poured out for others*.

**Listen to the song of the day "Pour Me Out" on the *Give Praise and Thanks*
album.**

LISTEN TO YOUR HEART

Psalm 40:7

Sacrifice and offering you do not want; but ears open to obedience you gave me.

God is interested in your *heart...* your desire to *spread the love of God*.
God is *not* interested in you *proving yourself worthy* of *anything*.

It's not just today's psalm that states God is *not interested in your sacrifice*.
The prophet Hosea also stated the same sentiment:
"For it is loyalty that I desire, not sacrifice,
and knowledge of God rather than burnt offerings" (Hosea 6:6).
Jesus referred to this twice:
"Go and learn the meaning of the words, 'I desire mercy, not sacrifice.'
I did not come to call the righteous but sinners" (Matthew 9:13);
"If you knew what this meant, 'I desire mercy, not sacrifice,'
you would not have condemned these innocent men" (Matthew 7:12).

**The message Jesus wanted us to hear is that we are
already *completely loved* by God *just as we are*.**

St. Paul said that God "chose us in Jesus,
before the foundation of the world, to be holy and
without blemish before him" (Ephesians 1:4).
God chose *you* "before the foundation of the world"!

**Instead of spending your time trying to prove yourself worthy of God's love...
try spending time in *silent acceptance* that *you are eternally loved*.**

Listen to the *yearnings of your heart* as to how God wants to love the world...
through you.

**Listen to the song of the day "Listen to Your Heart" on the *Listen to Your Heart*
album.**

301

25 | COMFORT

Psalm 124:8

Our help is the name of the Lord, the maker of heaven and earth.

The Creator of the universe...
made *you*.

You are part of the grand masterpiece that is *still unfolding*.

God (or whatever name you have for our loving Creator) is
sustaining and *holding it all together*.

**The *relational nature* of God is reflected in Jesus
who shared in humanity's joys and sorrows
while showing us the way of love, mercy, forgiveness, and compassion.**

He demonstrated the ultimate act of forgiveness when from the cross he said,
"Father, forgive them, they know not what they do."

That is the kind of Love that God has for *you* as well.

It's *unconditional* and *eternal*.
So whatever is causing you pain or uncertainty now...
call on the Maker of heaven and earth.
Help is as close to you...
as your very *breath*.

Listen to the song of the day "How Wonderful to Me" on the *Live to Love* album.

NEW LIFE AHEAD

Romans 8:28

We know that all things work for good
for those who love God,
who are called according to his purpose.

We are all *called according to God's purpose.*
Discerning this is a *moment-by-moment process* of opening ourselves
to our Loving Creator's will.

It requires being present... being awake to the moment.

Each of us is called to love God with *all our* heart, mind, soul, and strength...
as well as to love our neighbor (*everyone!*) as ourselves.

None of us do this perfectly.
But it is *in our* imperfection that God does the most glorious work of all...
gently loving us *in our* weaknesses so as to transform us into being the same
unconditional, compassionate lovers to the world.

Jesus gave us the perfect model to follow.
When hated...
he responded with love.
He showed the unconditional Love of God when hanging on the cross
when he forgave his persecutors...
Even when they had *not asked for forgiveness*!

Jesus showed us that if we follow him...
God would turn all the *grief, struggles, and pain* into
the glory of resurrection and New Life!

Listen to the song of the day "Radically Okay" on the *Mercy Reigns* album.

Romans 7:19

For I do not do the good I want, but I do the evil I do not want.

St. Paul is telling us about his *ongoing inner-conflict*.
It's no doubt familiar to each of us...
this struggle between *wanting to do what is good* and another desire to *do what is not*.
This is *not* the place to *hide* from God in *shame*...
but is instead the place to *surrender* to God's *grace*.

We are not involved in some "worthiness" contest to *achieve* or *merit* God's love.
Look at what happened to St. Paul.
When he was still known as Saul...
he was a persecutor of Christians.
His conversion came by the total *grace* of God... no *achievement* of his own.
Did it ever occur to you that God *wants to be with you in your inner turmoil*?
How else would you ever *experience* what Unconditional Love *is*?

Several verses after today's scripture above, St. Paul went on to write,
"Miserable one that I am! Who will deliver me from this mortal body?
Thanks be to God through Jesus Christ our Lord" (Romans 7:24-25).
The name "Jesus" literally means "*Yahweh saves*."
Jesus has already shown us that God is willing to go to
***any length* to show us Love.**

You do not have to prove yourself worthy.
God loves you *in* your imperfection.

You are enough.
Allow this Love to *transform* you.

Listen to the song of the day "Radically Okay" on the *Mercy Reigns* album.

WHOLENESS GUARANTEED |

Luke 13:32

"Behold, I cast out demons and I perform
healings today and tomorrow,
and on the third day I accomplish my purpose."

Jesus showed us that God wants to *heal* us and see us made *whole*.

We are being led to a *glorious transformation*.

It is a *process* in which we encounter struggles, pain, and infirmities.
We are invited to *let go* of *control* so that *in* our struggles...
in our weaknesses...
God can *lift* us and *transform* us.
Jesus showed us that ultimately death does *not* win...
but in fact leads us to *new life* that is *eternal*.

So what *appears* to be horrible...
what *appears* to be a horrendous end...
can actually be the *very thing* that leads to
our *transformation, joy,* and new beginning...
if we have *faith* and *cling to the hope of Christ*.

As St. Paul said in Romans 8:38,
"For I am convinced that neither death, nor life, nor angels, nor principalities,
nor present things, nor future things, nor powers, nor height, nor depth,
nor any other creature will be able to separate us from the love of God
in Christ Jesus our Lord."

This is *Good News*!

Listen to the song of the day "Heal Me" on the *Live to Love* album.

29 | LISTEN

Luke 6:12-13

In those days he departed to the mountain
to pray, and he spent the night in prayer to God.
When day came, he called his disciples to himself,
and from them he chose twelve,
whom he also named apostles.

Jesus often communed with God in silent prayer.
The Son of God apparently prayed in very human ways...
by being in the quiet Presence of the One he called "Abba".
Before making a big decision...
like picking the apostles...
Jesus went to the mountain by himself and "spent the night in prayer to God."

**How often do I set aside time to be in the *silent Presence of God* to
listen to the quiet inner voice of our loving Creator?**

That voice will *always* have your best interest at heart.
It will *always* treat you as "the beloved."

**The God who knitted you in your mother's womb...
wants a close, intimate relationship with *you!***

May we all set aside some silent time to listen for God's tender voice.

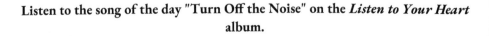

**Listen to the song of the day "Turn Off the Noise" on the *Listen to Your Heart*
album.**

RESTORATIVE JUSTICE | 30

Luke 14:5-6

Then he said to them, "Who among you,
if your son or ox falls into a cistern,
would not immediately pull him out
on the Sabbath day?"
But they were unable to answer his question.

Jesus had just healed a man in front of the Pharisees,
the religious leaders, on the Sabbath day.
This broke the Jewish law, which banned any sort of work on the day of rest.
However, Jesus tells them that *Love* takes *precedence* over the *law*.

The Pharisees (and many people today) are stuck in an "either-or" mindset:
Either you keep the law and are *in*... *or* you don't and are *out*.

Jesus is saying we need a non-dualistic, "both-and" mindset.
I can *both* keep the law as my foundation *and* break it when Love requires it.

Following the rules can make someone "right" but also quite *harsh* and *heartless*.
Compassion and forgiveness require a transformed, non-judgmental heart.

Think for a moment just how imperfect we *all* are and
how often we have turned our backs on God.

Then think how God loves us and forgives us *without exception*.
Allow that thought to settle in your soul.

Listen to the song of the day "Salvation" on the *Live to Love* album.

31 LOVE IS THE TOP PRIORITY

Luke 13:30

"For behold, some are last who will be first, and some are first who will be last."

Jesus says that the people this world might look down upon...
those viewed as being "last"...
might actually be looked upon as "first" in the viewpoint of God's Kingdom.
And the reverse is also true.

**What really matters is our motivation...
not outward appearances.**

What is in our hearts?

**If we are motivated by love, mercy, forgiveness, and compassion...
then the Kingdom of God is at hand!**

If those who are first would reach out to those who are last...
then being "first" or "last" would no longer matter.
Each of us is *first*...
in God's eyes.

Listen to the song of the day "God's Love Is All You Need" on the *Listen to Your Heart* album.

HAPPINESS | I

"Blessed are the poor in spirit, for theirs is the kingdom of heaven."

Everyone wants to be *happy...*
and in the Beatitudes, Jesus gives us the *blueprint* for *being happy.*
The very first line (today's scripture verse) is the key to having *life to the full.*

Cling to *nothing*!
***Do not hold on to anything* so as to be *attached* or *identified* by it.**
But, at the same time... *do not renounce* those things.

Be able to *both* accept and enjoy the blessings God brings into your life
and be able to *let them go...* passing them on to others.

When we are not attached to things that *don't last...*
we will be open to experiencing the things that *do last.*
We will be able to *begin experiencing* the *kingdom of God...* right *now.*

We will be able to begin experiencing the joy of the *Divine Presence.*

Unhindered by attachments, each of us is *free* to *love fully* and
to be the *unique, beloved child of God that God intended.*

As it says in the First Letter of John,
"Beloved, we are God's children now; what we shall be has not yet been revealed.
We do know that when it is revealed we shall be like him,
for we shall see him as he is" (1 John 3:2).

For when I am fully *me*... God's glory is *fully revealed.*

Listen to the song of the day "Glorify You with Me" on the *Give Praise and Thanks* album.

2   RESURRECTION AHEAD

Wisdom 3:2-3, 7

They seemed, in the view of the foolish, to be dead;
and their passing away was thought an affliction and
their going forth from us, utter destruction.
But they are in peace. They shall shine,
and shall dart about as sparks through stubble.

To those who have lost a loved one or are dealing with a recent loss
or an impending loss...
take comfort in today's scripture.
"Dying and rising" happens *over and over* throughout our lives.
Struggles and **defeats** are **transformed** into sources of **strength** and **victories**.

It happens when *seemingly* "bad" times are *resurrected* into "good" times
through the transforming power of Love.
**These transformations give us hope that when our physical life ends...
a glorious transformation is in the works.**

Cling to Jesus who showed us that the path to death
always leads to resurrection and new life.
Always!

Have no fear.
As Jesus said, "And this is the will of the one who sent me,
that I should not lose anything of what he gave me,
but that I should raise it on the last day" (John 6:39).

***Count* on it!**

Listen to the song of the day "Salvation" on the *Live to Love* album.

NEWS OF GREAT JOY

John 6:37-38

"Everything that the Father gives me will come to me, and I will not reject anyone who comes to me, because I came down from heaven not to do my own will but the will of the one who sent me."

Re-read these words of Jesus *several* times. These are words of great hope and comfort.
Jesus said that he will not reject *anyone* who comes to him.
We find this hard to believe because when we do wrong to others...
they usually *do* reject us.
And isn't that *our* reaction when someone does wrong to *us*?
How "conditional" is our fickle love!
But "God is Love" (1 John 4:8). Our Creator's love is *unconditional*.

Where are you broken?
What have you done that you regret or think is unforgivable?
What is afflicting you with inner turmoil?
While many people likely think that these are the areas that God despises in us...
it is actually the areas where God wants to *embrace* us,
***heal* us, and make us *whole*.**

These are the places where *we can't do it on our own*... the places where *we need God*.
The risen Christ wants to show you the Unconditional Love of God.
He promises to not reject *anyone* who comes to him.
***Accept it*.**

Jesus said, "Come to me, all you who are weary and heavy-laden,
and I will give you rest" (Matthew 11:28).
The most *incredible* Love... is *true*.

Listen to the song of the day "I Will Give You Rest" on the *Live to Love* album.

INFINITE ACCEPTANCE

Luke 15:4-5

"What man among you having a hundred sheep
and losing one of them would not
leave the ninety-nine in the desert and
go after the lost one until he finds it?
And when he does find it,
he sets it on his shoulders with great joy."

Jesus made it *quite clear* with these words that
no matter how *lost, broken,* or *unlovable* we might *feel...*
God will *never abandon us.*
As a matter of fact, God will *always pursue us* with open arms...
no matter what.

Jesus says God *delights* in seeking us out when we are lost.
How else would we experience being unconditionally loved?

Jesus talked in parables and metaphors to try to explain to us that
our Creator's love is *far beyond anything we can imagine.*

If you are at the end of your rope...
God is there waiting to *catch* you.

Why wait until you are at the *end* of your rope?
Why not let go and fall into the arms of Unconditional Love *now*?

Listen to the song of the day "God Is" on the *Give Praise and Thanks* album.

PEACE BE WITH YOU

Psalm 27:1

The Lord is my light and my salvation;
whom do I fear?
The Lord is my life's refuge;
of whom am I afraid?

What is it that you *fear* now?

**What if Jesus was standing *right by your side*...
with an arm around your shoulder?
Would you still be *afraid*?**

One of Jesus' most quoted lines was, "do *not be afraid.*"

**The One who would *lay down his life for you*...
will *surely not let you down now.***

What are the things distracting you from a right-relationship
with God and *others*?
Allow the light of Love to shine on them.

**Keep your eyes on Jesus...
follow him...
and he will *lead you* to wholeness and peace.**

Listen to the song of the day "Radically Okay" on the *Mercy Reigns* album.

6 | LOVE WINS

Psalm 98:2

The Lord has made his victory known;
has revealed his triumph for the nations to see.

We see dying and rising all around us.

Each day ends in the darkness of night...
but then comes the dawn of a new day.

Each year ends in the dead of winter...
but then somehow new life appears again in the spring.

Someone *dies*...
while a baby is *being born*.

We're surrounded by examples of this *cycle* where God is constantly telling us...
death is *not the end*.

God showed us in Jesus the ultimate lesson...
that death *does not win*.
It's a *passage way* into something better.

The crucifixion was followed by the resurrection!

In each of our lives we experience many deaths and resurrections...
many *struggles* that lead to new life if we have faith and
cling to Christ who will *never abandon us*.

Listen to the song of the day "Seasons" on the *Listen to Your Heart* album.

SILENCE SPEAKS

John 10:27-28

"My sheep hear my voice;
I know them, and they follow me.
I give them eternal life,
and they shall never perish."

How can you hear the voice of God if you are *not listening*?
It's not just the *cacophonous noise* of the *world* that distracts us...
but also the constant noise *inside our own heads*.
Most of the time our minds are running with *non-stop commentary*.

Thoughts after thoughts after thoughts, etc.
So *stop... be still...* and *be silent*.

If you *listened* you would hear words of unconditional love, acceptance, and forgiveness.
As Jesus said, "My sheep hear my voice... and they follow me."
Following the Good Shepherd would be a *joy*!

Notice that Jesus did *not* say that when his sheep follow him that
one day he will give them eternal life.
He said, "I give them eternal life."
It begins *now*.

If you want to experience a taste of this freedom,
if you want to experience amazing grace *now*...
listen for the voice of the Good Shepherd.
Read and meditate on the words of Jesus in scripture.
Follow where he leads and experience life that has no end...
right *now*.

Listen to the song of the day "I Will Give You Rest" on the *Live to Love* album.

Romans 11:32

For God delivered all to disobedience,
that he might have mercy upon all.

God purposely made us *imperfect* knowing that we would *disobey*...
so that God could show us *love, mercy, forgiveness,* and *compassion.*
Life is *not* about us being *perfect.*
That would set us up for *failure.*

It's about us being *perfectly loved by God.*
It's about us receiving love *in our imperfection*...
and then *sharing* it.

That's how you learn the depths of love. Someone has to *model* it to you.
God doesn't love us because *we* are good but because *God* is good.
It is *easy* to love those who love you back...
but what about those who *don't?*
What about those who are hard to love because of their imperfections?
Being a Christian is *not* about *being perfect* but *being in need of the Great Physician.*

It is only when we experience the love and compassion of God *in our*
***imperfection* that we can be *transformed* and be able to extend**
the same kind of love, mercy, forgiveness, and compassion to others.

As Jesus said, "When you hold a banquet,
invite the poor, the crippled, the lame, the blind;
blessed indeed will you be because of their inability to repay you" (Luke 14:13-14).

God is inviting *you* to the banquet.
Invite *someone else* as well!

Listen to the song of the day "All Are Welcome" on the *Give Praise and Thanks*
album.

GOD IS HOLDING YOU | 9

Behind and before you encircle me and
rest your hand upon me.

The psalmist goes on to write,
"Where can I hide from your spirit?"
Impossible!

God is *everywhere*.

God is like the very *air* we *breathe*.
God is like our *breath*.

**To speak God's ancient name "Yahweh" is the very *act* of *breathing*,
"Yah" (*inhale*)... "weh" (*exhale*).**

God is there *in* our joys and *in* our *sorrows*...
celebrating with us during the highs and *mourning* with us during the lows.

*"All are one in You.
You are all that's true.
May I find You in all I see...
breath of God breathe on me."*

Listen to the song of the day "Breathe On Me" on the *Listen to Your Heart*
album.

10 MADE FOR ETERNITY

Wisdom 2:23

For God formed man to be imperishable; the image of his own nature he made him.

This is Good News!

You and I are made in the image of God's nature...
and we were *formed* to be "imperishable."
So why worry?

The unknown nature of our mortality usually leads us to *avoid* this topic... but we will *all die one day*.

It may be *today... tomorrow... in fifty years or in eighty years... but it will happen.*
Even those whom Jesus physically healed... later *died.*
So physical death is inevitable.
But we have faith that while our bodies will *die...*
our souls will *never die.*

The Risen Christ *assures us of this!*

God is leading us to wholeness and completion in each *moment,*
which is the only time that is real.

**God *is loving us now.*
Each of us is God's beloved son or daughter.**

Open your heart to hear this message that I've been given *especially for* you.

Listen to the song of the day "How Wonderful to Me" on the *Live to Love* album.

HAVE FAITH | 11

Psalm 46:2

God is our refuge and our strength, an ever-present help in distress.

God *pervades* all reality.
God is not *out there*.
God is not *off in some distant place* coldly observing us.
God is *with* us and also *within* us.

"For 'In him we live and move and have our being'" (Acts 17:28).

God is *intimately* close to you...
as close as your very breath.

Our Creator is *Love* itself...
right now...
as in *"ever-present."*

So learn from the past but *let it go*.
It's *over*.
Plan for the future...
but do not fret over it as it is *not yet* and so it is *not real*.
***Now* is where you will find God...**
patiently and lovingly *drawing you to the future*...
inviting you to *co-create* what will be.

So in times of trouble, allow this awareness to *envelop* and *embrace* you.
God will *never* abandon you. *Impossible!*

So do not be afraid.
Be at *peace*.

Listen to the song of the day "I Will Give You Rest" on the *Live to Love* album.

12 | LIVE TO LOVE

Psalm 34:19

The Lord is close to the broken-hearted, saves those whose spirit is crushed.

We *hate* to *fail*.
We are taught from childhood that the objective is to *win, win, win...*
at all costs.
We must defeat the opposition.

But Jesus says the objective is to *love, love, love...*
at all costs.

He says the *top priority* is to *love God and your neighbor as yourself*. (Matthew 22:36-39)
He takes it a step further: We *must* love our *enemies!* (Matthew 5:44)

Jesus says that instead of winning...
your life's mission should be to extend
love, mercy, forgiveness, and compassion.
It's not a "win-lose" scenario but a "win-win"!

When we actually *join* the so-called *loser*, the outcast, the one who is suffering...
we know that Christ is near to us because
those are the people that he spent his time with.

It is also when *we* are at the end of our ropes...
that God is there waiting to *embrace* us.

This is the place where we *let go* of our agendas
so that we might allow God to begin *transforming* us and
take us to greater heights than we could *ever* imagine.

Listen to the song of the day "Changed" on the *Give Praise and Thanks* album.

TRUE LIFE

Luke 17:33

"Whoever seeks to preserve his life will lose it, but whoever loses it will save it."

A statement like this one from Jesus confounds our normal reasoning process.

**At some point I have to relinquish the *false self* built by my ego...
so that my *true self* can be realized.
We have to *let go* of the things that *won't last*
in order to recognize the things that *will*.**

What things in your life do you *hold onto* and become *identified* with?
It could be possessions, titles, positions, your profession, popularity, or abilities.
All these things will eventually *disintegrate*.
When we are willing to *let go* of such things...
we find our *true selves*.
It's hard.

**It'll feel like *dying*.
But the process *always leads to new life*.**

After I peel away all the *masks* I wear...
who am I essentially at the most basic level?
A child of God...
eternally and unconditionally loved for no other reason than that.
So are *you*...
and so is *everyone*.

When will the world awaken to this truth?
It starts with *you* and *me*.

Listen to the song of the day "God Is the Goal" on the *Live to Love* album.

14 AWAKEN

Wisdom 6:11

Desire therefore my words;
long for them and you shall be instructed.

In any close relationship we have intimate, *two-way* conversations.
Do *you* have such a relationship with God?

Or is it a *one-way* line of communication with *you* doing *all the talking...*
and *no listening*?
I believe that our Creator *yearns to speak to us in our hearts*
and *is always speaking.*

God's words come to us in many ways:
through silent meditation,
reflective scripture reading, nature, people,
music, art, books, etc., etc., etc.
But the question is: *Are we listening?*

Try taking some quiet time to simply sit in the presence of God.
God *is present...*
but many times *we are not*!

Our minds are *constantly chattering*.
***Stop* and observe your mind's *endless commentary* and *judgments*.**

Allow it to cease.
Practice *being still.*

Be present to the Divine Presence in times of silence and times of activity...
and then *listen to your heart*.

Listen to the song of the day "Slow Me Down" on the *Mercy Reigns* album.

AMAZING LOVE | 15

Titus 3:3-7

For we ourselves were once foolish, disobedient, deluded, slaves to various desires and pleasures, living in malice and envy, hateful ourselves and hating one another. But when the kindness and generous love of God our savior appeared, not because of any righteous deeds we had done but because of his mercy, he saved us through the bath of rebirth and renewal by the holy Spirit, whom he richly poured out on us through Jesus Christ our savior, so that we might be justified by his grace and become heirs in hope of eternal life.

Wow... that is a LOT to digest.
St. Paul's writings tend to ramble... but they are *filled* with *deep* meaning!
Paul's life was completely turned around through an encounter with the living Love of God... the risen Jesus himself.
It came at a time when Paul was *persecuting* Christians... not *loving* them.
He did not *merit* such a meeting with Jesus.
There is nothing we need to do to *earn* this Love.

You see... it is *freely given* to you and me by a God whose love is beyond our understanding.
That is truly *GOOD NEWS!*

Listen to the song of the day "Mercy Reigns" on the *Mercy Reigns* album.

16 | REDEEMER

Luke 19:10

"For the Son of Man has come to seek and to save what was lost."

If you've ever felt lost...
Ever felt like you didn't measure up...
Ever felt like you *let someone down*...
ever *messed up* in a big way...
did something hurtful...
or felt like no one could *possibly love you*...
then you are *exactly the one that Jesus is seeking out*.

**You are the one that he wants to *find* and *be with*
because God *could not bear* to see
a beloved daughter or son *lost*.**

**You see...
God's justice is *not punitive*...
but *restorative*.**

Jesus showed us that he would even *die* to show us
the love and forgiveness of God.
Take a few moments to bask in that knowledge.

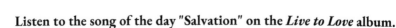

Listen to the song of the day "Salvation" on the *Live to Love* album.

STRENGTH IN WEAKNESS | 17

I call upon you;
answer me, O God.
Turn your ear to me;
hear my prayer.
Keep me as the apple of your eye.

There has been *much* to pray about.

Many people are suffering with illnesses.
Sometimes it feels like there is *nothing* we can do...
like we are *powerless* to help.

Indeed... we sometimes *are powerless*.

It is only when *we come to that place* of powerlessness that
we can *turn* to a *Greater Power*.
Faith tells me that God *does* hear me when I call.

**Jesus said that when we go to our *inner room* and
become *present* to the *Divine Presence*...
we *are heard and answered*.**

For *each* of us is the *apple* of God's eye.

***Cling* to that love and allow it to *transform* and *heal* you.**

Listen to the song of the day "Come to Jesus" on the *Live to Love* album.

18 LISTEN

Luke 19:48

"...all the people were hanging on his words."

What was it like to actually *hear* Jesus speak?
People were drawn to him and
his words *inspired, healed, brought peace,* and *transformed*
those who listened to him.

While we cannot hear Jesus speak in the flesh today...
we can still hear him speak by reading his words in the Gospels...
and then *ruminating* over those words in the *silence* of our hearts.
We can also simply *be silent*.
Find a quiet place and practice *letting go*.
Allow your thoughts to *cease*.
This will *not* be easy. You will have to let go *again, again,* and *again*.
Settle into the silence.
As St. John of the Cross said, "Silence is God's first language."
Be *present* to the *Divine Presence*.
Let that Presence settle into your whole being.
Allow that silence to *fill* you and *nourish* you.
You will find yourself *hanging* on each silent word.

"In the beginning was the Word,
and the Word was with God,
and the Word was God.
He was in the beginning with God.
All things came to be through him,
and without him nothing came to be.
What came to be through him was life,
and this life was the light of the human race." (John 1:1-4)
Listen.

Listen to the song of the day "Turn Off the Noise" on the *Listen to Your Heart*
album.

FREE LOVE | 19

Luke 19:45-46

Then Jesus entered the temple area and proceeded to drive out those who were selling things, saying to them, "It is written, 'My house shall be a house of prayer, but you have made it a den of thieves.'"

The only times we see Jesus *truly and justifiably angry* is either
when the religious leaders (Pharisees) are holding people
to the letter of the law while *ignoring* the *greatest* Commandment to love...
or in this temple area scene.
Here, Jesus sees the selling of small animals to people so that they might
take them to the temple for *sacrifice*.
What *infuriated* Jesus was that people were being misled to believe that *sacrificing an animal* would somehow make God forgive them...
pacify God's anger with them...
make God love *them*.

Jesus knew that God's love... was *free*.
God's love and forgiveness were *not for sale*.

Jesus said, "Go and learn the meaning of the words,
'I desire mercy, not sacrifice'" (Matthew 9:13)
when he quoted the prophet Hosea (Hosea 6:6).
Good works and sacrifice do not *make* God love you.
Knowing in your heart that God loves you
naturally leads you to good works and personal sacrifices.
Do you know that God loves you deeply... just as you are?

Listen to the song of the day "The Way You Are" on the *Mercy Reigns* album.

20 | SPIRITUAL RICHES

Revelation 3:17-18

For you say, 'I am rich and affluent
and have no need of anything,'
and yet do not realize that you are
wretched, pitiable, poor, blind, and naked.
I advise you to buy from me gold refined by fire
so that you may be rich, and white garments
to put on so that your shameful nakedness
may not be exposed, and buy ointment
to smear on your eyes so that you may see.

Those who are wealthy are not bad people because of their wealth...
as long as they keep God as their top priority as well as care for the poor.
But wealth *does* make this *challenging*.
It can make it quite easy to overlook or never even see the poor and those in need.
It's easy for wealth to blind us to the needs of the poor and to our need for God.

The book of Revelation is rich in symbolism.
The writer says we all need God's spiritual wealth so that
we may be healed of our blindness and see as God sees.
God scolds us to change our ways as a parent whose motive is *love*.

God wants to save us (as in *make us whole*) −not punish us.
As Jesus said,
"For the Son of Man has come to seek and to save what was lost" (Luke 19:10).

Listen to the song of the day "Love Will Always Lead You Home" on the *Mercy Reigns* album.

SPIRITUAL BLINDNESS |

Luke 18:41-42

Jesus asked him,
"What do you want me to do for you?"
He replied, "Lord, please let me see."
Jesus told him, "Have sight;
your faith has saved you."

When a blind man heard that Jesus was passing by he kept calling out to him...
even to the point where others in the crowd were telling him to be quiet.

**Do *we* pursue and call out to Jesus...
with the *same* persistence?**

More important than the *physical* healing was that
the blind man had *faith* that Jesus could help him.
He believed in a Higher Power.
The blind man wanted to *see*.

**The question is:
How are *we* blind?**

How can Jesus help us to see what we are missing?
Our restoration might not always come through physical healing...
but trust that God will make you *whole*.

Listen to the song of the day "Heal Me" on the *Live to Love* album.

22 | LOVE IN ACTION

Luke 19:41-42

As he drew near,
he saw the city and wept over it, saying,
"If this day you only knew what makes for peace –
but now it is hidden from your eyes."

Jesus shows us the face of a loving and caring God...
weeping over the sight of all his children turning away from him.
They were not following his example of
love, mercy, forgiveness and compassion.

**They just didn't see...
didn't realize that Jesus was showing them the way
that would lead them to peace and wholeness...
if only they would follow him.**

What would it take for them to realize how much God loves us?
It would take responding to persecution with
love, mercy, forgiveness, and compassion...
all the way to the cross.

Listen to the song of the day "Salvation" on the *Live to Love* album.

BLESSINGS ABOUND

Daniel 3:62-65

Sun and moon, bless the Lord;
Stars of heaven, bless the Lord;
Every shower and dew, bless the Lord;
All you winds, bless the Lord;
praise and exalt him above all forever.

All creation is a testimony to the glory of our Creator.

From the dew on the ground,
to the winds that blow,
to the sunshine,
to the vast galaxies of the universe,
we are immersed in the grand artistry
of a Benevolence beyond measure.

You and I are *part* of this *on-going* creation!

How *awesome* and *wonderful!*

Immerse yourself in this awareness.

Just *be.*

Then...
be thankful.

Listen to the song of the day "How Magnificent, Wondrous and Glorious" on the *Mercy Reigns* album.

24 TRUE WEALTH

Luke 21:5-6

While some people were speaking about how the temple was adorned with costly stones and votive offerings, he said, "All that you see here – the days will come when there will not be left a stone upon another stone that will not be thrown down."

All the *material* things that are very *expensive* and of "high value" today...
will one day *wither, decay, and be worthless.*
That beautiful, trendy sports car will one day be a
broken-down, rusted piece of *junk.*
God breathes life into all living things.
Just as God gives life in the spring and it flourishes in the summer...
life begins to slip away during autumn...
before ending in the winter.
But that is *not* the final word.
Spring returns! *New life* is ahead!

As Jesus showed us...
death does *not* win.
There will be *resurrection*!

God's *unconditional Love* will bring us through
any struggle, suffering, or death to *new life*...
if we simply have *faith.*
Ultimately *love* is the *only* thing that *lasts.*

Invest your life in *that.*

Listen to the song of the day "Seasons" on the *Listen to Your Heart* album.

BELOVED

Psalm 100:3

Know that the Lord is God,
he made us,
we belong to him,
we are his people,
the flock he shepherds.

I think the main reason we feel anxiety and despair is because
we don't truly feel the love of God.

It's there in our hearts...
planted there by our Loving Creator...
but we allow the sufferings of the world to smother it.

Just as a mother holds her newborn...
so God holds you and me.

**There is no way God could ever let go of us...
because "we belong to him."**

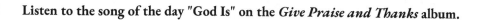

Listen to the song of the day "God Is" on the *Give Praise and Thanks* album.

26 | LOVE POURED OUT

Luke 21:1-4

Jesus saw some wealthy people putting
their offerings into the treasury and he
noticed a poor widow putting
in two small coins.
He said, "I tell you truly, this poor widow
put in more than all the rest;
for those others have all made offerings
from their surplus wealth,
but she, from her poverty,
has offered her whole livelihood."

Like this poor widow giving her *whole livelihood*...
Jesus gave all of himself as well.
He showed us true, *unconditional* love even unto death.
His love didn't change despite being persecuted.

Jesus is our example of *how to love*.

We are called to give of ourselves to others
even when it's not convenient or easy.
And when we fail...
it's good to know that God continues to love us regardless.

Take a few moments to contemplate such a love for you!

**Listen to the song of the day "Pour Me Out" on the *Give Praise and Thanks*
album.**

Luke 17:15-16

And one of them,
realizing he had been healed, returned,
glorifying God in a loud voice;
and he fell at the feet of Jesus
and thanked him.
He was a Samaritan.

Jesus had just healed ten lepers and told them to show themselves to the priests.
Only *one* of them, a *Samaritan*, returned to *thank* Jesus.

Samaritans were shunned by Israelites.
Jesus shows us again...
that God has *no* favorites.
Or should I say...
God has *ALL* favorites.

God accepts *all* people as one.
All are *included*.
Jesus shows us a God who loves, forgives, and cares for all without divisions.
He asks us to do the same.

And whatever it is about you that you think separates you from God...
bring it to Jesus.
He rejects *no one!*

Forgiveness and new life are freely given...
no strings attached.

Listen to the song of the day "All Are One" on the *Mercy Reigns* album.

28 GLORY TO GOD

Daniel 3:57

Bless the Lord, all you works of the Lord, praise and exalt him above all forever.

We are swimming in blessings.
I know we all have troubles...
but the blessings *far* outnumber the troubles.

**It seems we have a *choice* to either focus our attention
on the *blessings* or the *troubles*.**

Every sunrise, every delicious flavor, every aroma, every smile,
every beautiful song, *every next breath* is a *gift* from God.
Even when negative things happen...
God will *transform* them into something positive with *time* and *faith*.

All *deaths* lead to *resurrections*.

All the *little deaths* we must endure along life's journey lead to *new life*
when we *trust* and *go with the flow* of God's mercy and grace.

**And when we are open to that grace...
we can also be God's instrument
in turning a curse into a blessing by being a conduit of God's love.**

All of creation is involved in this *process* of *dying* and *rising*
as God transforms *death* to *life*.
As St. Paul said,
"We know that all creation is groaning in labor pains even until now" (Romans 8:22).
May we all join in a *universal* song of *thanks* and *praise*!

Listen to the song of the day "Give Praise and Thanks" on the *Give Praise and Thanks* album.

BE MADE NEW | 29

Matthew 8:8

The centurion said in reply,
"Lord, I am not worthy to have you enter
under my roof;
only say the word and my servant will be healed."

Jesus never seemed concerned about anyone's *worthiness*.
Never.
He never mentioned *worthiness* as a requirement of God's attention.

**In fact... Jesus reached out *to* and spent time *with* those
who were considered *unworthy*.**

No one had to pass any tests or answer any questions about *beliefs* and *doctrines*.
As a professional officer in the Roman army...
the centurion would have been an oppressor of the Jews.
But this was no obstacle to Jesus when it came to helping someone in need.
He simply *responded*.

As Franciscan priest Richard Rohr says,
"God does not love you because you are good;
God loves you because God is good."

God loves you *in your unworthiness*!
How *else* would you experience the *healing* of Unconditional Love?

Allow that knowledge to *sink into* and *saturate* your soul.
Be *healed*.
Be *whole*.

Listen to the song of the day "Heal Me" on the *Live to Love* album.

30 OUT OF THE COMFORT ZONE

Luke 21:17-19

"You will be hated by all because of my name,
but not a hair on your head will be destroyed.
By your perseverance you will secure your lives."

Jesus promised his followers that they would be persecuted.

But he also promised that if we persevere in following him...
we would be saved.

I believe that means we will have some pain and suffering in this world
but if we follow the Way that Jesus showed us...
we will also have inner peace and joy.

We will be on the path to wholeness and the discovery of our true selves.

We will become *fully alive* as we are present to God living fully in us.

Awaken to God's presence and eternal love for you.

And be freed!

Listen to the song of the day "Take the Road Less Traveled" on the *Live to Love* album.

UNCONDITIONAL LOVE

Matthew 9:10-12

While he was at table in his house, many
tax collectors and sinners came and sat with
Jesus and his disciples. The Pharisees saw this
and said to his disciples, "Why does your teacher
eat with tax collectors and sinners?"
He heard this and said, "Those who are well
do not need a physician, but the sick do."

Life is not a *contest* to *achieve worthiness* of *being loved by God*.
If that were the case... we would *all* fail.
We are *all* sinners.
At times we all choose our own selfish interests over God's interests for us.
**Jesus was *quite comfortable* sitting with all the sinners at table...
which would have been quite *scandalous*!**
The religious leaders took issue with Jesus sharing a meal with such people.
**But the only people Jesus seemed to take issue with were the *religious leaders*
who wanted to *separate* themselves from those they deemed *unworthy*.**

Who are the people *we* separate ourselves from today?

Jesus showed quite clearly that God *wants to be with sinners*.
**How else would each of us truly *experience* the
unconditional, transforming love of God?**

Jesus wants to sit at table with *you and me*.
This is *Good News*!

**Listen to the song of the day "All Are Welcome" on the *Give Praise and Thanks*
album.**

2 DIVINE PRESENCE

Psalm 27:1, 14

The Lord is my light and my salvation; whom do I fear? Wait for the Lord, take courage; be stouthearted, wait for the Lord!

Since God *is* Love (1 John 4:8)... *what* is there to *fear*?
"There is no fear in love, but perfect love drives out fear because fear has to do with punishment, and so one who fears is not yet perfect in love." (1 John 4:18)
We are God's children.

"You formed my inmost being; you knit me in my mother's womb.
I praise you, because I am wonderfully made; wonderful are your works!
My very self you know" (Psalm 139:13-14).
**Whatever *struggle* or *pain* you are going through...
know that God will *never abandon you.***

"Wait for the Lord."
**When you *wait*... you are *consciously present*.
And *where else* would God *be*... but in the *here and now*.**

God is an *endless* Source of Love shining *on* you... *in* you... and *through* you.
**Open yourself to this Love and know that it will *never waver*
based on whims or your actions.**

This love is *unconditional*.
***You* are the *beloved*.**

Just accept it.
Allow it to *transform* you.
Allow this Love to birth something *new* in *you* this Christmas.

Listen to the song of the day "God Is" on the *Give Praise and Thanks* album.

ETERNAL LIGHT

Isaiah 25:8

He will destroy death forever.
The Lord God will wipe away the tears
from all faces;
The reproach of his people he will remove from the
whole earth;
for the Lord has spoken.

Centuries before Jesus of Nazareth, the prophet Isaiah predicted
the coming of the Messiah...
the Great Hope...
God made flesh.

His birth would bring a Great Light into the world and
"the light shines in the darkness, and the darkness has not overcome it" (John 1:5).

Through the life of Jesus we see this Light shining
love, mercy, grace, forgiveness, and compassion **into the world.**

Through his death and resurrection we see that death has no hold on us...
it is merely a *passageway* to *eternal life*.
So why not invite the Light of Christ into your life more fully?

It is a Light of pure love and acceptance that claims you as a
beloved daughter **or** ***son.***

"God will wipe away the tears from all faces."

Listen to the song of the day "Make Your Way" on the *Mercy Reigns* album.

4 | LOVE IS BLIND

Isaiah 26:4-5

Trust in the Lord forever!
For the Lord is an eternal Rock.
He humbles those in high places,
and the lofty he brings down.

How often do those idolized by the world...
eventually fall.
It's a virtual *guarantee*.

***No one* is *perfect*.**
Eventually we see that anyone held up as an "idol" will show imperfections.

And the higher the pedestal we place them on...
the further they fall.

Before we pass judgment, aren't we *all a complex of contradictions*?

Don't we all have our inner *shadows*...
places of weakness that we just can't seem to overcome on our own?

Instead of pretending those shadows aren't there...
instead of trying to stand on a pedestal of adulation or
put anyone else up on that pedestal...
may we humbly let the Light of Love shine upon *us* and *all that is*.

God holds *each* of us, *contradictions and all*,
in a tight embrace of *unconditional love*.
Jesus showed us this is so.

Listen to the song of the day "The Way You Are" on the *Mercy Reigns* album.

TRUST IN LOVE

Matthew 9:28-30

When he entered the house,
the blind men approached him
and Jesus said to them,
"Do you believe that I can do this?"
"Yes, Lord," they said to him.
Then he touched their eyes and said,
"Let it be done for you according to your faith."
And their eyes were opened.

Do you ever think that you are just not *good enough* to be loved...
that you just aren't *worthy enough*?
Do you desire healing of some affliction or struggle but feel like
you aren't *worthy* of Jesus' attention?
If so... you are *not alone*.

It's a common misconception about worthiness.
Does Jesus question the two blind men about their *worthiness*?
Does he quiz them on their *beliefs* and *behaviors*?
Does he scold them or shame them about something they've done in the past?
No!

Jesus simply asks if they have *faith* in him... and then *heals* them.
This is what Unconditional Love *does*.

Jesus shows us the heart of God.
Invite Jesus into *your* heart... and experience *healing*!

Listen to the song of the day "Come to Jesus" on the *Live to Love* album.

6 GROUNDED IN LOVE

Matthew 7:24-25

"Everyone who listens to these words of mine and acts on them will be like a wise man who built his house on rock. The rain fell, the floods came, and the winds blew and buffeted the house. But it did not collapse; it had been set solidly on rock."

What is the *foundation* on which you build your life?
If it is material possessions, prestige, position, reputation, or anything else *human-made*...
there will come a time when it will all *crumble* and come *tumbling down*.
Troubles, struggles, and difficulties are part of life.

But when Christ is your foundation...
your life is built on an *Eternal Love*.

Such a foundation cannot be *achieved* by going to church once a week,
performing rituals, and following rules.

It happens not by *achieving*...
but by *allowing* or *surrendering* to a Love that is *unconditional*.

When you *listen* to the words of Jesus... ponder them...
allow them to speak to your *heart* and then *act* on them...
you will experience *transformation*.
Then you will have an *everlasting* inner strength and peace amidst all of life's storms.

It's never too *early*... or too *late*...
to stand on the firm foundation of Jesus.

**Listen to the song of the day "You'll Lead Me" on the *Listen to Your Heart*
album.**

COME TO JESUS |

Matthew 15:29-30

Moving on from there,
Jesus walked by the Sea of Galilee,
went up on the mountain,
and sat down there.
Great crowds came to him,
having with them the lame, the blind,
the deformed, the mute, and many others.
They placed them at his feet,
and he cured them.

What in your life needs healing?

**It may be a physical healing that you need...
or it may be an emotional, psychological, or spiritual healing.**

Do you carry resentments or deep wounds from something that
has been done to you in the past?

**Go to Jesus in prayer and ask for his healing...
then see what happens.**

But... be *patient*.
The healing that will come may take time and
might not be exactly what you want...
but it will be exactly what you *need*.

Listen to the song of the day "Heal Me" on the *Live to Love* album.

8   HOMEWARD BOUND

Psalm 23:3-4

> You guide me along the right path for the sake of your name. Even when I walk through a dark valley, I fear no harm for you are at my side.

Sooner or later you will realize that you can't go it *alone*.
If you think life is about being perfect...
you will fail.
The wheels *will* fall off somewhere along the line.
Something out of your control will derail you.
No one can make it on his or her own without *help*.

We are *all* flawed.
But that's not so we can feel shame or so God can punish us.
That would make God a cruel tyrant!
Jesus showed us that God will never abandon us and will do everything to save us.

After all... the very name "Jesus" means "Yahweh saves"!
Since God *is* love (1 John 4:8)... there is *nothing to fear*.

You are *loved* and *chosen* by God *from the very beginning of time*.

It is when we walk in the "dark valley" that we can truly experience the Great Light that will show us the way.

**In times of struggle...
know that you are being led safely home.**

Do not be afraid. *Love* is leading you.

Listen to the song of the day "Love Will Always Lead You Home" on the *Mercy Reigns* album.

PEACE BE WITH YOU

Matthew 11:28

"Come to me, all you who labor and are burdened, and I will give you rest."

Sometimes the struggles and stresses of life are almost too much to bear.
When this is how it feels...
stop.

Take a *deep* breath.
Know that you are held by a *Great Compassion*.

As Psalm 46 states: "Be still and know that I am God!"

Sometimes it takes being overwhelmed by life's circumstances before we are finally forced to *let go of trying to control everything* and to *surrender* ourselves into the *loving hands of God*.

Jesus gives us a gentle invitation to simply come to him and
place ourselves in his care.
Try it. Feel the *comforting peace* that will *enfold* you and *warm* you.
It is then that you will be able to hear the gentle whisper of
"I love you" in your heart.
Chaos and dismay do *not* win.
Even *death* is a *doorway to new life*.

Love will *always* have the *final say*.
You are in the *process of transformation*.

Be still... and find *rest*.

Listen to the song of the day "I Will Give You Rest" on the *Live to Love* album.

10 FEAR NOT

Isaiah 40:11

Like a shepherd he feeds his flock;
in his arms he gathers the lambs,
carrying them in his bosom,
and leading the ewes with care.

The prophet Isaiah described the coming Messiah
hundreds of years before the birth of Jesus.

However, this *long-awaited king* would be like a *loving shepherd...*
not some *war-like military ruler.*

Jesus compared himself to a shepherd
who leaves the ninety-nine sheep in the hills
to search for the *one* who has *strayed away.*

"And if he finds it, amen, I say to you,
he rejoices more over it than over the ninety-nine
that did not stray" (Matthew 18:13).

This reflects the God who shepherds *us!*

If you feel lost...
rest easy.
God will *never leave you*.

So... what is there to fear?

Listen to the song of the day "How Wonderful to Me" on the *Live to Love* album.

RADICALLY OKAY

Isaiah 35:4

Say to those whose hearts are frightened:
Be strong, fear not!
Here is your God, he comes with vindication;
With divine recompense he comes to save you.

First off... we know that God is love (1 John 4:8).

Secondly, we know:
"There is no fear in love, but perfect love drives out fear
because fear has to do with punishment,
and so one who fears is not yet perfect in love" (1 John 4:18).

Know this: **YOU. ARE. LOVED!**

The God of Love *loved you into existence!*

You are ***God's child.***

Jesus showed us the face of this loving God in all that he did.

And he said this:
"Everything that the Father gives me will come to me,
and I will not reject anyone who comes to me" (John 6:37).

The God of Love is coming to save you!

Listen to the song of the day "Radically Okay" on the *Mercy Reigns* album.

12 | DIVINE DELIVERER

Isaiah 41:13

For I am the Lord, your God,
who grasps your right hand;
It is I who say to you,
"Fear not, I will help you."

The prophet Isaiah lived 700 years before Jesus but he made some
incredibly accurate predictions about the coming Messiah.
The line quoted here may have been written by one of
Isaiah's followers who carried on his prophetic call.

**God was truly speaking through these prophets
who were passing on the messages
they were receiving through prayer.**

This message says that the God of the universe
is grasping your hand and is saying,
"Fear not, I will help you."
Is this *your* image of "God"?

Or do you have a *fear-based* image of a *judgmental taskmaster*?

**The reality is: God is intimately *with* you and *for* you...
and *yearns* for you to experience *unconditional love* and *acceptance*.**

Jesus reflects this God *perfectly*.
Allow him to take your hand.

Or perhaps Jesus' hand will reach out to you... through someone near you?

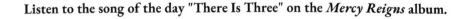

Listen to the song of the day "There Is Three" on the *Mercy Reigns* album.

TURN OFF THE NOISE | 13

Silence, all people, in the presence of the Lord! For he stirs forth from his holy dwelling.

The prophet Zechariah's advice from 500 years before Jesus
remains a profound one today.

How can we expect to hear God speak to us if we are
continuously bombarded with *noise...*
constant audio and visual stimulation...
not to mention our minds' *addiction* to chronic *busy-ness*?

God speaks in *silence.*

Only God can tell us *who* we are and *why* we are here.

**Why would we not create a space of silence
so we could hear what God is saying?**

It would seem that most religious leaders of our time have failed to teach us this...
despite the fact that most religions at one time were steeped
in contemplative prayer or meditation of some kind.

When Jesus was asked by his followers to teach them how to pray he said,
"When you pray, go to your inner room, close the door,
and pray to your Father in secret. Do not babble like the pagans,
who think that they will be heard because of their many words" (Matthew 6:6-7).

Advent is the perfect time to *stop... wait... let go...* and *listen*.

Peace is available... right *now*.

Listen to the song of the day "Turn Off the Noise" on the *Listen to Your Heart* album.

Psalm 34:19

The Lord is close to the broken-hearted,
saves those whose spirit is crushed.

Sometimes life deals us a bad hand.
Sometimes things don't go the way we'd like them to go.

**Sometimes we have to go through horrible pain due to either
our *own* actions or through *no fault of our own*.**

I know that in my life it has been the times of great suffering
when I have experienced the *most* transforming compassion of God.

**It's precisely when I'm *least in control* that
God is able to do what God wants to do...
rescue me!**

It's then that I can see that the love of God has
nothing to do with my earning it or my goodness.

It has *everything* to do with God *freely giving it* and God's *goodness*.

It's only when we reach the *end of our rope* that we have no choice but to *let go...*
and fall into the arms of a God Who promises to *never let us go*
no matter how *bleak* the situation may *appear*.

It's only in those times that we can experience the saving power of a
love *beyond our wildest imaginations*.

Listen to the song of the day "God Is" on the *Give Praise and Thanks* album.

BLIND TRUST | 15

Luke 7:22

And Jesus said to them in reply,
"Go and tell John what you have seen and heard:
the blind regain their sight, the lame walk,
lepers are cleansed, the deaf hear, the dead are raised,
the poor have the good news proclaimed to them."

John the Baptist was confronted in his final days with a
disorienting dilemma of uncertainty about Jesus.
The One he had been *certain* was the long-awaited Messiah... he now questioned.

Jesus did not come in *might* and *power*...
but in *peace* and *compassion*.

The Living Christ wants to bring you into a *deeper experience* of
love, mercy, grace, forgiveness, and compassion.

It is *not* about *certainty*...
but *faith*...
which is about believing and trusting
even when it doesn't make sense.

Why believe and trust?
Because Jesus opened the eyes of the blind and the ears of the deaf,
healed the lame and sick and proclaimed Good News
to those who had lost everything of this world.

When struggles come and life does *not make sense*...
trust in the One who *promises* to bring you to New Life.

Listen to the song of the day "Salvation" on the *Live to Love* album.

16 | BE OPEN TO GRACE

Isaiah 48:17

I, the Lord, your God, teach you what is for your good, and lead you on the way you should go.

At the time it happened...
suffering a ruptured appendix was seemingly one of the *worst* times in my life.

I now look upon it as one of the most *wonderful* times.

It was during that time of suffering and *loss of control*
that I came to know God's *grace*.

I came to know a Great Love *beyond all understanding*.

There was no hint of *quid pro quo*.
The Love was given *gratuitously*.
I experienced compassion at a very deep level.

It was *life changing*.

Wherever you are experiencing pain and hurt right now...
open your heart and allow God to enter in an embrace you.

You are already being held in an immense Love...
larger than you can imagine.

Trust.
God (Love) will lead you to a better place and *transform* you.

Listen to the song of the day "Make Your Way" on the *Mercy Reigns* album.

DEATH TO LIFE

Psalm 30:12-13

You changed my mourning into dancing;
you took off my sackcloth and clothed me
with gladness. O Lord, my God,
forever will I give you thanks.

God is in the *redemption* business.
The *whole universe* is participating in a great act of *dying* and *rising*.
All of it.

This is true for each of us on the *large* scale of our *birth and death*...
and also on the *smaller* scale of *each day* as we go through
little "dyings" and "risings" along the way.
There comes a time when we must *let go* of *one thing* so that *another* thing can *begin*.
When we *resist change*...
we *create suffering* for ourselves by *blocking the Spirit's
creative flow in our lives.*
Dying and *rising* is part of the deal. Love *requires* it.

Jesus showed us this quite clearly through how he *lived* and *died*.
As he stated, "No one has greater love than this,
to lay down one's life for one's friends" (John 15:13).
But he also showed us that death is *not* the *end*.
It's the door to *transformation* and *new life!*

So allow this knowledge to settle in your heart.
Accept Love's invitation to turn your *mourning* into *dancing*.

How magnificent, wondrous and glorious is God!

**Listen to the song of the day "How Magnificent, Wondrous and Glorious" on the
Mercy Reigns album.**

18 BELIEVE

Psalm 85:9

I will listen for the word of God; surely the Lord will proclaim peace to his people, to the faithful, to those who trust in him.

Are you listening for God's *silent whisper* in your heart?

**Whenever you feel any sense of fear or anxiety...
immediately listen for an *inner voice* of *calm*.**

When a violent storm was threatening to sink a boat carrying Jesus and his followers...
they cried out to him for help.
His response:
"Why are you terrified, O you of little faith?" (Matthew 8:26).
Then he calmed the winds and the sea.

**In Jesus...
we know *who God Is*.**

When John the Baptist sent his followers to Jesus to ask
if he really was the Messiah, Jesus replied,
"Go and tell John what you have seen and heard:
the blind regain their sight, the lame walk, lepers are cleansed,
the deaf hear, the dead are raised,
the poor have the good news proclaimed to them" (Luke 7:22).

This is a God of love who proclaims peace to us.

Trust!

Listen to the song of the day "Let It Be Done to Me" on the *Mercy Reigns* album.

GOD SATISFIES 19

Psalm 34:11

The powerful grow poor and hungry, but those who seek the Lord lack no good thing.

It's a paradox.

**The more *material stuff* you collect...
the more your ego *wants* and can *never* be *satisfied*.**

It will always want *more*.

**And so those who spend their time *grasping* for more stuff...
grow *poorer* and *hungrier* spiritually.**

But when we put God first in our lives...
when we *seek* God in *each* moment...
what is lacking?

Nothing.

When we empty ourselves of *our* desires...
and open ourselves to *God's* desires...
inner peace and contentment is ours.

***The kingdom of God...
is then at hand!***

Listen to the song of the day "Breathe On Me" on the *Listen to Your Heart* album.

20 YOU ARE SPECIAL

John 5:36

"The works that the Father
gave me to accomplish,
these works that I perform testify on
my behalf that the Father has sent me."

When Jesus was born...
God became one of us as a helpless, little baby.

God experienced everything we experience in human flesh.
God became one with us.
And then what did Jesus do?

He *healed.*
He *forgave.*
He *reached out to the outcast, the forgotten, the lost.*
He worked to bring all together as one.

If you are feeling like the outcast...
the forgotten...
the lost...
God wants me to let you know...
that *you have not been forgotten.*

God could never forget a precious son or daughter.

Listen to the song of the day "I Stand in the Light" on the *Mercy Reigns* album.

LOVE NEVER FAILS | 21

Though the mountains leave their place
and the hills be shaken, My love shall never leave
you nor my covenant of peace be shaken,
says the Lord, who has mercy on you.

How *quickly* we *lose* faith in God when troubles come or
things don't go the way *we want them to*.

But God *never turns away*!

Do we not actually put our faith mostly in things of the world?
It's only when some hardship comes along that we come to see that
all the world's possessions, prestige, or power will *crumble*.

We *cannot save ourselves*.

We are unable to control the *uncontrollable*.
It's in these times that God *remains present*.
Try this exercise.
In *silence* take a *long inward breath* while praying "Yah"...
and then let that breath *out* while praying "weh."
Yahhhhh... wehhhhh.
Yahhhhhhh... wehhhhhh.
Yahweh.

**God is as *close to you*...
as your *next* breath.
God will *never leave you*.**

Listen to the song of the day "Mercy Reigns" on the *Mercy Reigns* album.

GIVE GLORY TO GOD

Psalm 72:17

May his name be blessed forever;
as long as the sun,
may his name endure.

⌣

God has all the time in the world.

God is *outside* of our time.

Prophets *foretold* of the coming of the Messiah for
hundreds and hundreds of years before the birth of Jesus.

The Savior had a lot of *shady* characters as ancestors!

And when the Word became flesh...
it was not as a powerful, wrathful God...
but as a gentle, *defenseless baby*.

His words were not of retribution and punishment...
but of forgiveness and mercy.

God desires our wholeness and redemption.

How will the Word become flesh in *you*...
in a new way this Christmas?

⌣

**Listen to the song of the day "Glorify You with Me" on the *Give Praise and
Thanks* album.**

LET IT BE DONE | **23**

Psalm 34:7

In my misfortune I called, the Lord heard and saved me from all distress.

Is there something you are struggling with?

That *very thing* can lead you to your salvation.

It is the very place where you cannot do it on your own...
the place where you need God.

**It is the place where God wants to be *with* you...
not punish you.**

It is the place where God can help you grow and become whole.

Let God's unconditional love bring you relief and peace.

Listen to the song of the day "Let It Be Done to Me" on the *Mercy Reigns* album.

Luke 1:36-37

> "And behold, Elizabeth, your relative,
> has also conceived a son in her old age,
> and this is the sixth month for her
> who was called barren;
> for nothing will be impossible for God."

Where in your life do you feel *barren*?
Where is it in your life that you are struggling and in need of *new life*?

Trust that God is *able* and *willing* to do the *seemingly* impossible!

See that God gave Elizabeth a son in her old age...
a son who became John the Baptist.
And God gave Mary a Son who became the Messiah.
Yet Mary remained a "*virgin mother*".
Impossible?
Nothing is impossible for God!

**Allow this paradox of "*virgin mother*" to open your mind to
a *deeper mystery* and a *deeper truth*.
God is a God of "*both-and*" not "*either-or*."**

The Love that continues to create the universe wants to transform *you*...
but that can only happen if you have
an open *mind* and *heart* and
are *willing to be changed*.

Listen to the song of the day "Changed" on the *Give Praise and Thanks* album.

LIFE CHANGING

"And you, child, will be called prophet of the Most High, for you will go before the Lord to prepare his ways, to give his people knowledge of salvation..."

John the Baptist's father prophesied what was ahead for his son while John was still in the womb.
Are we not *all* called to do what the Baptist would do?

Aren't we all called to *prepare the way* for Christ to come into the lives of all people we meet?
We are called to be channels of God's *unconditional* love and *acceptance* of *all* people and *everything that is*.

Following Jesus truly brings peace and wholeness both *now* and *always*.
If you think that you don't have your life together enough to do this... relax!
Join the club of sinners!
We're all messed-up in some manner but Christ invites us... *one and all*... to his table.
It's a beautiful story!
What seems *too good to be true*... *is true*!

It has nothing to do with *merit*.
All we have to do is *accept* it.
Allow this Good News to settle in your soul!
Christ... Love incarnate...
becomes one of us.
Welcome this Love into your life on this Christmas Day... just as you are!
Now... invite someone else to do the same... because *all* are welcome!

Listen to the song of the day "All Are Welcome" on the *Give Praise and Thanks* album.

26 THE GREAT COMPASSION

Psalm 71:5

You are my hope, Lord;
my trust, God,
from my youth.

Loving God...
I thank You for all the blessings in my life.

**All my pain and difficulties I hand over to You knowing that
with Your help You will lead me
through them and *transform* my life.**

I can look back to my earliest days and see how you accepted me...
gently and patiently led me and opened my eyes to who *I am* and who *You are*.

You are my only true hope.

You are *around* me and *within* me.

I am so thankful!

I put my life in Your hands!

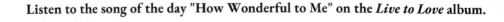

Listen to the song of the day "How Wonderful to Me" on the *Live to Love* album.

CIRCLE OF LIFE | 27

Song of Songs 2:11-12

"For see, the winter is past,
the rains are over and gone.
The flowers appear on the earth,
the time of pruning the vines has come,
and the song of the dove is heard in our land."

God is *perpetually giving life...*
pouring out love to fill all that is empty...
to *birth* something *new...*
to *re-birth* where new life is needed.
The cycle of the four seasons shows us this.

So do the *life, death,* and *resurrection* of Jesus.
**Each of us receives the gift of life and is invited into
the *cycle of receiving and giving*, gratefully *accepting* what is given...
but then humbly *letting it go...*
giving everything back.**

The gifts are *not* to be *hoarded...*
but *shared.*
**It is a beautiful *cycle of unconditional love...*
of *participating* in the very nature of God and the Trinity.**

The invitation is *always being given.*
What do *you* need to *let go* of so God can *give* you something *new*?

Are you allowing yourself to be a part of this *Great Flow of giving and receiving*?

Listen to the song of the day "Seasons" on the *Listen to Your Heart* album.

28 | HUMBLE AWARENESS

Matthew 2:13

> Behold, the angel of the Lord appeared to
> Joseph in a dream and said,
> "Rise, take the child and his mother,
> flee to Egypt,
> and stay there until I tell you."

How amazing is it that Joseph would uproot his wife and baby and make a *very difficult trip* to Egypt with *no idea* what awaited them there...
no plan...
based on a dream?

Joseph was *attuned* to God.

He must have had an amazing contemplative dimension that enabled him to *listen* with the *eyes* and *ears* of his heart to the directions of the Spirit.

**What humility and *lack* of ego...
to be able to *set aside* whatever *his* plans were...
and to follow God with such trust and *blind* faith!**

Could it be that God is speaking to *us* in *each moment*...
but our minds and egos are in such control that we are quite *unaware*?

**Maybe if we would take a *moment* to *observe* our
racing, non-stop thoughts and insatiable desires of our egos...
and *let go*...
just *maybe* we might *hear* the *gentle voice* of God.**

Listen to the song of the day "Turn Off the Noise" on the *Listen to Your Heart* album.

LOVE STORY | 29

1 John 2:9

Whoever says he is in the light,
yet hates his brother or sister,
is still in the darkness.

God is Light...
only Love.

Allow that Light to shine into the darkness *inside* of you.

We all have a place of darkness...
a place where we feel *we could not possibly be loved*...
a place where we don't *measure up*...
a place where we are *afraid* or are *embarrassed* because of shame.

Allow God's Light to shine into that area.

God's Light will not *condemn, accuse,* or *shame* you.
On the *contrary*...
it will *embrace, console, accept,* and *lift* you!

It is the *one place* where we know we *can't save ourselves* and
where God is the *only* One who can save us...
and *promises* to *never let us go!*

**Allow the Light to shine on you...
and through you.
Be a part of an *Epic Love Story*.**

Listen to the song of the day "May I Be Light" on the *Listen to Your Heart* album.

30 ALL ARE ONE

1 John 2:15

Do not love the world
or the things of the world.
If anyone loves the world,
the love of the Father is not in him.

First off, we know we *are* to love creation because
God *entrusts* us as *stewards* or *caretakers* of the "*world*" in that sense.

But we are *not* to love the "*world*" in the sense of
material possessions or in the sense of making objects
of other people or things for our own selfish desires.

It's all about *relationship*.

If we *give* of ourselves to God...
God *gives back* to us in an *endless circle* of abundant *giving and receiving*!

**The *more* you give of yourself...
the *more* God *gives back*.**

This is *mirrored* in the Trinity...
an *endless cycle* of a loving relationship between Father, Son, and Holy Spirit.

**The key is to *be present*...
and in loving relationship with everything in *each moment*.**

Listen to the song of the day "All Are One" on the *Mercy Reigns* album.

REASON TO REJOICE

Psalm 96:1-2

Sing to the Lord a new song;
sing to the Lord, all the earth.
Sing to the Lord, bless his name;
announce his salvation day after day.

As we ring in the New Year with celebrations...
let us be reminded that each moment is the eternal "now".

Each moment is all that is real...
the only "time" when God is with us.

It's *constant*...
just like God's love.

So let us celebrate our loving God Who holds all and embraces all...
Who does not exclude anyone for anything they've done...
but simply loves each of us for who we are:
God's beloved son or daughter.

This is what you are now...
and *now*...
and *now, etc.*

Listen to the song of the day "Sing a New Song" on the *Live to Love* album.

About the Author

Bill Tonnis' began his career delivering bad news on the radio, but now he delivers good news through ministry.

After obtaining a Bachelor of Science degree in Broadcast Journalism from Xavier University, Bill had a successful career as a news reporter/anchor at 700 WLW Radio for over twenty years. Emotionally drained by the job of delivering "bad news" daily, he had a life-changing epiphany in 1997 that led him to start writing spiritual songs and finding a new sense of purpose.

He completed a Master of Arts degree in Religious and Pastoral Studies at the College of Mount St. Joseph (now Mount St. Joseph University), left the radio station, and followed a new calling to be the Youth Minister at Our Lady of the Visitation Parish in Cincinnati. After five rewarding years in that role, Bill felt called to chaplaincy, and he completed the full training (four units of Clinical Pastoral Education) at Good Samaritan Hospital. He then began a new position at the parish as Pastoral Associate for Outreach, where he oversees social justice and service programs. Bill now provides pastoral care through words and music to shut-ins, hospitals, nursing homes, and jails.

Along with his work as a lay pastoral minister and chaplain, Bill shares his talents as a retreat leader/presenter, music minister, and a singer/songwriter with many organizations. His four original music albums entitled *Listen to Your Heart, Live to Love, Give Praise and Thanks,* and *Mercy Reigns* as well as all individual songs are available to download for purchase at various music service websites (such as iTunes). You can also purchase CDs of Bill's albums by contacting him at BillTonnisMusicMinistry@gmail.com.

Bill also writes a devotional blog at:
https://billtonnismusic.wordpress.com/category/todays-contemplation/.

Made in the USA
Lexington, KY
12 September 2018